PLANNING A SUCCESSFUL L·I·F·E

THINGS THEY NEVER TAUGHT YOU IN SCHOOL

AUTHOR

E. H. Timmerman

BS in Chemical Engineering and MS in Petroleum Engineering from University of Texas. Experience during 45 years with major oil company and as a worldwide consultant. Real Estate Broker in Colorado.

WITH CONTRIBUTIONS BY:

Nancy Montgomery

MBA Stanford Graduate School of Business
BA Wellesley College, Massachusetts
Certified Public Accountant in California
Experience with "Big 8" accounting firm and several business firms including Vice-President of Finance of a rapidly growing, mid-size company.

DuBose Montgomery

MBA Harvard Graduate School of Business Administration
BS in Management Science, BS and MS in Electrical Engineering from Massachusetts Institute of Technology. Experience as general partner of Venture Capital firm, management consultant and Director for about a dozen venture companies.

Erline Timmerman

Investor during thirty years.
Studied at Texas Lutheran College, Texas, University of Houston, Texas and University of Tulsa, Oklahoma.

Please do not duplicate without written permission. Advice can be good, bad and indifferent. You should study many sources and you alone are responsible for decisions.

R&E PUBLISHERS

Published by
R&E PUBLISHERS
P. O. Box 2008
Saratoga, California 95070

Typesetting by
Estella M. Krebs

Cover by
Kaye Graphics

Library of Congress Card Catalog Number
87-90652

I.S.B.N.
0-88247-774-9

Library of Congress Cataloging-in-Publication Data

Planning a successful life.

    Bibliography: p.
    1. Conduct of life. 2. Finance, Personal.
I. Timmerman, E.H.
BJ1581.2.P63   1987   158'.1   87-90652
ISBN 0-88247-774-9

Table Of Contents

Introduction

We live only once on this earth and the quality of our life depends upon our choices which are made daily. Each person over 12 years of age should ask at least once each year, *"What do I plan to do with the remainder of my life?"* A useful, happy and comfortable life might involve helping others, protecting our surroundings and making sufficient money to provide a desired lifestyle. We cannot all be president of our country and many of us do not wish the workload and responsibilities of being an executive of a large company. As a minimum, we should strive for inner peace and contentment with our life. Some individuals will also desire larger amounts of money, fame and possibly power. Our dreams and wishes should be practical and attainable so that defeats and frustrations are bearable. We must learn to say "NO" to miminize "hurts" of life.

The next question should be, *"How do I plan to reach my goals?"* Most adults have not answered this question and they do not organize their thoughts. They fail to:

1. Accept leadership roles and accept and learn the normal requirements of business and society.
2. Recognize the need for goals and the need to plan their lives and remain healthy.
3. Properly budget money and time rather than simply drift.
4. Learn the rules and techniques for generating enthusiasm, motivation and develop good habits.
5. Develop and build desirable character and needed moral values and guiding principles.
6. Create a method for saving, management and handling personal finances.
7. Study throughout life, make necessary changes and react to a changing world environment.

Society in the highly developed western nations allows us each to make many individual choices and our selections determine our lifestyle, our friends, our type of work and the place where we work. We determine our future and we are responsible for our own decisions. We each make decisions daily and these choices must be consistent with the plan for life if our wishes, desires and ideals are to be accomplished. Without a plan, decisions are not consistent and contradictions lead to defeat and despair.

Government or society has developed many laws, rules and regulations to protect us and our neighbors. Our choices must conform with these laws. We face jail, fines and supervision by probation officers when we violate laws. Most individuals learn from parents, friends and books so that dealing with the courts is not required. As we grow older and become more experienced, we recognize that rules developed by society during thousands of years are basic and meet our needs. Changes are made slowly by compromise between millions of residents living in our great country. We learn to work within the system to accomplish our desires and meet our true needs by making compromises with relatives, friends, neighbors and as a group between nations.

Help is available to guide us in making our decisions and choices. Friends, business leaders, associates, "How To Do" books, tapes, newspapers, and schools offer advice. We can solve our problems which we encounter in our social and business lives if we ask for help. Solutions are easiest if we accept help from the experienced. It is unfortunate when we refuse to listen to family and true friends and spurn advice. The advice obtained may be good, bad, sterile and indifferent. We should always compare advice from several sources before evaluating reliability. We individually make the final choices and we live with the consequences. Always get the facts, know what you are doing, decide using intelligence and common sense and then act. Your future is involved and this is not a time for being careless or lazy. Think and do not submit to peer pressure.

Most books study a single subject and we must read many texts if an overall plan for our life is to be assembled. Our plan should consider finances but emotions and feelings also are important. Our attitude affects our health, our decisions, actions and our relations with others in social life and in the workplace. Our financial well being and living standards are determined by how we handle our jobs or business and how we manage our investments. Management of our health is of major importance since we can work when healthy. A job enables us to buy food, place a roof over our family and pay for our pleasures. Our savings enable us to accumulate wealth which enables us to handle unemployment periods, live when we are ill and when we are old and retired. A fine balance between today and our future is essential. We need to understand the inter-relationships between our living habits, our jobs, our business efforts and our savings or investments. We can live a full life, be safe and have fun if we learn to earn money and learn how to make a few investments and manage for growth. We each need to carefully make our important choices such as selection of our mate, our lifestyle, our work field and location of our place of work. Other major decisions involve large expenditures of money such as buying a house and having children. We should select our friends with extreme care and we need competent specialists such as lawyers, doctors, accountants and bankers.

We must each be very competent in the use of writing, reading, arithmetic and job skills. These tools are useless unless we use them in the practical work and social environment. We must communicate with others and successfully live with associates and friends.

Selecting Your Lifestyle

Our lifestyle or way of living is determined by the money available and the location or environment in which we live. As an example, in most western nations where industrial plant is large, we have many choices which are very different from those in the "undeveloped third world" where earning money to buy food is difficult. In the west, most individuals seek luxury while in "poorer" countries, people strive to get away from hunger. The contrast is very severe as you will observe when you travel to poorer parts of Mexico, India, etc.

In the western world, we work individually to earn the money to buy the material items which we desire as part of our life. The goods are available in stores and most of us can earn the money to buy what we actually "NEED" plus luxuries. In underdeveloped nations, workers wages are small and material comforts may not be available to their "rich" because governments do not have money for imports.

Our characters, our habits, our work abilities and our social contacts are selected and developed by each of us as individuals. Our choices are many and we often find it difficult to decide. We should review our social and work abilities, our friends and our habits on a routine basis to decide whether changes are desired or needed to meet our constantly changing need, ideals and living conditions. We simply should not drift nor become creatures dependent upon our habits. Plan, control your life and create a better future by your deeds, work, actions and words. Recognize that the tenure system of the public school system often prevents you from hearing views of people with experience. You might read the following summary of notes collected during many years.

PLANNING YOUR LIFE

All plans must consider existing religious, political and economic conditions. The worldwide society in which we live is very complicated, is interdependent within the United States and with other societies throughout the world. All change slowly. Understanding our country, our nations history, the tools and methods used by industry and government, and our needs are all basic to successful living.

Ability to read and understand the English language and at least one other language, and an understanding of the complicated laws and regulations which control our activity and relations among each other are basic for living in the United States. We need the ability to express our opinions in the written word, spoken word and in computer-generated mathematical equations if we want a successful life in the western world. Cooperation with others, both socially and in the workplace, is basic. We create our success by influencing others, by our work, our intelligence, our decisions, actions and words. Advantage is gained over our competitors and possibly friends when we study and apply knowledge and common sense based on our own experiences and the basic knowledge learned by others during many past generations. Life should be fun but we each have responsibilities to ourselves, to our fellow man and to future generations. Rewards go to those who create employment, wealth and a prosperous nation. People who help others and who try to protect the environment also are admired. Society demands high ethical standards.

A plan makes our life more rewarding and useful. The plan must be actively lived and the plan for our life must be constantly updated to fit changing conditions. The value of any plan depends upon our actions, decisions and a strong implementation. Creature comforts are created only when plant and facilities are operated efficiently by cooperative joint efforts of both managers and the workers. Your job depends upon someone else buying your services and the products which you make at the plant. Competition for markets is worldwide and the world is becoming one large industrial complex. Finances, products and jobs compete worldwide.

Our choices are also limited by tradition which is not entirely included in our written laws. We learn these from our parents, by reading history and by listening to political, business and religious leaders. We need to appreciate the effort of our forefathers. They fought for freedoms and economic advancement during thousands of years. They gave us our life, our education, the benefits of freedom and the free enterprise system of business. Your ancestors made it possible for you to be born in the western world which makes the good life of the west available to you. We enjoy political, religious and economic benefits which are unavailable to most of the people in this world. Our ancestors denied themselves of pleasures so that money was spent on physical manufacturing plant, cities and training. Our creature benefits and standard of living are the direct result of the improvement obtained by working with machines rather than with bare hands. Our freedoms include selection of jobs, selection of place to work and selection of place where we live. We also inherited the freedom to worship as we wish, the freedom to express our ideas and opinions, and the freedom to select our friends. We have trial by our neighbors in our courts. These freedoms are not available in many countries where government is controlled by military or other dictators. Our parents paid a high price for our democratic form of government and competitive private business environment which has resulted in the high living standards which we so willingly enjoy today. We should be grateful to our elders and make every effort to pass the system to benefit our children.

Today, citizens of the western world travel the world to observe life in other societies. The real poverty shocks us and we are offended by the exploitation of the population by a few of their neighbors and by their governments. We learn to appreciate the benefits resulting from the location of our birth. We begin to understand why our ancestors braved hardships to obtain freedom, liberty and the economic benefits provided by the free enterprise system. We renew our effort to protect our life from the special interest groups who want excessive control and unreasonable change. We work to make our benefits available to everyone willing to work and earn. Excessive greed by our leaders in business and government become less acceptable. Ideas which are advanced to divide us are not tolerated. We really appreciate and like our country and its political-economic systems.

Many developing countries have natural resources which are needed to maintain the living standards of western nations who have depleted their better resources to support high living standards. Lower grade materials, including oil, remaining in the west are not economic in the world marketplace. A cheap energy source must quickly be developed. The undeveloped nations demand higher prices which are fair for their products. They expect grants, loans and aid to help them raise living standards in their countries. Unless the transition period is long, living standards in the western world may decline as this adjustment is forced upon the world by lower wages after inflation and taxes.

It is unfortunate that many countries cannot control the rapid growth of their populations. Higher living standards are not possible because additional people are born more rapidly than new plant can be constructed. The material wealth and living standard of the individual person cannot be increased under these conditions and the demands for economic aid are not effective. Nevertheless, their populations want more of the products which they see on television and in western movies. Their populations desire the benefits of the western world but population growth make the desire unattainable. The related political upheavals are now being observed in many countries.

These countries have the natural resources which must be purchased by the western world and their demands must in part be satisfied. The people are proud and they expect western creature comforts in countries other than Iran where religious concepts control desires as enforced by government or religious leaders. The result today is terrorism and large illegal immigration to the west. They also will rebel and go to war with the west if they believe they can win. These dangers can be controlled if the west uses common sense and if we select honest, capable, and intelligent leaders during elections. Unfortunately, we do not want to hear the bad facts and our politicians want to be re-elected for another term. Politicians often are lead and controlled by special interest groups who furnish money and staff for elections. Unless the average voter becomes less selfish and is willing to spend the time to understand the issues and facts, our great nation will face extreme stress and may collapse. We each need to assume our duty and look at the long term needs of our nation rather than simply enjoy todays pleasures. We elect our leaders by our voting records. We each individually are responsible for the result of our actions and inactions. We need to revive the political process by being informed and actively participating in the process.

We, too, have responsibilities to future generations. We need to work to protect and improve our great country, our democracy, its freedoms and the industrial complex which makes possible the benefits which we each willingly enjoy today. Our work, using many machines, enables us to produce goods and services in excess of needs. Our country can afford to take care of the ill, the handicapped and the elderly. In our parents time and in the underdeveloped world today, parents depend upon children to provide these services in ex-

4

tended family type of relationship. The world environment must be protected.

HOW DO WE ACCOMPLISH?

It is a sad fact but many in our country and the heads of governments in many nations are trying to reduce the living conditions in the United States. Loss of our freedoms is part of the scheme since we are unwilling to compromise. We fail to recognize that the poorest person in the United States lives better than the kings of a few centuries ago and that there is no real poverty here when compared with that found in most of the world population. We are all so very spoiled. A democracy depends upon cooperation and acceptance of the will of the majority. A few terrorists can take away freedoms of the majority. We might realize that many items which are used daily are luxuries. Government "doles" in the United States supply luxuries when many people of the world are actually hungry. We tend to spend money for movies and television that should be spent for food and housing.

Our young people need to recognize that lives of parents and children are intertwined until parted by real or imagined death. Parents give life to newborn at considerable physical and financial cost. Children grow slowly so that they can receive the training required for survival in a complicated, competitive and changing society. Such training and living expenses often cost $100,000 plus per child. We as taxpayers often pay the cost under various aid programs for the poor. The public also pays for schools, recreation facilities and many other facilities. In past times, children provided their own entertainment by being creative but today, everything seems to be planned by adults. Is this desired?

Some parents are capable but children often must obtain basic knowledge from teachers in schools and by personal study of books available in library and bookstores. Most older people are willing to help when asked but children must want to learn and listen. It is normal today for children to be unappreciative of the efforts of their parents and other elders. Teenagers often rebel and their future life is damaged by their refusal to accept advice. Fortunately for society, convergence of thought, ideal and actions by both children and parents usually occurs before children reach 30 years. The school of "hard knocks" causes children to learn to accept rules of society.

Workers pay very high social security taxes but the payments to the retired do not take care of their needs. We each must save a little while we are working. We need to learn management of money.

English is the language of the United States and it is also the business language throughout most of the world. Europe and many other nations force their children to learn English. The author knows two engineers from India who grew up 100 miles from each other but were only able to communicate with each other in the English language. In the United States, most newspapers and books are in English. It usually is impossible to communicate with your fellow workers and business associates in a language other than English. The parent who refuses to encourage children to learn English at home is handicapping children throughout life. Different cultures are desired but English is basic if the United States is to remain one strong unit. The educated throughout the world speak

English and our children will work in all parts of the world.

The computer and robot are changing the workplace and the types of jobs available. New devices are changing our lives at a very rapid pace. Think about the changes seen during the past ten years in the stores, the factory, the office and in the home. We individually must adapt, study throughout life, recognize trends and move to where there is work. Education in advance is the key to changes. Continue to study throughout life and be prepared for change. Learn to forecast short term.

Technology has, over the years, improved creature comfort living standards but it, too, does create problems. Burning of hydrocarbons in our plants and cars causes changes in the world's climate and must be controlled to protect trees, wildlife and humans. Nuclear energy might be the answer but its use today is very dangerous as illustrated in 1986 in Russia. New and safer sources of energy, probably fusion nuclear reactors, must be developed quickly if life is to exist over a long time period on earth. We also need to control wastes and use of chemicals. Genetics also present problems.

War is undesirable but protection of our nation is even more important. National interests need to be protected while we become part of a one world environment. The world will soon be one business unit and no country will be able to stop this trend. Anger, fear and other negative traits need to be controlled in individuals and between nations. Moderation in activities of life, in use of alcohol and in use of medical drugs, and compromise between individuals and countries are essential. Almost anything done in excess is harmful to health and excess emotions often cause fights, murder and disruption of local and international peace. Good health depends upon good thoughts and emotions.

Education, which is a process through which children and adults learn and acquire the experiences of others, is an important key to success in adult life. A valid high school diploma and a trade or profession must be truly earned by everyone. We also must learn to control our emotions, find personal values acceptable to society and find work which is rewarding. Our work also should be interesting most of the time so that we earn a living and relate to others in a friendly manner. Our friends and associates should not be allowed to make us feel guilty or inferior. Our peers should not control our life and actions.

Many teachers and workers do not wish to be informed. They do not admit their deficiencies because they wish to protect their jobs and do not want to admit that they are lazy and are not keeping up with the changes being made throughout the world.

The sources of information regarding jobs, investments and knowledge required to live a successful life are many. We each must constantly learn, study, read and listen and grow up and mature. We need to use various techniques to consult with the knowledgeable. Some are stubborn and lazy and fail to use the available tools. We thereby make our life more uncomfortable than necessary. Our lives are too short for us to learn all that is needed from our own mistakes and experiences. Learning from others and a strong faith in our ideals and abilities and faith in a superior leadership are often essential if we are to live a full life and control our emotions.

Many individuals tend to follow or worship "heroes" such as movie stars and athletes, and then become frustrated when they learn that their idols are arrested for drugs and sexual acts. They have admired poor characters. We are better individuals when we instead strive to develop our own abilities. We should develop our (1) understanding, intelligence and common sense; (2) physical attractiveness; (3) feelings and kindness toward others; (4) personality and enthusiasm; (5) ability to be creative and knowledgeable; (6) good health; (7) thinking ability and ability to. be adaptable and make changes; (8) desire for a good education including a feel for compromise and intuition; (9) earning ability with safety; (10) kindness toward others including children and the elderly; (11) moral and religious principles such as fairness and honesty; and (12) neatness and good manners. We might make these principles our ideal rather than people. We each need to be considerate, intelligent, understanding, honest and use good social graces. We need to work within the system and laws.

Reading, studying and managing our life and assets can be more fun and entertaining than a dull party or a movie. We should learn to enjoy our private hours. We do not always need to be with others, which usually is a way to waste time and energy. True change and accomplishment takes commitment, energy, patience and courage. Try and give life your best but keep expectations reasonable and practical. Learn to be flexible and adjust to new environments. Learn techniques which enable you to say "NO" gracefully. Have ambition, dreams and ideals and strive to make them become real so that life is interesting, but do not expect the impossible. Plan for the future but enjoy life one day at a time and combine work with play so that each day is a true joy. To obtain these goals, we must take charge of our life and time. We must honestly want to live a more successful, useful and enjoyable life. We must use our willpower and say "NO" to distractions. We must be friendly and cooperative with friends and family but we should do what is in our best interest.

TAKING CHARGE

We should take charge and implement the plan which we want to be the basis for our life. A plan is worthless if it is not used. The plan must be lived on a daily basis if it is to be a success. After a short time period, benefits of planning become so great that we wonder how we ever lived without a plan.

Only the very rich have the money to live a life of a "Playboy". As they grow older, they, too, want a life with more substance than simply playing social games with the opposite sex. They want to live rather than play. They want their life to be useful, meaningful and beneficial to society.

What do you want your life to be? Most people want a happy home, support from those whom they love, a broad education and an understanding of the country and the world, common sense, a desire to read, enjoyment of good music and a useful type of work. We also hope for a little "self-made" luck and a chance to accomplish to the best of our ability. We do not want either special favors or "handouts" from government. We want a fair break after we have made a real effort and have honestly prepared ourselves for work.

We each want success. Success often is defined as (1) a reasonable level of achievement, prominence and recognition; (2) an inner sense of satisfaction, happiness and fulfillment; and (3) a life which meets legal, moral and ethical standards as enforced by society, the church, our family and neighbors. We can attain most of these objectives if we simply try.

The life of our "grand parents" was planned by their physical needs, their religion and tradition. Religion was a major force in society during many past centuries. Parents taught children and they taught their children a need for learning, honest work and love for "GOD". Placing food on the table was a major task in the western world until about 100 years ago and continues to be so today in most of the world. Saving and construction of plant and machines has improved productivity above that obtainable with bare hands. Today, we in the United States have time, energy and money for worldly pleasures which we often use very foolishly. Theory of evolution, socialism, communism and excessive wealth and time have eroded basic principles used during many generations. Today we live with additional choices and our lives are controlled by our wishes rather than by what we need to live and enjoy our being. We each need to accept responsibility, plan our lives after careful thought and start living our plan today and continuing during all tomorrows.

Our recent ancestors enjoyed a simpler life with relatives and friends. They, too, were happy although life was more physical and hard work. A dollar of their low pay bought more goods than todays very inflated dollar. They had lower expectations and found happiness with fewer creature comforts. Government did not confiscate most of their hard-earned income and savings by assessing high taxes and inflation. Today the lifestyle of the rich and famous is shown worldwide on television and we each expect the same. We are frustrated and disappointed. The wealth of the world is simply insufficient to give such lifestyle to each of us.

There are at least three types of people. The *first classification* tend to be careless and possibly lazy. Some accept "doles" which are excessive compared with their ability to earn. Others do not take time to plan, develop strategy or reflect. They do not study agendas before going to meetings. They are afraid to speak and do not rehearse before speaking or making job applications. They simply drift and willingly accept what society takes and gives to them. They do not have ambition, energy, willpower and drive to study and work to improve their status.

The *second group* performs at a higher level but they are afraid. They do not reach decisions, act or take responsibility. They wish to be at the top but they lack the courage to take necessary risks. They always want to look good and they spend their time protecting their flanks rather than producing effectively. They do not make decisions or fight for their beliefs and rights. They become workers doing lower level work in offices, factories and in the community. They do not properly plan their life nor work because they fear the possibility of failure. Possibly they look toward the past too much and do not anticipate the future. They may work hard but lack in the application of effort. These individuals can be happy with life but they must accept lower objectives and adjust to a lower level in society. They are workers who are admired but they are not and maybe do not wish to become leaders. Most of us are in this class for various reasons. We are happy working for others and accept our lifestyle without regret.

The *third group* are leaders of our nation, our governments, our communities and our businesses. They are often the rich and famous. They constantly study, read rapidly and prepare for advancement by learning from others and from their failures and successes. They have no fears. They are interested in history. They have a broad experience and outlook. They thrive under stress, like to take risks and they make decisions quickly after being presented with facts. They use their past to screen facts and recognize errors in data and recommendations. They are confident and usually have the respect of their peers. They plan, delegate work to others, supervise, handle people well and get a job done by planning and controlling their work and lives. They organize, manage people and cause the company to make the money required to pay themselves and fellow workers ever increasing wages. They are leaders of business and the community. Leaders pay a high price in both time and energy.

In which group do you wish to belong? Are you willing to make the effort to be in Group 3? People in Groups 2 and 3 can accumulate wealth and become rich. After adjustment, people in Group 2 may be equally or even more happy. Members of Group 3 usually enjoy their work too much and they may become "workaholics". Time available often is devoted to society and their work rather than to family as leadership obligations are imposed by society and the workplace or company.

We need to make a plan for our life. Our plan should offer the chance or possibility of being successful. If we want wealth:

1. We might marry rich or inherit money. This approach might be too easy since character and ability to manage money might not be learned. Fortunes are often lost and inheritances may not occur. Learn to earn your own money.

2. We might learn what a major company has to teach. Learn the business. Thereafter, you have the alternative of going into business yourself for your own account. This can be rough but the rewards can also be high.

3. We can work hard with intelligence and fight for the top job where we can in part control our destiny. Unfortunately, there is only one president and he is responsible to the directors and stockholders. This method requires use of mind, tact and other god-given abilities for success.

4. We can make investments and supervise so that they grow at a reasonable rate. We might strive for around 15% growth rate at reasonable risk. Some borrowed funds may be used when risk is small. Most of us should use this approach.

We can have the same lifestyle with less income from jobs or business if we receive income from investments. Successful investment and its income offers the best chance of a pleasant future.

Thousands of people offer us services which promise to help us prepare our plan for our life. The phone book contains many names and the daily mail is cluttered with offers of seminar announcements and notices of new books. The newspapers contain many ads and papers and magazines often give advice on a wide variety of subjects. We are confused by the conflicting advice unless we study the motives of advisors. They all want to sell you something. Very few specialists have the expertise and practical experience necessary to give you practical, good, sound, reliable help. Advisors are interested in making money for themselves and some are outright frauds with no interest in your well-being. We need to check their records and most of us have bankers, lawyers, accountants and religious leaders whom we know to be honest, trustworthy and possibly knowledgeable. We each need to select specialists including medical doctors, and possibly psychiatrists, in addition to those mentioned above, with extreme care after careful investigation based on their past performance records. We also must read books and learn to be our own specialists so that we ask the correct questions. Our specialists work for us only part-time and cannot possibly know our needs and expectations as we do. The wealthy can hire full-time, good specialists in various fields of expertise to handle financial, legal, social, medical and public relations problems so that they obtain services which are not available to the average citizen. Most individuals must obtain the knowledge to handle our own simple affairs alone with the aid of part-time specialists. This need causes us to become better managers but we must make the effort. Be your own expert so that you properly evaluate your advisors and others.

We can make a plan for our life if we so desire. Many advisors will help the poor at reasonable cost. As a start, you might read the remainder of this text to become familiar with some of the basic concepts and basic rules needed to develop discipline and create your plan. No product is being sold and you alone must decide whether the suggestions made herein are of value to you. We each react as individuals and we each have different needs and desires. Our plans should differ to meet our needs as individuals. The advisor's need to make money causes him to concentrate on financial planning and few people help you by giving advice on lifestyle, medical and general living aspects of life.

Your plan should be in writing so that you can refer to it as needed and make revisions when necessary. Revisions should be few unless major changes have occurred in your life. Plans generated by computer do not meet your needs since no computer program can be flexible enough. Your plans must consider and be subject to restraints placed on it by your neighbors, law, the worldwide community, your developed social abilities, and by your business abilities which provide money for living and savings. Decide what you want. Your behavior will change when you realize that you will receive a benefit. The following ideas have been accumulated over a lifetime by reading.

LEADERSHIP TECHNIQUES

People, like all animals, have a "pecking order". There are leaders, there are workers and there are "drones". We are individuals with different ideas ideals, desires, habits, demands and goals. We each have choices and leaders have the most choices since they make and enforce laws and moral codes.

Leaders usually earn more money and they receive more honors. The leader is at the top of the human chain of command and exercises the authority associated with leadership. The leader makes things happen in our nation, community, schools and churches. Leaders also control the business world. Do you want to be a leader? Do you have the necessary discipline, drive and will to meet the challenge? Can you be considerate but firm and possibly harsh when necessary?

A real leader can change a community and nation. An example of the use of drive and willpower may be seen in public housing projects. Leaders may not have money or education but with drive and an ability to obtain cooperation, he or she can convert Federal Housing Projects into desirable places to live. The group simply generates a sense of pride which causes homes and apartments to be maintained and look attractive. They have no crime since the residents are appreciative of help given and strive to improve their lives and surroundings. They will not tolerate crime.

In other similar situations, houses and apartments have broken windows and crime makes living very uncomfortable. Leadership is simply lacking and residents do not join forces to maintain social control over their surroundings. Government bureaucrats often get in the way and keep the residents from developing the necessary organizations. As a result, the living standard of American Indians and Federal Housing Projects is extremely poor. The government experts mean well but they depend upon book knowledge and they do not understand the people nor their wishes. The experts do not use common sense and they have not learned skills of leadership which includes "how to handle people". Often the poor people know what they want and need and simply need to be motivated and shown "how to handle problems" so they can do it their way.

Poor leadership of nations can lead to worldwide disaster. The result may be war, famine, mass murder and worse. The common thread present usually is dictatorship, socialism, excessive control of people and business by a few managers, lack of savings, use of loans for food rather than industrial construction and a very rapid movement of people from the farm to the cities. Poor living conditions in cities causes civil disorders, repression of rights of people in an effort to control order and major corruption of government by a few leaders who seek wealth and power and are not replaced nor controlled by anyone. The government bureaucracy expands as leaders attempt to retain control by giving jobs which are not productive to everyone. Aid money is spent on food and the business effort and industry are restricted until it cannot function. Eventually the country becomes bankrupt morally and financially. The industrialized nations return to a rural economy with no exports or industrial goods. Is the United States drifting in this direction?

The number of great leaders is very few. Most people in leadership positions are average and many are inferior because most of us do not accept our responsibilities in the community. What does it take to be a great leader? A leader wants the job and accepts responsibility.

At the start of the industrial revolution about 100 years ago, owners and their managers used a strong stick and workers jumped. The worker did the will of the "boss" and did not ask questions. The "BOSS" had the money and he controlled the community.

Workers became more qualified with experience and began to question the methods used by the "boss". They continued to follow instructions but they tactfully made suggestions which honestly tried to improve the tools and techniques used in the plant and office. Leaders, too, recognized that many ideas of the workers were good and that productivity was improved. The "new ideas" made managers look good and they made money for the organization. Workers were paid for suggestions placed in plant "suggestion boxes". Workers did the will of the "boss" and the "boss" learned to pay by techniques known as "the carrot and the stick". The relationships often were verbal and based on "gentlemen's agreements". Union contracts became prominent in the 1930's depression to comply with new laws. The relationship between worker and management became more formal. With time, the process became wasteful as restrictive work rules and high wages were negotiated. During the 1980's, living standards in the United States are under severe strain as we try to adjust to lower standards existing elsewhere in our "one world type economy".

This Transactional leader, who developed to negotiate with unions, recognized what subordinates wanted and tried to accommodate union pressure with high wages at the expense of high prices to the customer. Efforts of subordinates were rewarded with money, promises of advancement, high status, praise and "feather bedding". Negative "rewards" were few since wages were based on service rather than on merit under terms of negotiated contracts. The leader could give merit raises to the management team and salaries, too, became very high. The leader could praise work "well done", he could recommend pay raises, bonuses for superior work if permitted under contract. He could also ask superiors for promotions and he could give public commendations and recognition. He was able to punish by calling attention, usually in private, for failure to meet standards and to withdraw management help. A worker might be dismissed when cause was sound and after following lengthy procedures specified in laws and contracts.

The "transactional management" works best when performance can be measured accurately, when results depend upon effort and skill and when work is repetitive and tedious rather than varied and dependent upon sound thinking and decisions. Well-defined goals and reward systems can arouse motivation in a worker providing the management is able to give tangible rewards for meeting the goals. Unfortunately, the leader must be very cautious and comply with terms of contracts when setting goals with workers, when explaining conditions, when checking progress, when encouraging, when criticizing, and when simply talking with workers. The relationships often are very formal and strained because implied terms of contracts are not well-defined and the legal consequences are very severe. In extreme cases, the entire process becomes a policy of confrontation rather than one of cooperation and quality and quantity of output deteriorates. The result is loss of market to foreign competition. The process can be reversed when all involved recognize that the group will destruct unless everyone works together to produce a product having good quality at a reasonable price to meet the competition in the worldwide marketplace.

In the 1980's environment, many employees are college educated and they demand greater independence. Many highly qualified specialists want to be treated as individuals. They are paid to be creative and think. Their best ideas often occur while they are in bed, while they are relaxing and possibly while driving a car. The "time card" check-in does not apply to them. Management must encourage them to think rather than to work during eight hours at a machine. Such workers must be stimulated intellectually, must be excited, aroused and inspired to a vision of what they might accomplish with extra effort. Workers must be encouraged to think independently and put in the extra effort to accomplish the impossible.

The leader of such a group pushes himself and his subordinates so that everyone works above normal levels of performance. They are so confident of success, they expect success and work to find ideas and tools which result in success. They have high objectives and find solutions to company problems. Everyone gives his best and beyond by extra effort. Such leaders are charismatic and workers develop intense feelings which result in a desire to work hard. They trust their ability and their leader and know that sound solutions to problems will be found. They know that people change behavior only when they are benefited thereby. Workers follow this leader when he changes jobs and companies. This type of leader is long remembered by those working with him because their life and thinking ability are substantially improved. The leader who uses the transformational system knows how to praise and reprimand in a courteous but timely manner. He deals with one problem at a time and he is always fair after listening and determining needed facts. He points out what was done right and what was done wrong, how another method could have been better and he avoids any hint of a personal attack. He always concludes all meetings and discussions on a positive note, is helpful and asks for greater, improved performance. No one is ever threatened and every effort is made to reduce hostility and apathy, and to increase morale and self-esteem. Everyone tries to improve the productivity of the team. The leader stands up for his workers and he works to improve his own knowledge and to help subordinates.

The transformational leader inspires subordinates by assignment of staffs to new projects, by asking for volunteers when projects are started, by allowing people to test new ideas in both laboratory and in the workplace. Communication is open between management and worker. Effort is encouraged by a feeling of confidence, trust and consideration for others. Such a leader does not meddle, dictate or interfere unless absolutely necessary. The subordinates are encouraged to think independently and new ideas are welcomed and tested until proven to be not applicable. Each worker is treated as an individual and is encouraged to contribute at his or her highest ability or beyond. Everyone is encouraged to work as a team member and think of new ways rather than simply use old procedures. He thinks and insists that others do likewise.

Some companies are forced to use both types of management styles. The transactional approach is used in routine plant operations while the transformational method may be used in research and management. Performance and keeping the company solvent are the goals and the management form is adjusted to accomplish this need.

Life forces each of us to be leaders. As a minimum, parents must lead their children to adulthood. Many people work in social groups and lead their community efforts and cause the groups to reach decisions. A few of us enter politics and some manage business and major community efforts. We all need to learn the tools used by leaders and we should accept our responsibilities to the community so that life is liveable.

All leaders like to work with people. They are honest and treat others as they would like to be treated. They are knowledgeable, know how to maintain discipline and they are good at communicating with others in both public and private meetings. Leaders lift our spirits and cause us to work with them as a team. They apply common sense in decisions, show appreciation for help from others and they inspire us to work beyond our wishes and ability. Leaders take risks and they motivate others by understanding their desires. They recognize the character and abilities of others and they ask others to work and to cooperate so that common goals and viewpoints are reached to accomplish projects needed by the community and nation. They inspire us to work with them.

A true leader has a sense of new visions, a sense of mission and a dream for the future. He is creative. He has a strong feel for values and beliefs. He has energy and is willing to work for others in a manner which benefits everyone. He enforces a desire for honest discipline in the office, plant and community in a routine, friendly manner. He knows how to see problems early and how to solve difficulties. He is able to use common sense and use both rational arguments and feelings to motivate people to act and follow his lead. A leader is a good manager who knows business techniques, knows facts when data are presented and he knows how to motivate others as necessary to develop new ideas and get decisions implemented into actions and accomplishments. He works for the community without monetary reward. He is proud and wants to lead others to make life more pleasant.

A leader knows how to get us to say "yes". He knows how to get us to work more often, with more effort than we wish and to get results.

Today's leaders must be alert so that unscrupulous people do not exploit others and divert our attention from defense of our freedoms. Also, to avert disaster we must make things but we must have moral control over all that is made. Society must always be in control.

A leader respects each individual employee and customer. Leaders demand excellence, superior performance and adherence to policy. Everyone feels good about themselves and their work and people want to help and contribute. A leader motivates others. Pay and rewards are made on the basis of productivity rather than on longevity. The leader is able to simplify problems, systematize the work and then delegate to others so that he can think and plan for the future. Leaders have learned that their actions speak louder than words. A leader accepts our society and its laws.

Leaders are able to combine the old with the new and are not fooled by "new ideas" which have been rejected in the past. He knows history and uses common sense. Leaders know "what to do" and "how to do". He works for people in a manner which is fair to all and uses what is good rather than "reinvent the wheel". He recognizes restatements of the old, previously discarded ideas advocated by writers, politicians and consultants. He realizes that 80% or more of what he hears is designed to serve "interests of the few who are looking out for special interests" rather than the good of all. He knows that most studies are approved to "cover up deficiencies" and cause delay in needed decisions. Many consultants are unreliable and state their views rather than search for facts. Special interest groups and politicians seek delay through studies which transfer responsibility to consultants. Studies can be "doctored" by using half truths and adjusted partial facts. Leaders use common sense and accept responsibility instead.

Good leadership results in good management. Good management considers the company money the same as their own money. They do not waste. A good manager looks for what is being done wrongly. He watches basic criteria and ratios for his company and makes corrections quickly before the damage becomes threatening. Long term growth with moderate debt rather than immediate dividends and profits must be the goal if a long-time future is to occur. Both are needed. A manager should do his job properly or new management should be found. Honesty is essential and detailed sophisticated calculations which can be manipulated suggest trouble to a good manager. He wants simple facts rather than distortions of data. If a decision is correct, execution will also be done well. Good managers try the practical but avoid the impossible and they know the difference. They know that technology is over-rated and they support only when risks are acceptable. Operations which are unsuccessful must be fixed very quickly or they should be discontinued immediately. Managers have visions but they do not approve fantasy. They know how to remove the dishonest and those who do not perform to obtain necessary results. Leaders know history and current affairs in many industries and politics. They have a broad knowledge so that they are not mislead. Leaders know that rules developed by society during thousands of years do not change very often.

It is unfortunate that you were not taught the rules of leadership while "you are growing up". Most adults do not know the rules. As a result, we do not know how to budget our time and money, how to motivate ourselves, how to generate enthusiasm, how to rid ourselves of bad habits and how to accumulate financial and personality-character assets.

Study and discard your fears. Please try. You will enjoy being a leader of your class, your social organization and your company job. Go to your library and read books related to leadership and management. Such books contain many ideas and give "how to do" ideas. Some will make sense and are good, while others will not work. After reading many books and some experimentation, you will recognize the good ideas. Make them work for you so that your lifestyle is improved and you have a better life while living on this earth. Try, act and accept responsibility. Educate yourself and keep "up-to-date" throughout life. Listen and read well.

RESTRICTIONS IMPOSED ON LIFESTYLE BY OUTSIDE FORCES
RELATED TO MAN

Outside forces such as neighbors, governments and worldwide competition influence our lifestyle. You are responsible for planning your life using restrictions placed upon you by both man and nature. If you wish to live like a millionaire, you must make millions to support your life using legal means. Competition is severe and those who start early and know what they want have a better chance of reaching designated goals. We must each recognize that our efforts will be restricted by our own ability, our emotions and our willingness to work as needed to achieve our goals. In addition, our lives are controlled by many forces which have been developed by groups. We are only one in these groups and our desires must adjust to meet demands of the group. Our income to support our desires is influenced by the economic and business environment in which we live. There are many restrictions imposed by society as represented by laws and political procedures. The natural environment, peer pressure and our friends often influence our health and moral character as well as our opportunities. We must understand and take control of these outside forces as we plan to improve ourselves to meet the needs of our proposed lifestyle.

Our ancestors were able to make a modest living — poor by todays creature comforts -- by working with their hands. Today this manual labor type of work is not available. We may work with hands with machines. Training and education are required for all work since we need to talk, read, write and handle money doing even the lowest paid type of work. The uneducated do not find work because people with education are available. Machines dig our ditches and the operator is highly skilled and paid. We should remember that many people worked for $1.00 per day during the 1930s. Inflation has changed the value of the dollar so that a dollar per day in 1930 may be around $11.00 per day in the 1980s. Taxes, too, have increased so that the proper adjustment might be about $20.00 per day. People in China are willing to work for $3.00 today and in many cases, we compete with them after they have been trained. Worldwide trading has changed the American workplace substantially. We must compete worldwide.

The economy of the United States in the 1980s is handicapped by many restraints. The first is very high wages compared with many parts of the world. We have very large debts of citizens, government and companies as evidenced by the large loans under default. We also have been depleting natural resources at a high relative rate. Our government also is unable to act and lawmakers often submit to special interest groups. We fail to understand or consider the religions and customs of other countries. We criticize our friends but overlook the same violations by our enemy. We should ask whether our free and somewhat irresponsible government can continue to survive the strains of inflation, deficits, and high taxes as we change from an "industrial" to a "service" economy. Can a "Service Economy" keep us free? People seem to have forgotten that we need to work efficiently as well as play. Everyone, managements in particular, have become greedy. Can we continue to pay $75.00 to $250.00+ per hour to managers, lawyers and consultants? Should we be making the investment in plant and machines to reduce management and labor cost so that we can again become competitive in the worldwide economy rather than allow our jobs to go to others who work in other countries? Is our entire system today a farce which cannot be sustained and needs quick correction? Will we have excess workers or will education solve unemployment as fewer people enter the 1990s workforce? Answers to these questions, decided as a group, will affect your life and life-style. We can remain prosperous.

The net results are expressed in part by the following trends. See chart on page 17.

Expenditure for much needed cleanup of the water and air environment, increasing government interference in people and company life, and excessive awards in lawsuits have contributed to fewer expenditures on new plant and equipment. A larger number of untrained youths and women entered the work-force which also reduced productivity. A change in attitude of worker also has occurred. The ethical work habits which were based on hard work and efficient production of quality products were eroded by a more carefree, fun-loving behavior of many workers. Excessive greed, lack of cooperation, and a careless attitude reduced quality and productivity. The resulting higher prices for materials of low quality contributed to purchases from other nations by citizens of the United States. New cars were imported in large quantities along with many products of lesser unit value. Imports into the United States increased rapidly while exports declined, particularly after the federal government eroded confidence by using exports in relations among nations. The United States is now the world's largest debtor nation and this debt must eventually be repaid while we pay other debts among ourselves. Although inflation is today at low values, the use of further inflation by politicians certainly must be tempting.

The gross national product and other business indexes continue to increase even after adjustment for inflation. However, the upward trends are at a slow rate when expressed in constant value dollars. Income from wages and salaries in constant dollars have often declined during years since 1970 and certainly are much less than possible maximums.

Analysis of the trends shown on the curves suggests that productivity declined from an average growth rate of 2.5% during 1948 to 1968 to around 1% during 1968 to 1984. The average income per family unit increased from $17,000 in 1955 to $26,000 in 1970, increased at a slower rate to $28,000 in 1972 and has since declined to about $26,000. Wages and salaries of many workers has remained constant or declined since 1968 when expressed in dollars having constant value. Most of us fail to realize that the dollar in 1986 will buy goods which could have been bought with $0.50 in 1967. The depreciation of the dollar has been very substantial regardless of the index and adjustment thereto made by various analysts. Savings of the retired often are eroded by inflation because they do not know about money management. The workplace has changed. Individuals today perform little "manual type" labor. Machines have improved living standards but the cost has been high in many aspects of life.

A fun-loving society causes low quality, low productivity, poor morale of

TRENDS IN PRODUCTIVITY, IMPORTS, EXPORTS
AND PERSONAL INCOME

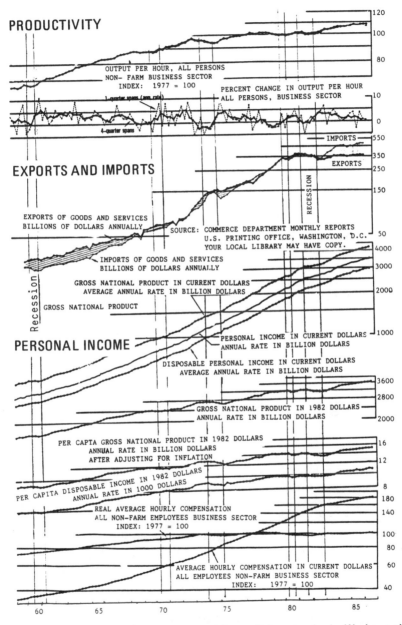

PRODUCTIVITY

OUTPUT PER HOUR, ALL PERSONS
NON- FARM BUSINESS SECTOR
INDEX: 1977 = 100

1-quarter spans (ann.rate)

PERCENT CHANGE IN OUTPUT PER HOUR
ALL PERSONS, BUSINESS SECTOR

4-quarter spans

IMPORTS

EXPORTS AND IMPORTS

EXPORTS

RECESSION

EXPORTS OF GOODS AND SERVICES
BILLIONS OF DOLLARS ANNUALLY

SOURCE: COMMERCE DEPARTMENT MONTHLY REPORTS
U.S. PRINTING OFFICE, WASHINGTON, D.C.
YOUR LOCAL LIBRARY MAY HAVE COPY.

IMPORTS OF GOODS AND SERVICES
BILLIONS OF DOLLARS ANNUALLY

GROSS NATIONAL PRODUCT IN CURRENT DOLLARS
AVERAGE ANNUAL RATE IN BILLION DOLLARS

Recession

GROSS NATIONAL PRODUCT

PERSONAL INCOME

PERSONAL INCOME IN CURRENT DOLLARS
ANNUAL RATE IN BILLION DOLLARS

DISPOSABLE PERSONAL INCOME IN CURRENT DOLLARS
AVERAGE ANNUAL RATE IN BILLION DOLLARS

GROSS NATIONAL PRODUCT IN 1982 DOLLARS
ANNUAL RATE IN BILLION DOLLARS

PER CAPTA GROSS NATIONAL PRODUCT IN 1982 DOLLARS
ANNUAL RATE IN BILLION DOLLARS
AFTER ADJUSTING FOR INFLATION

PER CAPITA DISPOSABLE INCOME IN 1982 DOLLARS
ANNUAL RATE IN 1000 DOLLARS

REAL AVERAGE HOURLY COMPENSATION
ALL NON-FARM EMPLOYEES BUSINESS SECTOR
INDEX: 1977 = 100

AVERAGE HOURLY COMPENSATION IN CURRENT DOLLARS
ALL EMPLOYEES NON-FARM BUSINESS SECTOR
INDEX: 1977 = 100

workers which results in lower wages and lower living standards. We hope that
the adjustment period will be long as the one world economy grows so that
others can gain while the United States remains stable with today's living standards. A rapid change will severely influence the life of each of us. Remember

the long lines at gas stations when the "oil cartel" increased oil prices and re-fused to sell us crude because of our relationships with Israel. These will occur again with oil and other minerals unless we pay a fair price for products critical to our economy.

The physical world and its population has changed with time. The inter-pretation of the Constitution of the United States evolves accordingly. Should the interpretations of various religions, most of which were created thousands of years ago, also change to reflect the needs of a much larger population and a smaller resource base which supports people? Ideals must adapt to physical needs of the world.

Some individuals place their personal beliefs above the law of the land. They simply believe that they are correct and are morally justified in doing what they believe. They fail to recognize that we all live together and that society has found that we do not live as individuals but we live as a group. If we all did our own thing, we would not have government or society. We would simply be selfish animals fighting each other for bare necessities such as food. We must cooperate and there are few places where we can live without aid from our fellowman. A very few people who believe that they are above the general will of society will cause all of us to lose our highly prized freedoms. Those who do not obey our laws cannot be tolerated. Our system includes procedures for legal change of law and these must be strictly followed. We do not allow our presidents to violate our laws. Why should we allow individuals to do so?

We shoot a horse after it has broken a leg. Are we correct when we force a terminally ill man who has cancer to suffer needlessly for months after he has asked to be put to sleep? Do our religious leaders interpret religions correctly or are they trying to cling to the past to exercise their authority? Doctors in some countries are beginning to take a more humane approach. The written requests of the patient are honored. He or she is allowed to die with the dignity expected by humans. Suffering and pain are reduced for patient, family and friends. Costs, too, are reduced and money is made available for treating people who can be treated so that they return to a useful life of joy. Are the nation, patient and public soundly served? Medical costs can bankrupt our nation.

The world needs high moral and ethical standards and these are usually based on religious teachings. Are moral standards lowered when religious leaders refuse to accept changing needs of individuals and individuals refuse to obey the details demanded by religious leaders? Is the acceptance of religion lowered? Can religion continue to be an important factor in the life of individuals and countries when leaders refuse to adjust to meet the needs of the populace?

The airline executive demands more runways, the motorist demands more roads, and the parent demands local schools; all to be paid by government. Soon we do not have money, land or airspace. We need to accept average need rather than "peak demand". When numbers are very large and increasing rapidly, there is a time when nature places a limitation on our desires. Certainly there is no way to find enough money. Society has always allocated its resources and that need should become more critical and difficult in the future. Proper allocation of resources is essential in both personal and group or government if we are to avoid bankruptcy, higher taxes and inflation.

Heavy industry such as manufacturing of steel, and labor intensive industry such as textile manufacturing is leaving the western world. Many questions as to the effects on our life are involved. Can our country survive in times of war and will we be held hostage by other countries when we no longer manufacture our cars and the energy to fuel them and our industry? Surveys show that Americans today are content to sit in their vibrating chairs and watch television rather than get involved with survival of our way of life and issues such as nuclear waste disposal and acid rain. Are we willing to protect our country or are we so afraid of war that we surrender without a fight? Will we allow excessive illegal immigration by people who refuse to learn English and join the American system of government and business to change our basic society? They do increase our costs as we educate them in their native language, give them health care and relief from poverty when employment is not available.

As an example of the problem, some schools are forced to teach over 75 different languages to immigrants and some of their leaders want no subjects taught in English. Such children can learn a new language quickly if given support in their homes but support is denied so that they are handicapped throughout life and never enter the American system. They want U. S. living standards but give allegiance to their home countries. Can we survive with such idealistic standards? During the 1980s, everyone would like to enjoy U.S. freedoms and high standard of living but these, too, will disappear with time if not nourished and protected.

People throughout the world seek short term solutions rather than long term.

Basic industry of the United States is moving overseas at the time when people with the fare for transportation clamor to enter our country. The reason is the differential in wages and lifestyle. We have major trade deficit because the world can purchase goods cheaper from other countries than from the U.S. Our wages are higher and our plant is older and less efficient. We also have forgotten what work really involves as we savor last weekend and plan next weekend while trying to work. As an example, South Korea manufactures the Hyundai car with $3.00 per *hour* labor while the American manufacturer pays $25.00. Robots in mid-1980s work for $6.00 per *hour*. American plants, which are inefficient, take twice as long to produce a car as modern plants. China has a billion workers willing to work for $3.00 per *day*. The problem is complex and it will be solved. The American standard of living will probably be reduced in the process as some labor unions are experiencing with de-regulation in the 1980s.

The western world needs raw materials of under-developed countries. We must pay for value received which means a major transfer of wealth. Will the time period be long so that the effects on the lifestyle of western countries is small? We should recognize our problems early and find solutions.

In mid-1980s, we have large trade deficits and large imports because our labor and management costs are very high relative to other countries. Robots, which eventually may work for $3.00 per hour, may decrease U. S. costs. We must ask, "where will be the jobs necessary to purchase products made by the machines?" We have troubles and no one has answers. Few people are aware of the problem and our leaders seem not to care. It will be too late when our nation reacts to problems and our jobs and investments will be at risk. Large inflation may be the first remedy to be tried. A depression may rapidly follow. Depending upon our government, the reverse is also a possibility. We must force our leaders to forecast trends rather than react too late.

The changes related to a one world economy are many. Questions regarding the allocation of resources among countries, the relative standards of living and allocation of creature comforts among individuals and among nations, the protection of national interests and ability to protect from aggressor nations all are involved. These are political in nature but economics, too, is involved. You can add to the list and you must help solve the issues by actively participating in the democratic political process with intelligence since your life is involved. We cannot ignore the political process in a democracy.

The political and military upheavals which will result from the economic changes could be severe or minor depending upon the time interval in which the changes occur. Unfortunately, the rate of change is largely controlled by people living in under-developed countries. The United States no longer controls its own fortunes in this worldwide economy. We have depleted many of our natural resources, including oil, and we are dependent upon other countries of the world until we develop a cheap energy source — probably atomic in nature. Fortunately, we do have food if we use our oil in tractors rather than in cars. The worldwide oil cartel is an example of what is expected.

Knowledge and a job in a "depression-inflation-proof business" is our most important asset even when we are 80 years old. We, too, need good health and management ability. Today the confusion is so great that futurists forecast inflation and a depression at the same time and suggest that this is occurring today. Certainly farming and mining, including the oil business, are in a depression while other parts of the economy in United States prosper. Everything is changing as government stalls and reacts to problems along party lines. All assets can be confiscated by laws, taxes and inflation-depression as politicians react to one special interst group and then another. A national policy is needed as a guide but not as law. Your freedoms, too, are involved. Long term political consensus is needed. We need the two party system but cooperation is needed.

The history of nations contains many examples showing the demise of countries which depended upon planning by governments. Enforcement of government plans always results in a stifled and handicapped business. Congressmen, Senators, and bureaucrats all like their jobs and pensions and they crave security. They are afraid of risks, they do not think creatively, and they pass and issue many new laws, rules and regulations to secure their advancement. Soon no one knows how the laws will be enforced and business ceases to function in a manner which meets worldwide competition. The few industrial entrepreneurs who are appointed to head agencies become frustrated quickly when the large bureaucracy refuses to move and take orders effectively and they resign to take more enjoyable work in industry. Government enforcement of planning is a sure way for a growing country to commit economic suicide. The treatment given the "Grace Commission" is an example of control by bureaucrats and defeat of reform.

Are we very selfish? We borrow as indivduals, as companies and as a nation and repayment of debt is of little concern, particularly at the national government level. Are we fair when we fail the future? What type of life do we leave for our children?

The competition everywhere is very stiff. This condition has probably been true during many past generations and we should not despair. Instead we need to exceed efforts by others and learn to succeed. Discrimination in the workplace is unfair but people perform differently.

Wages do depend upon supply and demand and what we actually contribute to company earnings and performance. A successful company must pay for what it gets in return. Each individual makes a different contribution and we should not all be paid the same except when doing work where we are paid by the piece of material made which is found to be of acceptable quality. There simply are no comparable jobs or individuals and the averages should not be made available to you. You need to exceed and excell above the average to retain and obtain work. Management rightly uses many critieria or items in the evaluation of its employees and we each must determine the criteria used and work to excell in every one of them.

Our sources of income are usually three. We can work for others, we can work for ourselves by owning a business, and we can earn money from investments which we make with our savings. Our efforts in each of these endeavors require many decisions based upon knowledge, sound analysis and actions. Time is simply wasted if we study and do not act. Our actions will be unsuccessful if they are not based on sound assemblage of facts, thinking, decisions and actions.

Americans also are idealists and they do not wish to understand customs and religions of other countries. Some religions do not like modern customs. Some business cultures have, for centuries, developed a habit of gifts and bribes to get things accomplished. Americans will not change the cultures of other nations and idealists in the United States must be controlled if we are to survive.

Your lifestyle is severely affected by both inflation and recessions. Recessions and depression result in less business activity and fewer jobs. Inflation reduces the purchasing value of dollar earned, which in part is offset by greater business activity in current dollars. In constant value or real dollars, wages often decline. Save a little. Never spend more than your income. Taxes and inflation damage you.

Most people are affected by taxes. If you work in the United States, you pay Social Security taxes and probably income taxes. Social security taxes are the principle tax for lower income earners. For the more affluent, Federal and State income taxes in 1986 can approach 50% of their last dollars of earnings. This severely reduces a desire to earn more and pride is the reason for being in management. Most people also pay large sums in taxes to state, county and city governments. Taxes limit our lifestyle by taking away needed money. Tax laws distort decisions.

Federal, state, county and city governments also pass all types of laws which restrict our activities. These laws and the tradition of society limit the choices of everyone. Car speed limits, drinking age of youths, bottle caps and packaging of foods and medicines, school attendance, drunk driver laws, pollution controls, taxes, planning rules for construction, condemnation procedures for taking private proverty, criminal laws and divorce laws all take away our liberty and restrict our ideas and actions. Idealists would wish many more restrictions, while others prefer liberty rather than protection from all of our sins and actions of neighbors. DO we have too many laws?

Most of the restrictions are made into law and enforced by the leaders whom we elect. Elected officials and their staffs like the power of office and sway with the opinion of special interest groups who offer money and workers for re-election campaigns. Hopefully, politicians will try to please the majority of the voters. Unless voters use common sense and elect honest, dedicated people who work for the average citizen, democracy is endangered. The country is endangered when elected officials vote only in favor of special business groups, welfare groups who want handouts without work, environmental groups who prefer animals to humans, peace groups who favor surrender rather than freedom, and church groups who favor a single religion, etc. There are all types of demands placed on elected officials and keeping a level and fair balance is difficult. Unless intelligent, knowledgeable voters support officials and make the demands of the citizens known at public meetings, our nation is at danger.

Society allows each of us to construct our own "sand box". We can play in it as we like if we do not infringe upon the rights of our neighbors and we must obey the laws of our system.

Television, newspapers, or "THE PRESS" exerts a heavy hand by influencing voters. The ordinary citizen can gain access only by using "letters to the editor". Voting is the tool of the average person.

We are each individually and as a group to blame. We do not want to know about the problems facing us and our country. We do not vote. Our "leaders" simply comply with our wishes as a group. They cannot be true leaders because we do not support them. We vote for the beautiful and attractive rather than the thinker and the person with the will to make us recognize our problems. We do not find solutions until we recognize a problem. We want to live for today and our children can "go to hell". We do not care about the future.

We should accept what government takes and gives if we do not vote. We can participate as a simple voter, as a knowledgeable worker and as a leader. If we want to have our way, we should be a leader, possibly an elected official of a city, country, state or federal government. We become leaders when we work, using principles developed by society. We volunteer to do jobs for the community, the school and the government.

We do not allow politicians to be honest. They are forced to make many promises in order to get elected. We accuse them of "mud-slinging" when they present an opponents record in an attempt to expose false promises by citing the past record of individuals. Many problems which are not recognized arise during tenure of elected officials. We need to elect honest, capable individuals who have demonstrated good judgment throughout their lives and trust them to act in a responsible manner. The voters are responsible when government is perceived to be extravagant, intrusive and possibly corrupt. Voters elect government officials. We should not allow the newspapers and television to control our opinions. They, too, are biased.

Politicians, too, are human and they must be supported and kept informed by the average voter. Support, inform and keep in contact with your elected officials by letters, phone calls and at meetings.

Beauty is in the eye of the beholder. The tourist and miner see a deep mine and tailings pile as a thing of beauty. It furnishes something different by reminding of the past and offers jobs today. Environmentalists see an eyesore.

Lawyers often are elected to office, they make laws, they practice before judges to enforce the laws and the judges are lawyers. All professions find it difficult to police themselves and lawyers are not the exception. As a result, we have complicated laws and the average citizen often finds it difficult to obtain justice under law. Crowded courts cause delays.

The courts or judges also cause restraints on lifestyle. Activist judges interpret the laws in a manner which makes new law rather than relying upon laws passed by elected officials. Lawmakers are often slow to react to public pressure for change and the deficiency is corrected by the courts. This distorts democracy which is based upon legislators passing laws, administrators enforcing laws and courts reviewing laws and enforcement of the other branches of government so that justice is available to citizens uniformly.

Many thoughtful individuals are concerned as to whether democracy and our right to make choices and exercise freedoms can be maintained when citizens are selfish, do not vote and seem to be interested in pleasures rather than in government. The voter turnout in some elections is so small that special interest groups control elections. We each need to study the issues facing our government and vote. We need to keep elected officials informed as to our wishes. The future of our lifestyle depends upon our actions rather than on our unspoken dreams. Make yourself known. Get the facts and make your views known.

We have many problems and most can be solved by individuals working together in local community groups. There simply is not enough money for national government to solve expectations of all people. Taxes are very high and such taxes influence all decisions related to jobs, investments and individual actions. Who will pay the taxes if everyone of us decides to retire or not work? At some point, higher taxes and inflation will not be possible and society collapses. Tax becomes unfair when people join the "underground economy".

Political decisions are often based on erroneous forecasts. As an example, on February 18, 1964, the American Home Economics Association forecast the use of dishes of plastic, paper clothing and electronic home cleaning on a routine basis. None have taken place to date and the homemaker uses the same techniques as her mother or father.

24

RESTRAINTS CAUSED BY CLIMATE AND NATURE

Fossil records show that many plants and animals have flourished and become extinct during geological time. This process will continue.

The climate of the world changes slowly. Some regions are too cold to allow growth of crops, others are warm and uncomfortable to humans. Other areas are dry and subject to famine because of droughts. Other parts of the world are very wet and all are subject to floods. Natural forces often cause destruction in most parts of the world and people are affected by loss of life and property. Working with, rather than against the laws of nature seems worthwhile.

The plant and animal species probably evolved in a process known as natural selection. Scientists in the 1980s are near processes whereby new species or variations of present life can be created by man in laboratories. This may be nature's way of practical creation which is described more generally by various religions.

Weather and climate control life of plants. Birds, fish and animals eat seeds and foliage of plants. It is natural for the strong to kill and eat the weak in the animal kingdom but man protects human life and spends billions of dollars yearly to care for the weak, old and ill. Is such protection desirable when the young are incapacitated for life, the hurt live a life of pain, and the old suffer and wish to die? These are moral problems but the money aspect affects the life of each of us and we, too, may wish to die rather than be kept alive by a machine when we are old. You are affected by the moral type decisions which often are made by church leaders who carry a bias based on their beliefs. Are their opinions correct?

Legally man is allowed to kill man only by accident and in war. Accidents kill over 12,000 annually in United States in homes, and our love for cars results in over 45,000 deaths per year.

Human population is growing rapidly throughout the world and futurists worry about long term food supply. Almost 100 years are required to change direction of such growth even when children are restricted to one child per family as is done in China today.

The oceans of the world touch all land masses and air circulates around the globe. Pollution created by one country affects all.

There are long term weather as well as daily weather patterns. In the past, the earth has become cooler as well as warmer. Dust in the air from natural causes such as volcanos and major windstorms and man-made dust caused by cars and smoke tend to cool the atmosphere. Escaping freon and other CFC's are believed to affect the higher thin atmosphere and may cause radiation changes. The CO_2 (carbon dioxide) which is added to the air by burning coal and oil is expected to create a "greenhouse effect" and warm the air. Cutting trees (trees reduce carbon products in the air and increase oxygen) causes change. Sulphur and nitrogen resulting from burning hydrocarbons by industry and cars creates acid rain which is damaging to man, plants and trees. There are many unknowns but man is polluting the air and causing problems for himself. Chemicals in water and in land also are troublesome. In the western world, billions of dollars are spent yearly in "cleanup" operations. Will man change the climate of the earth and cause his destruction? Atomic war and its dust and radiation clouds are not the only worry.

We need to find a new energy source quickly so that humans, other animals and vegetation do not become extinct.

RESTRAINTS CAUSED BY LOCATION

Living costs are lower in under-developed countries. Some people retire in such countries.

Warm climates require less clothing and fuel. Moderate climates may be more comfortable. Air conditioning and gas and electric heat have moderated these effects when costs are of little importance.

Salaries are often lower in country areas in the United States but living costs are rather constant since food and materials flow freely throughout the states. As an example, school teachers in rural areas may be paid about $15,000 while teachers with the same qualifications and experience in more wealthy urban areas may be paid over $30,000. Living in small towns is appealing but a more simple lifestyle should be expected. Larger cities do have smog, traffic conjestion, noise and people, and have more restaurants, movies, and entertainment of all types. All places offer advantages and disadvantages. People have different desires. Adjustments are necessary when moving from one environment to another. The change is most noticed when moving to foreign cultures.

In todays changing world, every worker must constantly expect changes and prepare for new types of work. Changes such as loss of work, transfers within a company and the entry of robots into the workplace can severely affect lifestyles. Study and be prepared so that the changes for the worse are few and hopefully none. Be prepared to move to jobs.

We are a nation of extremes. At one period of time, we create huge piles of garbage, mine tailings and chemical residues. Later we expect people who had no part in creating the problem, and which was not recognized as a problem initially, to spend billions of dollars for cleanup. We endanger national security by vacillating between a strong military and no real protection. We seem to want the ideals of special interest groups 100% at one time and later discard the ideal completely. We do not develop a consistent policy within our country or in relations with other nations. How can we survive as a great nation when we are divided on basic needs and principles? We do need to control the greed and self-interests of our leaders, politicians and business people. We also need to decide our future. We must insist on facts, be willing to read and learn, decide and make our leaders act.

RESTRAINTS IMPOSED BY OUR ABILITIES

Our democratic society gives us an equal opportunity to strive for goals.

We are not born equal since mental and health abilities differ. We do not equally take advantage of help and knowledge and thereby further handicap our lifestyles. Our mental attitudes and the principles which we have established as guideposts of life control our instinctive reactions to problems. They also control our thought process which determines our decisions and related actions under more normal conditions. We need to improve our habits and at times re-think our objectives and our use of the tools available for our achievements.

We must interact with our friends and associates in the workplace, in social activities and in community efforts. However, our character, moral values, emotions, thoughts, words and actions are largely under our individual control. We can improve these traits if we think, reflect and work on each individual item. We can make the effort and improve our life and lifestyle. Improvements are possible. We can improve our social life and our business abilities.

Look around you. Ask your true friends for suggestions. Study your behavior so that you find items which need change. Then act to improve your ability to do your job and ability to live with others.

A willingness to work with intelligence using an ever-increasing base of knowledge is essential. Social graces and the ability to handle people are im-portant parts of any effort. We need to create an environment in which others sincerely wish to help us accomplish our goals. We need to show others that we sincerely want to help them as well. Such mutual admirations will be helpful to everyone.

We are the sum of our physiology, our experiences of life, and our values. We have knowledge, impulses, feelings, relationships, and actions. Human beings, like other animals, respond to rewards for good performance and be-havior, and we also react to penalties for poor performance. Society punishes criminals and rewards people for behavior and performance useful to others. Children at an early age learn to fear punishment and they love favors and re-wards. So do adults.

Technology has improved living standards. We also need to remember that a pleasant, comfortable and enjoyable life existed before the days of television. Social life and basic values may have actually declined because of television. It does rob us of valuable time which is needed for living a full life. We miss many of life's pleasures when we become a slave to television and sports. These tools delay the improvements in our life. We should use them for relaxation but we should keep the time spent to reasonable amounts. Everything in excess is harm-ful to you.

The world has always solved its problems. Todays problems are different but they, too, will be solved. Plan your life so that you enjoy it to the fullest. Read and keep informed so that you react. Recognize opportunity.

Our decisions and actions as a group in our community and nation will determine the overall environment in which we live. We, as individuals, control our participation in that environment. The world will continue to spin around the sun and you will be part of the "one world" society. Control your future and make the changes required for you to prosper and enjoy high living stand-ards. Learn to perform better. Go to school and read books if you want a better lifestyle. Try to simplify problems. Use your knowledge and common sense in your work and life.

Social abilities are basic to a successful life. We constantly need to review our social and business contacts and our relationships with others. We should strive to improve socially, emotionally, healthwise, and intellectually. Look around you and consider whether any of the following concepts can be used to improve your life. We each have different needs but we must recognize that society will impose its rules upon us and our actions. Also, if we manage to avoid illness and accidents, old age will eventually impose restrictions on physical abilities.

SELF-ANALYSIS

What are your desires, habits and abilities? How can they be improved? How do you improve relationships with friends, neighbors and fellow workers? How do you improve your personality? You might consider the following concepts.

We each must frequently analyze our abilities and the abilities of others. Such analysis may be private but it must be frank and honest. The dream world will not suffice. The leader must often formally review performance of others, estimate future ability. He is responsible for guiding workers. He must encourage those who underestimate their ability and he must be frank and tactful when correcting those who are overconfident. A leader improves the performance of both groups. Each of us should review each step in our work procedures and try to improve. We should recognize that self-satisfaction stifles our progress. To know ourself, we have to be ourselves. We cannot long survive when we imagine that we are someone else. Use of role models may be good but you must apply the model to yourself and be yourself. You should have ideals and dreams but your daily life must be very practical.

We must know ourselves and correct our faults, bad habits and undesirable personality traits when necessary. Do not pretend. Self-analysis gives us confidence in our natural assets and gives us the urge to correct or improve the things which we find to be weaknesses. When you give yourself a thorough, honest examination, you are thereafter able to show others the benefits of such test and they, too, may see you in a different perspective. We are wiser if we spend time analyzing how people are rather than how we wish them to be. The analysis must be honest and truthful. No lies and deceit are permitted. Analyze yourself so that your work and the handling of relations with others is improved. If we see ourselves as others see us, we know whether we are doing a good job and giving our best effort toward helping others in our family, our community and workplace. Ask true friends for ideas. Accept their criticism with goodwill and grace.

Are you charismatic? Physical appearance, enthusiasm, good humor, animation, zeal and presence of character are all essential.

Studies show that you will not change your ideas to satisfy others. You will change only after you alone decide that a change is in your best interest. As a minimum, you might read thoughts of others and use what you believe to be beneficial to your future. Please give it a try. As a start, you might read the following comments relative to character traits and general living habits. Habits related to work and jobs are discussed in that section.

Go to bookstore and library and ask for books and tapes on subjects which interest you.

Always remember that most of the good and pleasant things in life will happen because you honestly and sincerely want them to happen and you willingly and forcefully spend the time and effort using both intelligence and common sense needed to make them occur.

APPEARANCES

The world is influenced by advertising. In politics, appearances seem to be more important than facts. Many billions of dollars are spent on beauty aids and skin care. Stylish dress is in vogue by the rich and by those who wish to feel superior. However, many people are comfortable and well-dressed with more routine clothes which have been tastefully coordinated. It is required that we be attractive but "show-off" is not necessary and is often harmful. True beauty comes from within when we find contentment and happiness and exhibit these pleasant feelings in our smile, words and actions. Try to be energetic, happy and feel good and you will dress and look attractive.

There is a time for blue jeans and there is a time for formal dress. There is also a time for business wear. Know the times for each and ask associates and hosts when you do not know what is expected.

Everyone can learn how to coordinate clothes and wear jewels in a tasteful manner. Practice so that facial expressions and actions appear attractive. We become older more slowly if we eat properly, avoid excesses, take care of our skin by avoiding sun and wind, use creams and makeup. Appearance can be created with moderate expense of time and money so that you look well, are full of energy and feel a desire to cooperate. Common sense rather than vanity is the key. Do your best but remember that the person who demands perfection is often unhappy because perfection is not attainable. It causes unnecessary worry.

ATTITUDE

Our attitude determines "How we get along with others." We need to interfere less. Develop a habit of saying less than you think, particularly if you are involved in controlling others in your job, at home and during play. We should cultivate a low, persuasive voice which sounds pleasant, and we should always use tact and courtesy, with a feeling for others, in relations with others. Make few promises and you must keep your promises. Learn to be kind and encouraging, helpful and show an interest in others dreams and desires, work and play. Learn to be cheerful and help others solve problems when possible. We must keep an open mind, make decisions and take action. Explaining decisions and why to affected individuals is good tactics. Do not gossip and do not brag. Keep confidences. Do not become discouraged nor despair — learn to smile instead. Do your best and be patient. Forget about yourself and do not expect credit. You also must learn to take care of yourself while being kind to others. Learn to negotiate your salary and your relations with others. Development of confidence in yourself and knowledge of your abilities are very important.

BOREDOM

Avoiding boredom is one of our important tasks. Boredom is a state of mind that includes a number of feelings, including an inner pain and a sense of being lost in time. We are agitated in a manner similar to being lost in a forest without direction. We might feel cut off from ourselves and others, and cut off from life.

Lack of activity may be part of the problem. Our ancestors worked long hours at physical labor at the workplace and in maintenance of life, health and their property. They did not have excessive free time and they often were physically tired. Without television, possibly without radio, they depended upon family and friends for their limited entertainment. They usually were mentally and physically healthy and they had loving connections with others. Even when alone, we can have thoughts, plans, fantasies and things to relate with our present and future life. We can stand happily in long lines or sit alone thinking, reviewing memories and planning the future.

Boredom is exhibited by our actions in many ways. Some people undertake excessive risks, such as diving from airplanes, investing in very risky ventures to obtain "cheap thrills". Unfortunately, thrills are not cheap and the high risks mean disaster. Excessive risks usually end in early death or physically painful accidents which place us in a wheelchair for life. Most accidents result from automobile accidents. Failure to think before acting increases our risks at home and in the workplace.

Other people who are bored disconnect themselves from the world by excessive reading and other very private activities. They go to a party and crawl into a corner rather than mingling with others and having a good time. They refuse to help entertain themselves and others at the party. Make friends with yourself and enjoy the fun of life.

Another group always lives by the rules. They are so conservative that their lives never have any excitement. They worry too much about what might happen and their life becomes a routine chore doing the same things every day. Allow yourself some stimulation so that life becomes enjoyable; force yourself to mingle with people; use different approaches to problems; develop hobbies; go to the store by different routes and enjoy the changing scenes caused by both man and nature. See the details surrounding you. They can be interesting and stimulating. Join a group — have fun.

CHILDREN

Commitment, kindness, communication using common sense rather than emotion, tolerance, shared values and desires, mutual respect and loving keep two people married. Children need to be nurtured in a two parent home which is based on love, encouragement and a desire to help.

Children can be a joy but they are expensive in both time and money. In developing countries which do not have retirement plans, children are believed to be a source of security since they are taught to live in extended families and everyone tends to take care of each other.

Relationships with others, including spouse and children, depends upon agreement on fundamental beliefs and living habits, mutual belief that you and your spouse and children are best friends, a shared sense of values and humor, and calm management of disagreements and conflicts.

Children are expensive in both time and money and should not be conceived because of carelessness. Children require training, love and affection and usually give more to parents than the children receive.

Children are the result of sexual relationships. The unmarried should ask each other, before having sex, whether children are wanted. The following questions might be worthwhile:

1. Am I selfish?
2. Am I ready to sit home at night with wife/husband and child.
3. Am I ready for home with rent, insurance, car payments, doctor bills, sick children, dentist bills and other family expenses? Can I pay them?
4. Am I mature enough to be a parent and handle children?
5. What would parents and friends say if children are born?
6. Do I really like children?
7. Do I want to be married or at least assume its responsibilities?
8. How does my sex partner answer these questions?
9. Do each of us like a good time or will we accept adult responsibilities?
10. Am I ready for diapers, washing, ironing, cooking and family life? Answering these questions may have cooled your desire for sex. At least, you have decided to use protective devices so that pregnancy is avoided. Use condoms, which have an 85% success rate, or use other devices in combination, such as the "pill". Condoms and other devices often are not used properly. Follow instructions carefully.

Go to your library and ask for *Young Man's Guide to Sex* by Holt, Rinehart & Winston and *A Young Woman's Guide to Sex* by Henry Holt.

Do you smoke or drink? Studies show that both are harmful to fetus and young children. Do you have sexual diseases? They can be transmitted to young at birth. Do you have genetic defects? Check with your doctor to determine chances of transmitting to your children.

The pill and various shields can prevent transmittal of sperm necessary to fertilize a woman's egg in most cases and abortion is available to some so that children can be avoided. You should really be willing to spend time, money and energy required to raise children before having them. Children need two parents.

Sexual intercourse is not always safe since many diseases can be transferred between man and woman. The worst is AIDS, which can kill you within two years. These can be avoided in most cases by using shields which do not permit direct contact of body parts and do not transmit body fluids between the partners.

The unmarried, as a minimum, should take precautions to protect themselves from disease and unwanted children. Then they do not face decisions as to abortion and the possibility of AIDS, herpes, warts, syphilis, gonorrhea. Do you want these risks?

Parents must support and encourage children if their education is to be successful. Schools cannot do the job of educating children without help from parents.

COMPLAINTS

A complaint, no matter how trivial, can grow to giant proportions if it is ignored and brushed aside. The time to handle complaints and grievances is while they are small — while they are a complaint and not an important emotional issue. This rule applies to complaints made by customers, government, wife, children, husband and employees. Listen attentively to what people have to say and do not argue. Tell others what can and cannot be done about the complaint. Give others a chance to air their complaints, try to understand the others viewpoint and be certain that others, too, understand your reasons. Try to reach a compromise where everyone, in part, wins. Possibly both viewpoints are extremes to stake out positions. Every complaint is serious to the person who makes the complaint and each individual and leader also takes it seriously. Honestly talk it over and let people know that you, too, recognize the problem. Talk things over, put others at ease and try to reach an understanding. If you can use the suggestion, do so by placing it into your operations. If there are reasons for not adopting a suggestion, tell others of the reasons and try to get them to understand. Answer real complaints with action or an explanation. People who constantly complain usually have mental problems and professional advice might be helpful. No company can long tolerate a person who exhibits a constant negative to job and management. Control your complaints. Watch for recurring hints which may indicate frustration and result in severe actions. Learn to cooperate instead. Do not show temper.

CONFIDENCE

You should be confident and feel secure. You should have confidence and believe in yourself. You do have the ability and skill to handle people and solve your problems. You can properly perform any task and be successful if you use your ability and really try. You will fail if you do not honestly believe that you can do the job. You simply must enthusiastically tackle the problem with all of your energy, believing that you can solve your problem within a reasonable timeframe at acceptable cost. If you do not have the knowledge today, start your task by reading, studying and contacting others who have the knowledge to solve your problem. Do not run away and admit defeat without trying. Each solution by your efforts and every success increases your confidence and makes solution of the next problem easier.

The author recalls the experience of a friend who needed a job during the 1930 depression. During a telephone call on a Friday afternoon, he made an appointment with a prospective employer for the following Monday. He also learned that the job required skill in typing. He never had used a typewriter but he did call a friend and he practiced 20 hours each day of the weekend on a borrowed typewriter. During the Monday interview, my friend passed all tests and walked out with a permanent job. His determination and drive resulted in a management position with a major company within a few years. Success goes to those with confidence, ability and the drive which results in efficient work. You should always try, learn and be willing to work honestly.

The timid and those with limited confidence, enthusiasm and drive should immediately study — read and reread — several of the many good books which are available in libraries and bookstores. Several classics are listed below:

How to Win Friends and Influence People by Dale Carnegie

The Power of Positive Thinking by Vincent Peale

Succeed and Grow Rich Through Persuasion by Hill and Harold

Doing a job the first time is hard but the second time is easier. We learn by doing.

You should be motivated. Learn to take necessary risks. Change your life or actions and raise your goals. You, too, can reach reasonable goals if you try hard enough, using legal means. Be confident. Stand tall, walk erect, look others in the eye, keep eyes level and hold your head level. Do not look down. Do not be cocky. Instead, be friendly, smile often and use a firm handshake.

You are urged to supplement your education in the "Art of Living" by studying books available from your library and bookstore. *The Book of Inside Information*, published by Boardroom Books, 500 Fifth Avenue, New York, New York 10110 is recommended. Also, *Living Through Everyday Crisis* by Ann Stern, Thomas More Press, 223 West Erie Street, Chicago, Illinois 60610. Also, use *The Great Book of Personal Checklists* by Boardroom Books. Subscribe to the publications *Bottom Line, Personal* and *Boardroom Reports*, Box 1027, Milburn, New Jersey 07041, so that you keep informed of changing views and new techniques.

You alone can change your character, personality and confidence in your-self. No one else can do it for you. Others can be supportive and helpful but they cannot cause you to make a change. Please work on the changes which make you a better woman or man. Create confidence in your abilities and thought-processes. Try.

CONTENTMENT

We are individuals and have different needs and desires. If we want to be happy, we must make peace with our mind, needs, ambitions and desires. Money helps satisfy physical, creature-type needs but you cannot buy happiness. You must want to be happy and adjust and work to accomplish that goal.

You might learn the art of living with others in a complicated and populated world using the rules developed by society during thousands of years. To live peacefully with others, you must give up a lot so that you eat, love, have shelter and safety. You probably have to give up your resentments, your anger, your annoyances, your desire to punish and your need to blame others. You may even give up resisting and others may at times win and you lose. Learn to admire and respect elders and the "boss" rather than feel contempt and hatred. You may have to cooperate and accept others as they are rather than trying to change them to your model and method of thinking. Your peace of mind, your love and work relationships, your aliveness — health — probably are at stake.

Ask yourself:

1. Do you feel free of expectations and obligations to others? You should be yourself but you must cooperate.
2. Can you make a mistake without excessive self-criticism and remorse? Do you feel guilty? Why?
3. Are you able to express anger without turning inward and reacting with blind rage? Have you learned to control your emotions?
4. Are you able to nurture yourself emotionally and support yourself materially?
5. Are you comfortable with your sexuality? Are you in control or are you drifting? As an adult, do you play too much?
6. Do you work well with bosses, teachers, landlords, and authority figures? Do you have trouble with law officers? You must cooperate.
7. Are you free from fears of rejection, disapproval, or abandonment? Always be in control of your mind, words and actions.
8. Are you fearful of being trapped by love relationships and marriage?
9. Do you strive excessively and have unrealistic expectations? Are you a slave to your work?
10. Are you good at setting limits on those who impose on you? Do others control your life?
11. Do you work through arguments rather than hold resentments? Have you learned to forgive yourself and others?
12. Do you appreciate and love life and yourself fully? Do you like yourself?
13. Do you feel fulfilled and comfortable? Do you like your house, family, environment, and work?
14. Do you enjoy being responsibie for your happiness, emotions, and quality of life?
15. Have you accepted the responsibilities of adulthood? Have you truly grown up? Are you living with rather than against accepted society? Are you part of a mature group or are you still acting like a spoiled child?

An adult has handled these questions and more, and decided to live with the world.

Our ideals must adjust to our capabilities, willingness to work, education, and our ability to live in a practical, competitive world. We must have goals and strive to accomplish. We must also recognize that goals need to be reasonable and that many of our expectations and dreams cannot be satisfied. Life includes both disappointments and success. You must want to live a happy life. Laugh and smile often.

COOPERATION

In todays complex world, we must cooperate if we are to eat, have shelter and be secure. Teamwork results in the maximum individual strength from effort expended. Our spirits are lifted when we work in harmony with others. Cooperation is vital and is the result of everyone pulling together to accomplish a desired objective. Teamwork requires and utilizes the fullest talents and ability of the group. Learn to praise others skillfully and assure them of your confidence and backing. Make reasonable requests for help if the group faces an emergency. Tell the group about the problems and work as a team to find a solution. Train subordinates and delegate responsibility and authority as justified by ability and mental attitude of individuals. Give every member a feeling of belonging and being an important part of the team. Inspire others to do their best for the good of all. A team effort is more important than modern equipment and business methods when combined with old, accepted common sense.

Few problems can be solved without cooperation, a desire to solve a difficulty and a willingness to listen and seek a mutual solution through honest compromise. These become most difficult when trust and confidence are lacking due to your past actions and words. If you have lied, stolen or otherwise "double-crossed" another, you rarely reestablish a sound relationship. The subordinate must always recognize that a supervisor has been given authority inherent in his position because he is deemed capable and that his will and viewpoint will prevail unless you can convince him that your ideas are superior. He should have an open mind but his decisions include past experience and company policy. He has the power to hire and fire and you should show respect and "goodwill". You, too, can learn the art of compromise, be cooperative and use the art of "selling". Hatred, lies, fraud, theft, and jealousy will hurt you. Do not allow these negative emotions to control your life. Each of us is only partly correct and we should all listen to others. Try to understand and compromise.

One can cooperate and, at the same time, be creative, protect self-interest, and do the correct thing. You might study:

> *Your Aging Parents* by John Deedy (Thomas More Press, $7.95)
>
> *How To Talk So Kids Will Listen and Listen So Kids Will Talk* by Adele Faber and Elaine Mazlish (Avon, $5.95). Good communica- makes every family work better, and this book teaches.
>
> *Living With Your Teenager* by Marlene Brusko (McGraw Hill, $15.95) is the book for parents of teens. Its positive approach will make adolescence much smoother.
>
> *Listen To A Child* (Addison-Weseley, $8.95); it helps parents listen to themselves, too.

COURTESY

Courtesy is good manners and is needed socially, on the job and in the home. Management should be courteous so that others will follow. Know fellow associates and be friendly. Courtesy denotes self-confidence and inner strengths needed for self-discipline. Treat everyone — from the boss to the janitor — like you would like to be treated. People who possess dignity and self-respect want to associate with others who are friendly, have manners and are courteous. Good manners develop into a habit slowly throughout life and require effort and practice. Show respect and be courteous to others if you want to be successful. Read texts by Emily Post and Miss Manners.

CRITICISM

Know how and when to criticize. Errors must be corrected immediately. Efficiency and high morale are achieved when criticisms are properly handled. Do not be a scolder but do offer constructive suggestions — not negative criticism. Talk to offenders in private — not before a group. Everyone makes mistakes, forgets and overlooks some details. People also are offended and get into arguments with others. The leader must handle such difficulties as part of his job and leaders must willingly accept suggestions and honest criticism with friendliness and grace. Instructions must be clear and given with tact. Never criticize until you have assembled all facts related to the problem. A person does not listen when criticized in public. Leaders should not be sarcastic or rude. Always try to make useable suggestions. Be friendly and let the other person know that you are trying to help him or her do a better job and become a more useful person in the workplace. Show how the suggested changes will help him advance — how company policy is involved. Sandwich criticism with praise. Be positive in attitude and try to gain confidence and respect of other person.

Use sentences such as, "I wonder what went wrong?", "One of us must have misunderstood the goals", "Possibly I failed to communicate effectively".

DECISIVENESS

Leaders and management operate in the spotlight of employee and public. Snap judgment is neither necessary nor good. However, after careful analysis of all details involved relative to a problem, decisions should be made without hesitation. A severely qualified decision often is worse than no decision. A willingness to make decisions and accept responsibility for its outcome is one price tag attached to the job of manager. Decisions and supervision are the basis of progress and success of a company. Management should quickly announce policy and decisions which set precedent. The sign of a good leader is being able to lay his hand on needed facts, have self-confidence and use his ability to grasp a problem. He then makes a decision and acts to implement it. Being indecisive can cost respect of employees and the public and often makes others reluctant to decide and act. A leader is paid to make decisions without stalling nor passing the buck to others. Committees seldom serve a useful purpose but may assemble data and viewpoints. The leader thereafter must act. When suggestions are made, welcome them. Listen to everyone and praise resourceful work and then as leader, make the decision, which is your responsibility. Insist on all pertinent facts. Make certain that they are true facts. Then analyze, make the necessary decision and act.

Our lives are determined by our decisions as individuals. Use the above process in your personal life. These techniques often work in relations with spouse and children.

DISCIPLINE

We must use discipline. The tendency to eat and drink more than needed, to over-indulge physically and emotionally, and to take excessive risks is human but all are to be avoided if we are to avoid accidents and poor health. Excesses of all types are to be avoided. Learn moderation. Learn to say "No".

Discipline is teaching and letting others know what is expected from them. The leader who establishes the right kind of relationships at the beginning will have few worries about its maintenance. Discipline is essential in any group since it is necessary to obtain effective use of time, materials and talents of every member of the work team. Learn the satisfaction of knowing that a job is well done. When discipline is based on the best interests of the people as well as the job, good discipline is automatic. Leaders in every capacity and activity must know how to take discipline as well as how to issue instruction. We must discipline our thought, deed and action if we are to relate well with others. Without judicious discipline, progress and security is impossible for either leaders or workers. Never be a fault-finder but do seek to improve and be a team member. To get what we want for ourselves, we have to help others get what they want. In so doing, we lessen the need for disciplinary action. We each find it necessary to correct people at times so that we can live in peace and conform to policy of company and society. This requires tact and courtesy on the part of the leader. Correction and criticism should take place in private between two people — not in public. We each must share the work load and operate as a team so that there is less friction. The morale of a group declines when one or more individual is allowed to not conform to the rules. A good leader is tolerant but he, too, is always alert to any attempts of people who try to take advantage. People react favorably to strength and they respond to it. A leader must live by the rules and set an example. Others will follow the lead and this reduces the need for disciplinary action. Discipline is self-control and associates with confidence. Have confidence in yourself and in those with whom you associate — be a leader.

We must teach and discipline children.

EGOISM

Egoism is an exaggerated sense of self-importance and conceit. We have developed habits so that we are haughty, inconsiderate of others, and we like to talk too much and take advantage of others. We become very self-centered and damage ourselves because our neighbors and friends do not like our habits, or character. They may refuse to work with us, not trust us and avoid us when possible. They cross the street to avoid saying "hello".

Some egoism and pride are essential to success and well-being. We need drive to accomplish and strive for our goals. However, control of our words, actions and emotions is the key. As in all of life, moderation, a little thought about effects on others and a concern for nature are essential. The egotist needs help but help cannot become available unless he recognizes difficulty and asks for help. Often we have the willpower to help ourselves and make necessary changes in our thoughts and actions.

EMOTIONS

We each, at times, become upset with ourselves and those around us, usually because of events which occur to disturb us. Others should not be allowed to cause us to feel guilty. Tempers, words and actions must be controlled. We should not raise our voice, frown or otherwise become upset. A solution to our problems must be found immediately and we should not blame others for our upsets. Get upset if you must but try to do so in private and work so that an immediate solution to the problem is found. Being mad — possibly being in a trance-like mood — will cause others to avoid you. Smile. Temper, lack of emotional control and tears should be used to relieve stress but please do so in private. Write your thoughts and then tear up the paper. Do not talk with others when angry or when depressed. Be cheerful instead.

Think of nice things and work out a joint solution with others. Like yourself and your life and little problems will not upset you as much. Be happy and joyful as you spend each day to lessen your tensions at home, at office and at play. Try not to show your damaging emotions in public except when absolutely necessary for effect and control. Get the bad emotions out of your system before relations with others and your health are affected.

EXPECTATIONS

Our expectations usually far exceed our income and ability. Our role models, the movie stars and sports figures, disappoint us when they take drugs and become greedy after they have millions. We can improve ourselves and become our own role models if we really try. Fortunately, the young rebel is often tomorrow's conservative. We grow up and mature so that we can face the real world. With age, we tend to recognize that the privileges of youth also include adult responsibilities as we are forced to depend upon ourselves rather than our parents. World hunger, disease, drug abuse, violence, greed and corruption are problems which have plagued many past generations and they will not be solved until the entire world accepts similar ideals and agrees to accept democratic principles. This is an unlikely prospect and we must strive toward the ideal but be content with reality. Life becomes easier after we learn to handle ourselves in difficult situations by showing confidence, dignity and class. We use words which reduce tensions between people and within ourselves. We respect our dignity but also respect rights of others and find ourselves making compromises rather than fighting. We work for good but accept the practical.

Problems encountered when raising our children cause us to appreciate our parents past efforts when we were the children. Criminals seem to accept the world as it is after age 40 years. They take jobs which were unacceptable during youth. We each seem to learn and attain a degree of common sense as we age. We recognize that society and its rules are good.

EXTREMES

Individuals and our nation are severely handicapped because we act as if every idea is a matter of black and white. Most ideas and facts deal with "grey areas" and often there is no true answer. There are always many qualifications or alternate solutions to our problems. Often several methods reach the same benefits in about the same time period. The solution often is to take some action which creates movement in proper direction so that problems are finally solved.

We react to a "new idea" by demanding immediate adoption without any amendments or changes because some study — often made by a very biased special interest group — seems to prove the idea desirable. A few years later, the study is discredited by a better designed study. Newspeople blow a study out of all proportion because it sells advertisement time. As an example, 15 years ago everyone agreed that selling dry foods out of the barrel was unsanitary although practiced throughout many generations when packaging materials were not readily available. The idea made sense but in mid-1980s, we see the practice again in all large grocery stores. We are forgetting common sense and inviting poisoned food by "cranks" as our stores follow the leader for customers. Competition is good but it, too, damages when common sense is forgotten by the buyers.

Another example involves our garbage. In past years, we have created large piles of household waste, industrial chemicals, mine piles, etc. without any complaints. Today we expect them to be "cleaned up" immediately. Some are real problems. Others are in the eye of the beholder and special interest groups and really are not troublesome to most people. The backpacker wants wilderness for his personal use and does not care about the needs or use of the majority who may not be physically able to see the scenic spots unless transportation is available to it.

We need to use a little common sense and recognize the needs of the majority rather than minorities. Everyone should have a chance to use our public land, its laws and the benefits of society if they honestly make the necessary effort in a reasonable manner. We need to set priorities and common goals and then act to attain them rather than vacillate between extremes. Being "hot" today and "cold" tomorrow is not desired. Good personal and country-wide policy is not created by such actions. They also are costly and confusing.

Voters need to change the attitude of both politicians and business executives. Politicians need to think about the long term good of the United States rather than getting elected. Voters need to do the same. Business leaders also need to think about the long term needs of companies rather than selfish interests. Maximizing stock values today may not be good when long term debt damages well-being and future of the company.

FEAR

We each live with some fear and moderate fear is desirable. Most of us fear the courts and we live legal lives. We fear disappointment and find success. We want friends so we cooperate. We fear being lonely. We fear the unknown which may be a mixed blessing.

Fear can be very damaging when we fear the imagined and fear events that never happen. A vivid imagination can cause us to fear life. We must control our fears and try to relate our life with other emotions if we are to remain in good health — mentally and physically. We should train ourselves to want to do good because of enjoyable feeling rather than because we fear the condemnation of our peers. Uncontrolled fear leads to extreme stress. Good health requires that we recognize that most of the events which we fear will never occur. Our fears and concerns should not cause us to worry unnecessarily. Do not allow fear to interfere with a useful lifestyle. Reduce the risks instead.

Take charge of your mind and control your fears.

FRANKNESS

Good leadership is good salesmanship. There is a vital difference between brutal frankness and tactful honesty in contacts with people. Being straight-forward counts heavily in human relations and is essential when getting others to work as a team. We each need to admit mistakes when they are made and mistakes must be corrected. It is not necessary to discuss faults with others, if they have not caused a problem. Instead we should privately correct our faults. We should clarify our thinking process and develop better habits so that our mistakes are reduced. Be honest and frank but do use tact, goodwill and be decent when dealing with others. Define problems in utmost detail, think clearly and treat others as you would like to be treated under the circumstances. Being frank, honest and straight-forward with people is being fair and decent. Discuss the facts with others in a calm, collected manner; get the others view-point and explain reasons for your actions with those affected thereby. Cus-tomers and employees and friends will understand and respect you when you are honest, sincere and decent in your relations. Do not be blunt, curt or tactless. Be friendly and considerate.

FRIENDLINESS

The one thing that the whole world wants and will pay plenty to get is friendliness. Make being friendly a daily habit. Smiles, guarded speech, and discretion in your actions should be a habit. Feel good and do not complain. Act like a friend and others will be friendly, too. People will overlook many faults if they can be among people they like and people who show an interest in them. Workers help leaders who are friendly. Confidence and mutual respect are based on friendship. To have true friends, you must be a good friend who is believed and trusted. A company financial statement often is sound because a friendly management instills a high morale in the workplace.

Do your friends have desired qualities? Men and women seek (1) kindness and understanding, (2) intellligence, (3) physical attractiveness, (4) exciting personality, (5) good health, (6) adaptability, (7) creativity, (8) desire for children, (9) good education, (10) good heredity, (11) good earning capacity, (12) neatness and good manners, (13) religious principles, (14) moral principles – honesty.

We may rebel but in the real world we are judged by our friends and associates. Choose carefully.

Others look at the company you keep as part of their judgment of your reputation. Your friends also influence your thoughts and actions as well as your lifestyle.

FUN

Life is full of pleasures but we must make the effort to make them occur,

40

to recognize the beauty and pleasures and to participate in life. Fun is one of such pleasures but usually involves entertainment and amusement. Fun has an important place in our life since it furnishes relaxation from stress but we also must recognize that life needs more substance than fun. All work and no play makes Jill a dull girl but all play and no work usually means a low standard of living — often no food. We must earn the money to live and play. If your work is not fun and pleasant, change your attitude or find other employment. Life does include disappointment.

Life is more pleasant when we have a number of interesting activities. We might read, listen to good music, join a discussion group, play games, participate in active sports, listen to radio, and see movies and television when programs have substance. Learn to enjoy as many activities as needed but do remember that excesses waste time and money. Select with care. All of our efforts should be analyzed at routine time intervals to determine whether some habits should be discontinued and replaced by more entertaining and useful activities. A reasonable question is whether or not an activity results in true joy and pleasure. Do our actions fit into our changing lifestyle or are the activities simply "holdovers" which are continued because of peer pressure? As an example, skiing may be a joy at age 20 years but skiing may be a fear of broken bones at age 70.

Most of us enjoy the fun parts of our lives. We often return to work tired and unable to do a days work after a weekend. Also, our work may be less than expected because we plan our fun while at work. We discuss past fun with others at the workplace and we make future plans when we should be devoting all of our energy to our work effort. We thereby jeopardize our employment and we increase our chances of an accident. Such waste of time is not fair to our employers and if not limited can cost us promotion and our job. Like everything else, our fun and pleasures should be reviewed routinely and must be controlled.

Joy and pleasure often result from an unexpected hug, by being with loved ones, loving others, seeing sports on television and on the field, by catching a fish and doing a good days work at the office.

A day at the beach or lounging around the pool is relaxing and is required to relieve stress. Accidents and sunburn must be avoided so that pleasure is not replaced by suffering. Fun is enjoyable but it is a rather shallow effort to displace our worries. We also need to handle our problems and worries so that stress does not occur and the need for relief does not exist. Remember that pleasure and joy can be obtained from a good book, discussions with friends and some of these activities can be beneficial during a lifetime rather than just a few hours.

HAPPINESS

Happiness is an idea referring to the state of the human mind. The hermit and the poor have been very happy when a fence is placed around the world and individuals honestly believe that they are doing what was intended for them to the best of their ability. They truly enjoy their work and life. Often the rich, particularly those with an ambition and an inquiring mind, are very unhappy —

largely with the world around them — although they live in utmost luxury.

Most individuals recognize that we each have an obligation to use our intelligence and ability so that the world is a better place when we die than when we were born. To do otherwise equates us with other animals. Fun has its place in each life but we also have responsibilities to the world.

We are happy because we strive for happiness. We are pleased and happy because we want to be and because we direct our thinking and work habits so that we are mentally capable of being happy. We must learn to smile rather than frown. Look for the pleasant side.

Learn to be happy with your decisions. If results indicate an error, make necessary changes as soon as possible. Change of job and location become difficult with age. There are many reasons for individuals and companies to hire the young rather than the old for most work.

We each need to "keep up-to-date" and accept change if we are to find contentment. The world changes and we must adapt to new inventions, discoveries and ideas while fighting for our moral standards.

HEALTH

Your health is your greatest asset since with health you usually can find work. How do you protect your health? Our bodies age with time. Physical hurts and pains cause us to change our physical and mental activities.

Our health is the result of a complex interaction of our foods, exercise, emotions, fears and actions. Sometimes disease and a breakdown of our defense mechanisms causes us to be ill. We often can be more healthy if we follow practical rules developed by man during thousands of years.

A.   Avoid accidents. Live your life so that you reduce chances of being hurt. Foolish actions — not thinking before you act — often cause accidents. Most accidents occur in and around the home and yard but the car is the cause of serious accidents. We tolerate 45,000 auto deaths a year but we often spend billions to avoid a few deaths in industry and on items which cause many fewer deaths from disease. Our love for cars distorts our thinking but we should each individually recognize the car problem. Excessive thrills such as jumping from airplanes and riding motorcycles increase your accidents.

B.   Avoid extremes. Extremes in living habits do reduce your life. Excessive weight, smoking, unrelieved stress, etc. reduce health and life. Excessive alcohol and smoking have been related to heart, liver and lung diseases. They cause physical abuse of men, women and children when control is lost over mind and emotions.

C.   Favorable image — like and believe in yourself so that you achieve goals and have confidence.

D.   Exercise. Walk and use your limbs in daily activity. Workout regularly if possible. Aerobic exercise reduces depression and is helpful if properly performed.

E.   Love. The warmth and enjoyment of other people is desired. Like the companionship of spouse and friends. Many women enjoy love-making without sex.

42

F.　Sex. Most healthy individuals dream of sex and enjoy memories. Learn to trust, touch, tease, take time and talk about sex in bed with your partner. Saliva is a satisfactory lubricant.

Sex between many partners in our liberated society reduces our ability to love and increases spread of diseases such as AIDS, which can cause death in a few years, herpes, warts, chlamydia, papilloma virus — cancer and other sexual diseases which have always plagued man. Use shields so that no body fluids are exchanged and there is no body contact of sexual organs, mouth, etc. if you make love with people whose history you do not know.

G.　Eating. Eat frequently in small amounts. Your largest meal should be at the beginning of the day. Eat light evening meals. Eat a variety of foods and eat balanced meals as suggested in nutrition books available in your library and bookstore. Do not be a faddist nor food stuffer. Use your willpower and keep down weight. Limit alcohol to rare special events. Don't drink as a habit. Limit drinks to one or two times each week or for special occasions with friends. Diet has been linked to heart disease, stroke, diabetes, arteriosclerosis, liver diseases and other ailments.

H.　Drugs. Never use drugs except when absolutely necessary under the supervision of your doctor. Drugs usually are harmful to you even when prescribed by a doctor and they reduce the effectiveness of medicine when actually needed.

I.　Sleep. People who live a long, happy life do not have sleep problems. You must respect your rest needs and be certain that you sleep as needed — usually 7 to 8 hours daily for most people. Do not borrow from your sleep time. Organize your day and work schedule instead.

J.　Leisure time. Enjoy the outdoors and do some work with your hands. Do not ignore a necessary balance between work and leisure or nature will take control with a heart attack, an accident or other calamity. Learn to read, watch television, relax, exercise, play games so that stress is removed daily. Visit with friends.

K.　Work. We must work to finance living and play. Try to find work that is enjoyable most of the time. You must develop habits so that you enjoy work, savings and play.

You need to enjoy your life and this requires that you:
1. Do not allow things to drift. Do something about your unhappiness immediately. Settle an argument quickly and learn to live with other people.
2. Confront your fears as they arise. Once you decide what is bothering you, do something about the situation. Take required action — solve your problems immediately.
3. Don't blame others. Take responsibility for yourself and your thoughts and actions. Get a perspective on your problems — be objective and find solutions.
4. Live your life so that you are comfortable. It is easy to find happiness for a brief time by ignoring your troubles and avoiding situations which cause discomfort but this is no solution. Seek long term

solutions to problems and do not simply walk away if the problem is important. You grow by solving your problems and using the experience another time.

5. Do something for others. If you concentrate on others, you will not have time to think about yourself and largely-imagined problems. Join a service group and help mankind in need.

6. Arrange for some privacy. Everyone must have someplace where they can be alone and relax and think. Do not allow others to demand all of your time. Have some space where you can be alone.

7. Learn to think and make decisions. An error can be corrected but constant worry will kill you. Get facts, decide and act today rather than worry.

8. Give in to others even when you think that you are correct. We all make mistakes but a grudge is very dangerous. Try to negotiate a compromise where everyone wins.

9. Work off anger quickly. Face the problem and find a solution. Take action, take a walk, punch your pillow, do some physical labor but get anger out of your mind.

10. Do not be afraid of failure. Take a few risks but try and do your best. Plan, work hard, think and look forward to success.

11. Don't be a perfectionist. Do your best but be reasonable. Others will do things somewhat different than you but their job, too, can produce good results.

12. Respect yourself. Others tend to accept your opinion of yourself. Be proud, feel worthy and good about yourself. You earn this right by good work and relations with others. Study the third edition of *Take Care of Yourself* by Drs. Donald M. Bickery and James F. Fries (Addison-Wesley).

13. Find security. You need to find someone upon whom you can depend emotionally. You have to find a way to survive and save for a "rainy day". Work or go to school to survive. Don't despair.

14. Take action. Assemble facts needed to make a decision and act instead of worrying.

15. Change your environment. If you cannot stop worrying, break your living cycle with a vacation. Release a tense feeling by going out for an evening. Take a walk in the park in the daytime. Avoid attacks by being careful.

16. Learn to relax. If you feel fatigued, stop what you are doing and relax for 15 minutes. Release your tensions by letting arms and legs go limp. Continue with other parts of body. Close eyes and allow mind to wander. Relax.

17. Do one thing at a time. You can really only think about one thing at a time, so close the door and tackle the important project. Complete it and go on to the next. Reach a decision and then live with it until experience proves it wrong. Then be flexible and change.

18. Change your routines. Change the route you take to work, change

supermarkets, etc.

19. Talk to a friend or read a book. Stop thinking about your problems except at your office.

20. Make overtures. Others, too, are lonely. Seek out a friend, go out and greet the world. Be sensible in your actions and be careful. Do meet people in safe environments and try to develop sound friendships.

21. Stop feeling guilty. Stop feeling sorry for yourself. You may not have caused the problem. Others may have contributed. You never should blame others for your unhappiness and dark moods. Cheer yourself and start looking ahead to new experiences. Do not look back except to avoid the same mistake another time. Do your best and have no remorse for failure. Learn and try to do better next time. Be confident.

22. Learn to be fair. Treat the "boss" and the janitor as you would like to be treated. They both should like you and you should like them. You need each other for mutual success.

23. Be friendly. We need the help of others. To remain healthy, we each must learn to enjoy our work — at least tolerate it — and we each need true friends. Friends help us to experience what it means to be alive. True friends enjoy each others company and do not need to always be doing something. The need for excessive outside activity such as parties, going to movies, going to the beach and mountains, etc. usually indicates a lack of true friendship. True friends exchange understanding at a deep level and truly enjoy being together without need for outside activity. Going places together is supplemental when admiration, trust and other emotions have been established. Friendship is built upon acceptance of ourselves as we truly are and then presenting ourselves to others in a way that they believe to be genuine and real. The selfish and those who emotionally and intellectually never advance beyond adolescence seldom have true friends. To sustain friendship, you have to be vulnerable and make sacrifices. If you choose isolation from hurt, you are also choosing loneliness rather than true friendship. Happy people are optimistic, courteous, well-adjusted, socially active and think highly of themselves. They are not braggarts nor overly selfish. They are confident, competitive, energetic, self-reliant and have the drive necessary to be successful. The main reason for unhappiness is expectations which are unrealistically high and unattainable. Strive for a better life but do be realistic. Attitude controls emotions and life.

24. Control fear. Too much fear is not good. Recognize that some fear is good. Fear keeps us from commiting crimes, taking unreasonable risks, etc.

25. Organize. Plan your day in advance. We need to protect our health by being smart. We need to force computer personnel to furnish a

list of desired data on a single page, possibly on a graph, rather than hiding the data within a hundred pages of figures. We become frustrated when we search and read too much data to find desired information.

26. Do not overwork. Recognize your limits. Most people who work long hours are not properly organized and do not delegate properly. Some jobs require work weeks of 60 hours because of the mass of data needed to make decisions. They should hire people whom they trust to prepare shorter summaries and delegate authority. Good decisions require a clear mind which often relates with adequate relaxation and rest.

You can overwork and worry so much that mind and health are affected. A good worker may lose interest in the job. You, as supervisor, must determine the cause and find solutions. The causes may include:

(1) A change in interest of the employee. Alcohol, drugs or a simple change in mental attitude may occur. The employee may have accepted a job for the wrong reason. As an example, he may have wanted more money and status but he may not want the added responsibilities. The employee may actually "NOT WANT TO PERFORM".

(2) The employee may not be properly trained for the job. He simply "MAY NOT KNOW HOW TO DO THE JOB".

(3) The employee may be frustrated because "HE IS NOT GIVEN A CHANCE TO DO THE JOB". He may be intimidated by others, colleagues and subordinates may not cooperate, he may lack authority to do job, incentives may be insufficient, others may play favorites, money to do job may be lacking, information to reach decisions may be withheld, other demands of the job may not allow time to do all the needed work, others may not do their share, etc. Always remember that superiors, including teachers, business associates and community leaders, want you to be only average. They, thereby, look better and often their job is easier. Try instead.

(4) The employees stability may have declined because of stress such as a death, overwork, lack of organization and many other factors.

(5) Workaholics may simply burn out due to excessive work which may be perceived or real. Better training and organization, other help by specialists may solve the problem if recognized by supervisors. Unresolved stress can kill a good worker. A true vacation is needed when the employee shows such strain. Ask yourself:

Is pressure to succeed always present?
Does a feeling of being tired always exist?
Is fatigue rather than energy present?
Does boredom exist? Can a feeling of job excitement be created?

Do friends annoy you? Do they ask about your health because of concern about your health and behavior?

Are you working harder but accomplishing less?

Is one area of your life disproportionately important to you? Is your life un balanced?

Are you increasingly cynical and disenchanted?

Are you unable to truly relax?

Are your opinions more inflexible?

Are you sad but cannot find reason?

Do you forget appointments, deadlines, personal possessions? Are you absentminded?

Are you irritable? More short-tempered?

Are you disappointed with other people?

Do you fall apart when job activities do?

Do you worry about your image excessively?

Are you too busy? Do you return phone calls, read required reports, newspapers, etc.?

Can you laugh at a joke about yourself?

Have you been saying less and less about people?

Do you feel disoriented?

Do you continue to work when others go home?

Are your goals unclear?

Do you work on one job at a time? You always should.

Do you jump among jobs and ideas?

Is joy elusive? Work should be fun. More fun than play.

If there are many "YES" answers, arrange for a change, a vacation, determine what is wrong. Replacement of a trained and trusted employee is costly and a supervisor should seek out the cause so that poor performance can be corrected. Likewise, loss of job is costly to the employee and he should improve his performance. The same naturally is true regardless of gender, race or creed. A trained employee is valuable. The income is essential. Enjoy your work.

Maybe exercise will offer a change of pace. Write for "Getting Fit Your Way", Dept. 36-TL, Superintendent of Documents, Washington, DC 20402.

We might benefit from reading *Intervention: How to Help Someone Who Does Not Want Help* by Vernon Johnson, Johnson Institute Books, 570 First Avenue N., Minneapolis, Minnesota 55403.

27. Control stress. Reduction of stress is important. The medical profession is again relearning that our health and well-being are controlled by our individual actions and emotions. A happy mental attitude is essential. We need friends, ambition, pride in our work, a desire for accomplishment and must actively work at being happy and healthy. We must have faith in our ability and strive for goals which are reasonable. We must have reasonable desires and lifestyle.

We must learn to live in an adult world. We must grow up and not react as children. We must accept rules of society to further our interests. We cannot walk away from life and others who live near us. We simply must adjust and live as happily as possible in our environment. The world does not depend upon us for its existence but we individually need neighbors.

Human beings must have some stress to function. The stress response galvanizes us to action. Stress is the spice of life because it makes life more interesting. However, unrelieved stress can be very harmful. Success during our work and play relations is dependent upon control of excessive stress.

Stress is caused by change and our failure to accept change. Divorce, disease, death, sex, challenge at work and home, fear of events, unresolved fantasies all contribute to stress. Failure to face life as an adult and many other factors contribute to our emotions and create stress. We need to anticipate our difficulties and to expect failures. We need to have reasonable expectations and we need to match ability with expectations.

The human body reacts to stress in three stages:

a. The alarm stage causes the body to react to perceived danger. The endocrine glands release hormones which cause a burst of energy so that the body can either fight or run away. Usually, the body thereafter reverts to normal after the emergency has disappeared.

b. A resistance stage appears if the source of stress and the perception of fear does not go away. The body does not heal itself and remains tense and alert.

c. The exhaustion or burnout stage occurs when stress is unrelieved over a long time. Your body simply runs out of energy and body functions are affected. The symptoms of too much stress include lowering of productivity, procrastination, tension, fatigue, headaches, being nervous, poor appetite, sleeplessness, worrying, abuse of drugs such as aspirin, abuse of food and sex, difficult relations with wife, children, boss and friends. Doctors are again learning what the old family doctor knew — excessive stress is the basis of many health problems. Disease is a mirror of your lifestyle and many health problems can be prevented when proper living habits are followed. Proper food, sufficient rest and sleep and control of emotions are essential for a happy, healthy, long life.

Feeling happy is the best key to alleviating stress and maintaining good health.

You can learn how to make yourself happy. Happiness is a mental attitude which can be learned and controlled. You must learn how to bring yourself joy. Do not continue to think about your hurts and upset periods. Experience the emotions of hurt and thereafter do something to eliminate the thoughts. React to your discomforts and thereafter make a decision and get the unpleasant thoughts out of your mind. Take charge of your emotions and mind rather than being a victim. You must decide that you want to get rid of undesirable thoughts and then do so by control of thoughts, words and actions. Review the situation and your thinking and determine the real cause of your unhappiness. Determine what needs to be done to correct that situation, take required action to prevent recurrence and get the situation behind you. Grow in character from the experience and try not to let a similar situation disturb you again. New ideas and thoughts in the identical situation can produce new feelings. You might even discover that the other person's approach and idea may be as good as yours.

Stress often is caused by fear. Fear usually is fantasizing about something that has not happened and probably never will happen, but you experience it as if it had happened. It is like a bad dream but it occurs only in our thoughts and we are alert. Control thoughts and live in the real world instead. You can control your thought-process if you really want to do so.

There are only two very basic emotions. These are love and fear. Anger is feeling out of control or being afraid. You should not try to control someone else. You may not be correct. Also, you should respect another's judgment and you should tactfully correct so that acceptance rather than argument occurs. If you do not like what someone is doing, tactfully try to reach an understanding with that person. Do not allow the situation to upset you. Find a mutual solution instead.

We naturally want people to like and love us but we should not make other people responsible for our happiness. Base your relation on mutual respect and immediately work out your differences as they occur. You generate your own happiness. Tolerate others or seek other company. Live at peace with your thoughts, live with your willingness to work and your ability. Accept the fact that you must live with others — work with others — in a cooperative lifestyle in this dependent and complicated society.

Most job-related stress relates to abilities of people to work together. How well people work together depends upon their ability to handle themselves and their emotions — both within themselves and in others. You, by your word and action, can provoke others and you can create calm. You and your boss must agree to get along and respect each other. Show your boss that you truly want to help him be a success and he may work for your advancement. Fighting with your boss causes trouble and you eventually will lose your job if the fight continues over extended time. Same applies within family.

Stress reduction techniques follow:

a.   When you are confronted with a stressful situation, first be aware of the building stress. Next say to yourself, "I am in charge". Then take a deep breath, determine the exact problem and find a solution immediately.

b.　Learn to smile more often. It is difficult to feel bad or be angry when you smile. You can do only one of these at a time. A smile reduces anger and disarms the other person as well so that his anger, too, is reduced. Many people want to feel bad and they create their own misery which often results in poor health. Some want to complain to gain attention. Some even go to the doctor for company. Find friends instead. Smiling will surprise you. You will feel better and your good feelings will influence your relations with others. They, too, will catch your smile and feel better. Be above the average. Smile freely, contagiously and often. You will grow older more slowly.

c.　Breathe slow – learn to take slow, deep breaths.

d.　Learn to think in a positive manner. Look on the good side of each situation. Your thoughts are creative for yourself and others. Your mental attitude and thought determine your response to situations which confront you during the day. If you are happy, you react more favorably to disappointments. Pleasant thoughts solve problems and make you feel good. Learn to be happy so that you make others happy. The cup is half full – not half empty.

e.　Forgive others and try to create situations in which everyone wins. Forget about having your way every time. Learn to be considerate of others. You, too, may be wrong part of the time. Inquire why others have a different opinion and reach different conclusions. You may reach wrong decisions because you have not listened and have used part of the facts. Listen, acquire all the facts, think, decide and then act.

f.　Learn to feel loved and be pleasant. Create a world in which feeling good is normal. Feel good rather than sorry for yourself. Enjoy life as you live it. Plan for the future but live each day separately – one day at a time. Read *Coping in 1980s – Eliminating Stress and Guilt* by Joel Welk, Mooer Press, 223 W. Erie, Chicago, Illinois 60610.

g.　Be proud of yourself, your family, your friends, the company that employs you and the country in which you live. Defend your basic principles and each of the above with both intelligence and vigor so that you continue to enjoy a safe, pleasant and useful life. Your failure to do so may make you a slave.

h.　Reduction of emotional stress is important. You also may wish to reduce physical discomforts by wearing proper clothing, using proper equipment such as chairs and floor coverings, assuming proper posture, etc. As an example, use of a chair might involve keeping your neck and back in a straight line with your spine, using a footrest to keep knees higher than hips, regular movement at intervals of feet, neck and shoulders. There are many ways by which you can make both the workplace and home less stressful based on physical conditions. When you hurt, every upset is a greater strain on your temper and emotions.

28. Control mind and emotions. Control your life.

Research shows that control of the mind can be used to relieve pain and anxiety, to overcome smoking, to control overeating and drinking, to conquer insomnia, to control headaches, to control emotions and blood pressure, etc. Most people simply use strong desire and willpower. Others try self-hypnosis, which may not be entirely safe unless performed under supervision of medical experts.

You should be aware of the techniques of hypnosis so that others do not use the method on you to control your actions and mind. Usually you must want to cooperate before others can hypnotize you and that is the best cue to defense when others try to influence you. Hypnosis places your mind in a trance and you must be absolutely certain of recovery before you try to use the methods on yourself and others. Always be in control.

You should not use the tapes available for self-hypnosis unless suggested by your doctors. You always should be certain that you can remove the effects when you wish. For your protection, you probably should be aware of the methods. *Consult your doctor before using.*

You should be certain that you can bring yourself out of hypnosis. You should tell yourself how you will come out of the "trance" before you start your hypnosis procedure.

Be comfortable and use normal procedures for relaxation. Sit in a soft chair and use a soft light. Thereafter, pick a spot near eye level and stare at the spot. Take a deep breath, hold it and tense your entire body, especially your hands. Then slowly let out the air and relax all muscles. Repeat the process. Count backwards from 300 slowly and tell yourself to relax your feet — concentrate on your feet until you feel them becoming limp. Continue upward by relaxing your ankles, calves, thighs, buttocks, abdomen, chest, hands, arms, shoulders, neck, face. By this time, you should be at low numbers, your eyes should close and your head should fall gently forward. This is a sign that you have induced the start of hypnosis. This should be the end of the relaxation techniques.

Please stop here. Think. If you have the willpower, you can accomplish the same objectives without going through the hypnosis procedure. Use self-discipline and accomplish your desires the easy way. Convince yourself that a change for the better is necessary. Then use your willpower to accomplish. Doctors may say that you have a "disease". They do help you.

You should have your doctor show you hypnosis methods in detail before starting self-hypnosis. Do not try it until you are certain that you know how to bring yourself out of the "trance". This deep relaxation can be deepened by repeating a simple word and seeing it in your mind. There are other similar procedures.

The person with adequate willpower who does not need hypnosis and the person in a "trance" each suggest to their brain the facts which are to be impressed on their memory. Facts and supporting detail are repeated many times. As an example, if you are trying to lose weight, imagine that you are looking at a large mirror. Admire your new trim figure and tell yourself how good and energetic you look. Convince yourself that you can become the imagined figure by eating only enough food to maintain that figure, that you are not hungry after eating that many calories and that you can leave the remainder on your plate or take smaller servings next time. Learn to say, "I am full and actually mean it by not eating another bite." True, you are imagining a mealtime event but make it seem real. Feel good about your new imagined figure and be proud of your accomplishments. Impress these pictures and ideas on your mind while you are in control. True, you are not at a real feast but if you truly impress the picture in your mind, you can accomplish the same in real life.

You need to bring yourself out of the trance state and this should be possible if you use the procedure you designed and told yourself before starting the procedure. Count slowly and feel your body regain your normal muscle tone. Become aware of sounds, raise your head, open your eyes and begin to feel good in your non-trance condition. The process should be repeated during other days until your mind accepts your desires and you are in control of your actions using the desired "new you".

Again, seek medical help before you try hypnosis. Be sure you can come out of the trance before trying. Do not allow others to use you as an hypnosis subject. Always be in control of your life. In the 1980s, others will use you if you allow them to do so. They may use hypnosis, threats, and physical force to cause you to submit to their wishes. Always be alert and wary. Know how to defend yourself. Learn when and how to say "no". Know how to escape from physical harm.

29. Be comfortable. Our creature comforts in our home, cars, and office can reduce stress and improve our health.

Most office and plant employees will be using computers in a very few years. Also, our children are using computers in both home and school. We should protect ourselves by:

Buying screen sizes of 9 to 14 inches.

Working so that eyes are about 24 inches from the screen. Center of screen should be about four inches below eye level.

Checking with eye doctor before use and at routine intervals, particularly if eyes strain.

Tri-focal lenses may be desired when glasses are worn.

Eyes should be rested at intervals — break for 15 minutes each hour, etc.

Using overhead lights over computer to avoid glare from screen.

Buying a chair with good back support and a height so that feet are flat on floor.

Buying green and amber tone screens to reduce eye fatigue. Be comfortable at all times.

30. Use our knowledge and instincts of good habits.

Separation of truth from falsehood is a problem throughout life. Determining what is fact is very important in medical advice. Doctors and many others seem to forget the public good and instead tend to try to increase their income and prestige. They may even try to create a disease. Genetic research is changing the medical profession and we need to keep informed and use common sense so that we have the knowledge to know when to trust our advisors. Ask for second opinions by seeing a second doctor if you have major medical problems. Drugs have many harmful side effects and they can kill you when they interact wrongly. Doctors, too, are not always fully informed of the many details and progress in a changing world.

Those who fight for personal freedom should carry adequate insurance to pay for the results of accidents when they violate rules of common sense. It is not fair to take cheap thrills and expect taxpayers to take care of us when we are in a wheelchair. We should always consider the probable risks resulting from our actions. These involve ourselves and others, including our surroundings. Are we willing to accept the consequences without complaint or excuse? Consequences may include physical hurts, mental adjustments and cash costs. The medical question of our century is, "Should the religious zealots be permitted to force their beliefs on those who have other beliefs and desires?"

American Association for Counseling and Development, Department U, Box 9888, Alexandria, Virginia 22304 offers names of practitioners in fields such as mental health, social work and career guidance. Many state government agencies also can be helpful. You might want to read *Modern Prevention — The New Medicine* by Dr. Isadore Rosenfeld (Simon & Schuster).

HONESTY

Business groups and schools today are again demanding much higher moral standards. The world cannot operate without basic principles and standards. Unfortunately, the words and principles differ in relationships in various parts of the world. Have you tried to operate in a country where cancelled stamps are stolen by postal employees to make another penny?

There is no degree of honesty. You must have moral and intellectual honesty to be successful. Buck-passing, blame-shifting, idle promises which are unkept and incomplete or misleading statements are all forms of dishonesty. They are not tolerated and are not practiced by a good person. Honesty is vital to self-respect and cannot be bought by any amount of money. A person who makes either vague or firm promises and thereafter does not fulfill them is not an honest person. Be tactful at social and business functions but do not create or leave the impression of lying. Telling good stories, discussing personal experiences and using harmless jokes are good at office and social gatherings. Make certain everyone realizes the nature of your words and actions. Never tell a lie and be certain that no one is hurt by you. Consider your words carefully and always ask yourself whether your reputation is being damaged.

There are people who will give a complete accounting of money entrusted in their care but they do not show moral honesty in dealing with others. It is dishonest to claim credit when credit is due others, to pass the responsibility to others or to blame others when you are responsible. Others, including workers, like to be treated fairly and receive credit for good efforts. We all like to feel important and be thanked for a good job as part of a team.

Respect and speak the truth. Be bold and fearless in your rebuke of error and in your keener rebuke of wrongdoing. Be human and loving, gentle and brotherly at all times but do be careful so that others do not take advantage or hurt you. Be tolerant but honest with yourself and your fellow man. Learn to be kind to man, animals and the environment. Make the earth a safe and pleasant place in which to live in peace but do not harm yourself or our nation. Be prepared to defend both. Sometimes a simple answer like "yes" or "no" can be misinterpreted by your listeners. Coverups and words which mislead are not to be tolerated in your relations with others. Watch your actions and body expressions so that they do not mislead. Your words are not believed nor accepted as truth unless they are supported by your actions, deeds and living habits. Your reputation is established slowly but it can be lost very quickly. Once lost, re-establishment is very slow. Guard your reputation as jealously as your life. Good luck.

Social and business decisions must be based on fact or unbiased and truthful information. Untruths are considered as fraud and deceit. Intentional fraud is a serious crime and misunderstandings cause lawsuits. In shallow social contacts, pertinent details may be left unsaid but in business discussions, all important considerations must be presented. When people know that you lie or are untruthful by your statements or omissions, you are no longer trusted and no one will believe you. You are forced to change your habits and find new associates who do not know your past. Also, watch your close associates since you may be judged by actions of those whose company you keep. The practical joker is always out of line in the business world and he can create a menace to health and safety. A sense of humor is valuable but it must be controlled. Pranks simply are not permitted. A supervisor should call the practical joker and the lying person into his office and tell the person that such acts are not tolerated. He should point out that lies and practical jokes interfere with production and waste time of other workers. Both embarrass others and jeopardize group morale. Having fun at the expense of others is a form of cruelty and must be stopped or the offender must be replaced. Act immediately when horseplay is noticed so that the waste of time is reduced.

Petty thefts are not permitted since that, too, is a form of dishonesty. Good humor and responsiblity are needed to create a sense of friendliness and goodwill but the extreme of jokes and lies are not tolerated. Our own good spirit and smiles set the tone of the group. People who are so insecure that they must lie and horseplay need advice and guidance. Make it clear to them that they can gain more recognition by becoming mature and reliable. Also, inform them that lies and practical jokes are not part of policy because they create hazards and are unsafe. Most people can grow up into adult behavior. They learn responsibility and do not need to be fired. They simply must be made aware of policy and the reasons for same.

People are often lying when they physically distance themselves from others, when slumping in posture, when head nods unnecessarily, when smile is erratic, when body activity is abrupt, when eye contact is infrequent and when actions are not usual for the person, based on past experience.

INDIVIDUALITY

No two people are exactly alike. Think of people as individuals rather than as groups. The knack of sensing the reactions of individuals and tailoring supervisory methods to specific personalities pays off in many ways. Be objective in your analysis and decisions but do not play favorites. Try to avoid a clash of ideas and personalities. Try to anticipate reactions of others. Bring out the best in everyone with whom you associate. Do not jump to erroneous conclusions. React slowly and assemble related facts before acting. Develop policies for a group but use some consideration for each individual in the application. We each want to be provided with a sense of importance, significance, interest and dignity. Treat people as individuals.

Friends will not remind you of your faults. You must ask them. Individuals have differing needs and beliefs. We all need to be more tolerant. Moral values may differ when others are not harmed.

LONELINESS

Individuals of all ages become lonely and one can be lonely even when at a party with friends. Loneliness is often caused by a lack of self-esteem, a poor self-image and self-flagellation — a feeling of not being secure. We each enter this world alone, are alone most of our life and we die alone. We should think positively rather than negatively, should take life one step at a time, should not over-generalize in opinions and when making decisions. You should realize that you and others share blame and praise for happenings and events, should not jump to conclusions without adequate investigation, evidence and thought. We should learn to recognize mistakes without feeling depressed and we should think, develop plans and act to solve our problems logically rather than continue to worry. The problems may be within ourselves and in our relations with others. You may be the cause and others may be the cause but you must try for solutions. Learn to love yourself, think highly of yourself without being haughty or boring. Read, study and develop confidence in your ability to act intuitively, rationally and logically, to be friendly but not overbearing, to be happy and to be successful. Try to forget your problems by keeping busy and working with others with confidence in your ability. Overcome your indecisiveness, your embarrassment about your failures — admit failures with good grace. You should not fear the unfamiliar since most fears never materialize and you should never develop a martyr complex. Instead, do the things necessary to increase your ability and self-worth. Recognize that you, your friends and even your boss put on pants one leg at a time. Be confident and believe that you, too, can accomplish your goals if you try in a competent manner by using your intelligence, being friendly and entertaining, being punctual, considerate, and using good taste in bearing, voice and dress. Cooperate with others while being honest with your moral principles, ideals and basic desires. Learn to be practical and, if possible, adjust your concepts of perfection so that you are able to live with others in fairness and grace in a changing world. Recognize that true change in yourself and others takes time, commitment, energy and courage. Do not feel deprived and learn to expect only that which is reasonably attainable. We cannot attain all our expectations. There will be some pain and we will at times lose. Find activities which are of interest and make life worthwhile. Wake up each morning with happy thoughts and a desire to get on with the projects assigned or desired by you. Enjoy managing your assets so that you overcome loneliness.

Our last days are often lonely. We no longer go to the office, our friends are dead or have moved and our children are busy with their problems. We need hobbies and interests. We no longer fear death since it, too, is recognized as part of the life cycle. We do fear a long illness and being kept alive by a machine to satisfy ego and financial needs of a doctor or to satisfy the moral needs of a preacher.

In some parts of Europe, the old and feeble can die with dignity. After long consultation with doctor and friends, the elderly can ask to have their doctor legally inject fluids which grant death without pain and suffering. Such alternative can remove the fear of suffering. The fear of lost independence and of imposing on loved ones for emotional, physical and financial help is also eliminated. Old people have a choice regarding the future. In China, where population is large, cremation is essential.

LOVE

True love is more than physical attraction. Honesty, friendship, cooperation are involved. Lasting love is an attitude rather than an attraction of body needs. We need to control the mind and have the willpower to forgive. Cooperate and believe that you like and love someone.

Some researchers relate all human reactions with fear and love. We each desire to be liked and loved. We often act very foolish and are harmed because we want love even if only for a few moments. Most important is the love for ourselves which is necessary in moderation. We should not be self-centered or haughty but we must feel good and like ourselves so that we have confidence necessary to believe that we can accomplish our objectives.

Most individuals also need support and a feeling of being liked by family, friends and business associates. Excessive love of children causes us to spoil their character so that they find it difficult to gain the independence required for living a successful life in the adult world. We each need to be loved and feel liked and confident of support as we seek our identity and lifestyle throughout life. Look for and always discuss complaints.

A firm love relationship is required between mates — a man and woman living together. Submission of one personality to another is wrong and eventually leads to severe trouble for all. We need to love and cooperate but we also need to be ourselves. Many couples separate and the emotional strain is severe and almost impossible if we do not have our resources both emotionally and financially. Learn to be independent but loving and caring. Confidence in a relationship must be maintained but too much "togetherness" results in loss of personality and character which often defeats the kindness and caring. Each party must give in to the other "75 percent of the time — actually 50 percent of the time" to maintain the relationship but they each must demand privacy, respect and independence. Learn to demand your basic rights and privileges at all times.

Each person must always be prepared to live a separate life at all times. Never allow love to cause you to give up what is needed for you to meet this possibility. Separation by death and divorce is a likely prospect for each person during a lifetime. Fifty percent get a divorce and death removes one person from each permanent long-time relationship. Love but always look out for yourself while living a caring and cooperative life.

LOYALTY

Everyone likes to follow a good leader of the community, state, nation and of business.

People are loyal to those who represent the ideas in which they believe and have faith. People cooperate with the men and women in whom they have confidence and those who show interest in others. Loyalty in leaders and the company for whom we work is essential if we are to work as a team in a successful operation. We need to have pride in our work and those for whom we work. Loyalty is earned through fair treatment and fair dealing. Indifference will crush goodwill and the spirit. To obtain loyalty from others, be loyal to them. A leader builds up the ego of the person who has not cooperated without inflating the individual. Praise work of others when good effort is indicated. Let others know how you feel about them and that you understand the feelings of others. Give others a feeling of security and that you both belong to the same group with comparable objectives. Do not be too hard-shelled nor cynical. We all must recognize the ordinary virtues of work, truth and honesty. Workers must be loyal to each other if the organization is to work as a team and be loyal to the company. Workers cooperate with the supervisor in whom they have confidence and when supervisors show an interest in subordinates. Without individual loyalty to the head of a group, there can be no loyalty to the company. Loyalty is not a slogan. It is a feeling and an inspirational force which cannot be simulated and for which there is no substitute. Appreciation, opportunity, a feeling of security and caring for each other make a loyal group. Loyalty within a family is desired.

MISTAKES

We each make mistakes and we should determine the reason for making them. What thought processes and handling procedures caused the problem? Guard against repetition by making yourself and your group mistake-conscious. It pays to be careful in the car, at home and at the office or job. Be aware of the cost of even the smallest mistake and be certain that your fellow workers, too, are careful and do not cause accidents which involve you. When a mistake is made, due to carelessness or indifference, everyone should point out to the offender, in a polite and man-to-man manner, that mistakes are not tolerated. Other mistakes may involve finances, paperwork, etc. which hurt company profits and your job security.

We each make mistakes but they should be infrequent and the same mistake should not be made a second time. We should appeal to our self-respect and develop a habit of being careful through good housekeeping, accuracy and clear instructions which are followed with utmost care in great detail. A good leader should accept the overall responsibility for mistakes of his group but the individual should be made aware of the problems caused thereby so that greater care is taken to avoid duplication of the mistake. It is human to make mistakes and they are bound to occur, but careful training and careful compliance with detailed instructions and procedures can be helpful in limiting their number. Do not be careless or lazy. These are weeds which will grow rapidly unless controlled and they can bankrupt a company. Being careful can be learned and a sincere interest in the job and a happy attitude will pay off for all involved. Convince yourself and those working with you that mistakes are harmful and that they must be kept to a minimum.

One method used to avoid mistakes is to have the lowest ranking member at a meeting give his comments on a problem first, the next second and the top ranking last. Then ask for discussion and later decide.

NEGOTIATIONS

Life is a series of negotiations with wife, children and business associates. There are many rules and these include techniques used in social and business life. Before starting any discussion with others, we need to determine (1) the maximum which can be asked without getting laughed out of the group; (2) the minimum which can be accepted; (3) the maximum that can be given away; and (4) the least that can be offered without getting laughed out of the room. With these values, we are prepared to use our negotiating abilities.

Ask your library for texts related to negotiation skills. Use variations of the "IF" technique — "If I could do this, what will you be able to do?"

POISE

You cannot have poise without self-discipline. Keep cool under fire and when angered. Be calm and use sound judgment and you steady others. Learn to take all things in stride. Show the group the importance of their contribution to progress of company operations and profits. People will not let you down if they feel that you appreciate their efforts and that you are counting on them. We each need to develop poise and learn to control our anger and temper. Learn to roll with the bad times and do not get flustered when the going is rough. The people who have balance rarely have health problems. Use of poise enables everyone to work in an atmosphere which is pleasant and easy on the nerves. Learn to handle your problems without disturbing others. Avoid depression and poor moods and try to be cheerful.

PRAISE

We are each expected to perform in a satisfactory and acceptable manner. We should not expect praise for doing average work. Praise should be used to encourage us to do superior work. Expect criticism when performance is poor but expect praise only when performance is exceptional. Control of our ego is expected — we should not need constant praise. The leader should recognize, with praise and advancement, superior work whenever possible but the employee should not constantly demand extras. The person who expects praise and favorable comments for everything that he does will be disappointed. No leader can meet such demands and the person who has not adjusted his demands to reasonable levels expected as an adult is never satisfied nor respected by his peers. He probably is doomed to failure and will find life somewhat disappointing.

PEER PRESSURE

Pressure is present from friends throughout life but it is most severe during high school and early college years. School teachers, possibly parents and your friends help you select job fields, colleges or commercial schools and, probably, marriage partners. These selections determine our future but we often are truly only drifting. Many of us do not take the time from pleasures to analyze and really select our future. Too bad if friends give poor advice.

We need to individually analyze and seek our own identity. Friends should give advice but they should not influence decisions. You live your life and your friends most likely will disappear from your life as you go independent ways in the work world. Think for yourself and analyze yourself — your hopes and ambitions as well as what you like to do and are capable of doing with your life. Certainly alcohol, drugs and crime should not be considered. Do not pick up sexual diseases for a few moments of affection from those who want your body for only one night.

We must impose limitations on ourselves and friends. We should interact with friends and associates but our character, our moral values, emotions, thoughts, words and actions should be under our individual control at all times. We do depend upon others for food, construction of our homes, manufacture of our cars, and for many items which influence our health and safety. You depend upon strangers everytime you drive a car. We must live in hope that others, too, want to protect their lives and that they will do the correct thing. Sometimes we are wrong and we need to have the willpower to turn in the criminal and poor driver to the police.

Everything we do is somewhat influenced by others but we should try to act in a manner which is good for us as an individual using cooperation. We individually can control our emotions, words, thoughts, actions and behavior in a manner which makes us and our neighbors better individuals. Together we set social values and keep our homes and neighborhood attractive. Peer pressure can work for the good of all.

You simply must learn to say "no" graciously. You can always find an excuse for your actions and inactions but that does not enable you to live a successful life. Learn how to say "no" when offered drugs and alcohol. Learn to say "no" when invited to waste your time and energy. There are many other times when you need to say "no". Do so. Learn to use your limited time doing things that are worthwhile to you and your neighbors rather than waste time in useless chatter with others. Convince your friends to do likewise. Keep relaxation to time actually needed to protect your health and emotional well-being.

PERSUASIVENESS

Communication with others is essential. You become more persuasive when you:

1. Meet in friendly surroundings such as your office and your home. Work where you feel most confident and comfortable.
2. Always look your best. Smile and be friendly.
3. Try to identify with your listeners. Show others that you are similar to them and that you like them.
4. Create trust and empathy with those that you wish to convince. Try to reflect your listeners experience and use negotiation. Try to be one of the group — be a leader. Speak and write effectively.
5. Make a strong presentation of your recommendtaions. Use facts and figures in a convincing manner.
6. Use stories and examples which relate with experiences of your listeners. You will be happier and more friendly if you make important decisions with care. Select your mate and job carefully and wisely after you have determined what you want from your journey on earth. Plan your future but live one day at a time. You cannot be all things to all people and you cannot do all things nor can you always be efficient and undisturbed. Control your problems and do not blame others. You alone can solve your problems in a friendly manner. You can give up any addiction if you really want to do so and if you make a sincere effort. If you cannot handle it alone, seek professional help.

Learn how to close a discussion by asking "closing questions" such as "are you, would you, can you, could you". Do not overuse nor appear dictatorial. Try to obtain "yes" or "no" commitments.

PUNCTUALITY

Tardiness and punctuality can become a habit. Being on time at work and in social activities is a mental habit or attitude. Chronic tardiness indicates a lack of organization and lack of planning. It is discourteous and unfair. You are selfish when you are late for appointments. It is the responsibility of fellow workers and supervisors to convince others that it is highly important that personal schedules are planned to insure punctuality — not a little late. The teaching must be individual since no two people respond in the same way.

PRIDE

The right to excel is desired by most individuals. Recognize those who perform above average — those who use quality thinking and pride of performance. Constructive thinking and planning, good training and careful supervision unite in a group which can beat the competition by improving yesterday's methods. Watch the work of new people and make sure that older employees remain honest and enthusiastic. Look for and praise points of excellence but correct mistakes before they become work habits. Praise when work is exceptional and do not discourage by excessive fault finding. Discover problems while they are unimportant and make corrections in a most friendly manner. Good leaders emphasize the importance of each job and inspire pride of performance by creating work as a team effort. A job should be discontinued if it is not important to the operation. Convey the importance of each job during training. A feeling of satisfaction is present when people are interested in their work. Pride in the workplace inspires initiative and creates a spirit of enthusiastic cooperation. Everyone feels good and this asset lifts the organization high above its competition so that the company prospers and jobs are secure. Pride in your home helps create a beautiful neighborhood.

PROCRASTINATION

It is easy to delay decisions and put off doing a job. Delay ruins your work efficiency and lowers your ability. Such action is very poor leadership and affects work of larger organizations. Learn to handle problems immediately after they are called to your attention. Handle paper and make decisions when paper first comes across your desk. Do not allow work to pile up and complicate your operations. Arrange your work in order of importance and make a schedule of work to be done and promises to be kept. Nothing hurts confidence of coworkers and customers more than poor performance caused by putting things off to another day. Handle problems today. Tying up loose ends on schedule each day makes work easier and enables you to get a fresh start each day. It is easy to set things and decisions aside but very tough to fit the problems back into the daily work pattern.

We may not simply be lazy when we delay. We may react to fear and obsessive perfection. We delay because an uncompleted project cannot be judged. We may fear failure and we may fear success. We fear envy and simply want to be one of many. We may not perform because we want to show the "boss" that he is not in charge but we do so by delay rather than open confrontation.

We may be seeking help and hope that others will be forced to help if we do not do our work on time. Education and experience are important but they do not insure that people are capable of working or solving problems.

RELATIONSHIPS

You, at an early age, must learn the rules developed by society during thousands of years. Failure to do so makes one an outcast and life becomes difficult. You must make an effort to be happy, learn to smile and you must accept your job as useful and hopefully a pleasant part of your day. You simply must adapt and get along well with others at all times. Doctors do not expect to develop a pill which will make you get along better with your spouse, children, or fellow man. Pills do not resolve the problems experienced during childhood and that continue to influence emotions and attitude today. We are more agreeable, relaxed and good natured when we feel good and like ourselves.

You should learn to have complete control over your emotions and your dislikes. Medicine can help with the problem of depression. To change your mental attitudes, rough treatment at times is necessary. Techniques developed to cure drugs, alcohol and cult thinking may be used. You will not stop your habits as a result of pleading by friends and family but you can do so if you alone decide the change to be necessary and then use willpower to accomplish that change. You should recognize that your actions are harmful and really want to change your life patterns. Then, family and friends, including support groups, can be very useful by enforcing your will to continue your new habits. Often you realize that you have talents, that you are worthy of a better set of habits and that your future life can be much better if you want it to be so. Your undesirable habits must be recognized by you before they can be changed or altered. Professional help often is necessary and you, individually, must seek that help when the problem is substantial and you do not have the willpower to make long-term changes for the better by your own efforts. Do constantly try to improve your mental and living habits. You can accomplish if you really try.

Learn to treat yourself well — do something nice and special for yourself often. Chat with a friend, curl up with a book, read about self-respect and confidence and make life pleasant. Make your life happy and enjoyable by physical and mental actions. Use sound judgment and common sense in your work and relations with others. In moral theology, one finds that "All true needs such as food, drink and companionship are satiable but illegitimate wants such as excessive pride, envy and greed are insatiable."

Confidence, tact, trust and cooperation can be learned, are required and are expected by others with whom you associate. You must, in general, conform with the rules of society if you want friends and if your life is to be lawful. You, by your actions, must prove to be worthy of respect and trust of others. You must be honest and keep promises.

Learn to smile. People will think that you are friendly and will talk with you. Don't allow shyness to limit your activity. Most people are shy and they appreciate your taking the first step in trying to be friends. Learn the social arts, participate in social activity at least once each week. Enjoy the many people you meet and make them friends. Always call people by their correct name. Be sincere if you want true friends. Friendships offer an antidote for loneliness. If you want a friend, you must be a friend. If you want a successful love life, you must treat your partner the way you want to be treated. When meeting people, you must anticipate a few rejections. People simply do not all think alike nor like the same things.

If you are single, frequent singles groups — no bars. If you want lasting relationships, you need to meet people who are sincere and who are looking for long term relationships rather than "one night stands". Men and women both want love and relationships. They want friends. To get love, you must give love and understanding. You can always get sex but getting love, friendship and true understanding requires much effort by two people. Others respond to your efforts when made in a friendly and understanding manner. Be careful in your approach but do take the first step to a more happy life by being friendly. Life is filled with risks but you should manage them.

You also need to be consistent in your relations. Friendship cannot be turned on and off like water from a faucet. Instead you must control moods and emotions. Be prepared for some disappointments so that you take the good with the bad without becoming upset. Always show an interest, have a glint in your eye, try to feel good and smile.

Being friends is not easy. After a long relationship, each party will believe that he has given in to the other about 75% of the time. Of course, the actual figure probably is about 50%. You must be forgiving and considerate.

Develop an outgoing personality and a cheerful, positive attitude along with the ability to meet strangers. Make contacts with others and use their referrals in your social and business life.

Learn to be gracious, charming, exuberant and have good taste in manner, dress and carriage. Be impressive without being distasteful. Go to the library or bookstore and read several recommended books on etiquette and protocol. Be sincere but be polished. Study books by Emily Post and Miss Manners.

Progress occurs when an idea from one specialty is transferred to another field of endeavor. Without broad knowledge, we simply "reinvent the wheel". Everyone can find or plan a "study" which supports any desired idea and with talk shows and reporters, many "false studies" receive publicity. Recall that most new ideas have been tried before.

You will find that "boss", parents and friends will hesitate to give you advice unless you ask. They hesitate to be helpful unless you accept advice in a friendly manner. True friends may offer suggestions or hints but you must be alert or you will miss their aid. Unless you grow up and learn to accept advice graciously, your mistakes will "hang you". Learn to ask for and seek advice by obtaining opinions from those you truly trust to be honest with you. Learn to ask for the views of friends and associates whom you trust to be helpful but be aware of those who give false advice to hurt you. Friends can make or break you. You need their feedback but you must decide whether they are giving good responsibile direction to you. You are responsible for living your adult life but society will impose its laws so that you recognize the rights of your friends, associates and neighbors. Your boss expects you to be friendly and understand your job. Know what he expects. You must be enthusiastic and ask questions necessary to understand your job and any instructions given you. You are expected to complete an assignment efficiently and correctly. Thoroughly understand how and why you did the assignment so that you can repeat it when necessary. The teacher and even the company executive does not increase his competition when he exposes his operating methods and experiences to students. Their listeners will not use the information given because they did not listen, they are too proud, they are too self-centered and lazy and they simply are not motivated. The few who listen and think will succeed. They apply sound judgment. Always look for better ways to do a job and to sell. You will not be friendly unless you feel comfortable and secure. Life is a mass of decisions based on "grey areas of information". Knowledge is not complete and experience is important. There often is no completely right or wrong in human and business relations. In business, whether in the plant, in the office, or in contractual relations between parties, everyone must believe that a fair and equitable relation exists. In work relations, one person must have the responsiblity for assigning work, supervising so that work is completed in a cost-efficient and timely manner. Such supervisor also must set quality standards and negotiate relations between employees. You, as an employee, must accept your "boss" and his instructions in a friendly manner. You have to develop an attitude which permits you to be an enthusiastic worker who is willing, friendly, and cooperative. You also must be sincere and honest with yourself and fellow workers. You must be trustworthy and be part of a team effort. The overall effort must show a profit and make money for the owners in a competitive worldwide marketplace or there will be no work for anyone. You are competing with fellow workers for advancement. Simply stated, you must perform your work in a friendly, pleasant manner and do the best job to advance. You should be confident in your ability and feel good about your work. You also must have and retain the confidence of superiors and fellow workers. You must be trusted and remain trustworthy. You, too, can win the competition if you:

1. Assume responsiblity for your actions and gain the friendship of fellow workers.

2. Discover your abilities and use them as you strive to accomplish your goals. Know what you want; work and accomplish in a friendly manner.

3. Accept work willingly and adapt to your environment. Running away from problems is never successful.

4. Success is 99% work and 1% inspiration. You also need a little luck but you create your luck by work, deed, thoughts and actions. You and your neighbors need to be aware of what is required to make your neighborhood and schools useful. You must each be honest, generous and just. You need to be kind to those whose lives you touch and you should make creditable use of your time and talents. You need to be part of society and make a friendly free society continue to give you the highest social, moral and physical standards

possible. You must cooperate with others in a friendly manner. You need ambition but excessive drive, aggression and ambition can be a handicap to success and happiness. You should want to be successful while being friendly and considerate of your fellow man and nature. You obtain your goals if you learn how to handle people — win others to your sound and well-considered point of view and ideas. Study tapes: "Vocabulary" by Evans and "Listening" by Montgomery from Learning, 113 Gaither Drive, Mt. Laurel, New York 08054

REPRIMAND

Scolding hurts morale. It is easier to find the cause and emphasize more stable and practical living habits. An increased interest in the job and a greater spirit of teamwork are helpful. People do not realize that coming to work late is disruptive. People do not realize that the practice is very costly to company and employee because it disrupts the flow of work of others in the workplace and reduces morale. Leaders who set an example and sell the importance of each individual to the group's performance usually get cooperation so that good discipline is maintained without use of a club. It is equally important that each individual pull his load by reducing lost time and motion while working. The individual who shirks his load will be looking elsewhere for employment. Always do your part.

RESPONSIBILITY

You have volunteered to serve on a community committee and you were employed to willingly do a job in a workmanlike manner within a specific time-frame. If you repeatedly do not perform adequately, your job should be forfeited. The owner-invester, too, has a right to a reasonable, long term return on his money the same as when you are paid for working. An entrepreneur devotes his ideas, money and long hours to his business hoping to gain a profit for his efforts and risks. By giving you a job, he has made you a part of his team and effort. You should expect him to be fair but you in return should help him obtain his objective. An occasional expression of gratitude on the part of both would seem appropriate.

Similarly, parents have spent long hours and much money and energy, which they could have spent on their pleasures and activities, to make children's younger days safe, informative and enjoyable. Hopefully, their efforts gave you the base for your present lifestyle. They prepared you for adulthood. Do you show a little appreciation for their past efforts by being respectful, courteous and helpful as they grow older? Do you devote a little time to them to show your appreciation for 20 years of their life given you? It is normal for children to be unappreciative as teens but children and parents ideas and ideals usually converge as children mature. They reach mutual understanding, friendship, devotion and respect for each other before age 30. Suggestions made by parents as friends do not imply a desire to control children's lives. Children should not feel sorry for parents but they should treat their parents well — maybe as special friends. Children have a life to live but friendship and, hopefully, love toward parents is a reasonable and normal expectation.

We also need to be honest and fair with everyone, including friends and business associates. Man is responsible for the protection of planet earth — its beauty, its plants and animals. Nature tends to restore itself and this fact must be recognized by all since man, too, must live. Man is at the top of a food chain and many animals eat other animals and most eat plants. To eat is essential for all animals but we should try to make animal's life as pleasant as possible, using laws of nature involving hunter and hunted.

We are masters of the earth and should be respectful of its needs. Your greatest responsibility is to yourself. You alone are responsible for your way of living and you must conform with the rules of our society. You also are responsible for your health and you must work and play safely and rest and relax to be fit emotionally and physically. Take some time each evening and weekend to meditate, listen to music, exercise, reflect and "unwind". Make your life pleasant and enjoyable but do take care of yourself. Parents should control accident-prone thrills desired by children and adults should work and play safely.

SALESMANSHIP

Every contact between people involves salesmanship. Directing and obtaining cooperation from others is good leadership. In all contacts between individuals, someone is buying another's thoughts and ideas — possibly products. Skill is required to convince others to follow your lead — willingly and intelligently. Selling requires consideration of the needs and feelings of others. People cannot be led or sold the merits of your ideas or product until they are convinced of the value. Sell others. Learn to sell others your ideas and products. To sell, you must convince others that your product and ideas are needed and that they serve the best interest of the other parties. When selling a product, each party to the sale must be convinced that the deal is fair and of benefit to all parties. Salesmanship is nothing more than tactful and convincing persuasion. Selling is convincing another person that what is being sold is good for buyer and seller — serves a common good. Use of salesmanship is essential in our personal relations but it should not replace the need for technical skill and job knowledge. It is simply one of the tools necessary for all jobs and social activities. There is no substitute for knowledge and know-how. Salesmanship is a tool which is required to encourage people to use their skills and talents — it convinces others by selling them the importance of their job and its value to company profits so that raises in salary are possible. Raises are the result of good performance in the highly competitive marketplace. We should all be good salesmen and learn to use the needed techniques. We need to phrase our words so that sales occur. As an example, ask the prospective customer, "How may I help you?" rather than "May I help you?"

You should always ask the prospective buyer questions which cause him to think favorably about the product being sold. Such questions involve the buyer favorably without leaving the impression that a salesman is bragging. You should always ask questions which attempt to close a sale. Both buyer and seller must believe that the deal is fair to all parties if later trouble is to be avoided.

The sales techniques are somewhat different when selling a home compared with the sale of a dress. Space does not permit proper discussion in this text and you should learn to sell the product which you are actually selling.

Experience has shown that 80% of all sales to new customers are first made after the fifth contact or sales attempt. Most salesmen give up after the second attempt. Thus, about 70% of new sales are never made. Success goes to those who have learned to sell and who have the drive to make many contacts. Buyers need time to accept your sales pitch and must be convinced of your sincerity and willingness to stand behind your promises.

We are each salesmen. We each need to sell ourselves in our work and business and we sell ourselves to our spouse and children and to our friends. Some individuals also sell products to customers.

You may wish to investigate Dale Carnegie courses, courses offered by schools and seminars. There also are many "do it yourself books" which should be on your bookshelves. Tapes, too, are often available.

The following characteristics are often exhibited by good salesmen:

1. Posture should be springy in step, balanced and noble in carriage. Chin, chest and shoulders should show thrust. Be alive.
2. Eye gaze should be good, open and concentrative. Look the buyer in the eye. Do not be shifty, scowling, staring, dreamy or narrow-slitted. The good salesman has a steady eye, a steady nerve, steady habits and a steady tongue.
3. You should smile. The good salesman turns up with a smile and smiles even when he does not make a sale.
4. You should understand people and make others understand you. Be considerate and helpful to buyers.
5. A good salesman strives to out-think rather than out-talk the prospect. Keep alert and think how you can help the buyer so that he buys from you.
6. The salesman's world is interesting. He enjoys meeting new people, new points of view, new problems, new facts. He takes firm interest in his company and also looks out for his customer's interests. He is honest with all.
7. A salesman knows when to be silent. He is silent when he has nothing to say and when the prospect is talking. He does not argue but he does point out benefits of his product and how it will help the customer make money and stay in business. Allow the buyer time to think.
8. A salesman needs to be truthful. He keeps his word, his temper and his friends. He likes others.
9. A salesman has a sense of humor. He uses this balance wheel but he uses it with care. Never use coarse jokes nor embarrass your prospect.
10. A salesman wins respect by being respectable, he respects others and

is respected by all.

11. Temper is never displayed. Be coureous in the face of discourtesy. The more the provocation, the more you must bridle your temper. Exhibit self control and respect for customers moods and habits. Respect his views, religion, etc.

12. It is wise to have great self-confidence but you must not brag or show ego.

13. A salesman must know his product and the needs of the customer. The customer will not spend time and effort making you understand his problems.

14. A salesman must have plenty of energy. Everyone notices it in his walk, talk, habits, ideas and plans.

15. Control of ego is critical. Too many salesman "I" themselves right out of an order. A sale is pulled to its goal by the prospect's ego and needs. The seller's ego is harmful and unnecessary.

16. Friendliness is basic. Be loved by your fellow man and your customers. Selling is a human relationship. Basic, sincere friendliness is worth more than tricks, which usually kill a relationship. Be a good mixer, have many friends on your own and higher levels of management.

17. The test for brains is not how much you know but how you use your intelligence. Use common sense.

18. A prospect or customer must believe that the salesmen will and is handling the buyer's interests scrupulously. Any neglect of customer will kill the relationship.

19. A good salesman is a born communicator. He is a natural talker, teacher who honestly helps. His enthusiasm shows in his voice, his flow of words, his convincing approach, his power of graphic expression, his clear delineation of facts, and his urge to convert others to his way of thinking. He is believed.

20. A salesman must be well-rounded, must be wholesome and must be naturally liked by everyone.

21. A good salesman knows his products, what he is selling, what his products can do for each customer and he must know all the sales material. He is helpful to the buyer.

22. A salesman must be honest, respect others and be helpful to others. He must have endurance and unyielding stamina, he must have ability to hold a line, work a plan and stand up to punishment. He is an honest and willing worker who works for himself on commission.

23. A salesman is resourceful. He jumps hurdles in his job using resources from within himself; he is a quick thinker. He also shows originality, daring, adaptability and good judgment based on common sense.

24. Business usually is practical and the buyer must have confidence that the seller, too, is practical and that advice given is based on cost/benefit analysis.

25. A strong salesman is a self-starter. He avoids slumps and keeps a high level of interest.
26. Selling is often debating logic and orderly analysis of ideas and use of clear speech. Presentations must be clear, the reasoning must be persuasive so that fact is soundly considered and fact, truth and honesty lead to conviction and the inevitable conclusion and closing of a sale. Everyone must be convinced that your product is the best available for the job at hand.
27. A good salesman likes to sell ideas and products. He loves his work, likes people and likes to help them buy his products. He believe that he is doing a good favor for his customers by his actions.
28. Salesmanship is nine-tenths good relationship. Manners are often as important as sound argument and good logic. Watch selling style, manners and dress.
29. Develop sound discipline. The successful salesman works in all kinds of weather. He plans his work, works his plan and makes enough calls. He toes the line under difficulties without any urging from others. He likes his work and people and it shows in all his actions.
30. A good salesman investigates. He knows that time is wasted if he does not make a sale. He never uses undue pressure. Every person must develop these traits and be a salesman. Your future depends on it.
31. He knows how to find clients and how to determine their needs and determine sales possiblities.

SECURITY

During youth, our energy and ability to work give us confidence and a feeling of security. For most individuals, these assets become less as we grow older. We need to think a little about our life when we become older and when we might have an accident. Someday, we each must retire and we may even be ill. We must save a little during younger days and learn to manage our savings regardless of money being made, where we live or our lifestyle. Start your savings plan today. Money increases options and gives a sense of greater security and independence. You will experience greater happiness with a "nest egg". You learn management of your life and investments which you need for daily living today and during your retirement. You develop a long-term interest in life which will help you stay alive during emergencies and during your retirement. Money saved will give you a more comfortable lifestyle and a reason to want to live. Management of your affairs forces you to keep informed so that you are a citizen capable of voting honestly. If you "cop out", others will take your inheritance and your freedom. As a minimum, you become poor and you might become a slave doing the will of others. Your forefathers fought hard for the American ideals and so should you. Be informed.

Social security is an insurance policy and is valuable in protecting your family during younger years. It will not take care of your needs.

Our individual security never exists. We may lose jobs, our mate may leave us, someone may break into our home and we may have an accident. We may die or someone dear to us may disappear. The risks can be reduced by eating properly, by using reasonable precautions, by being friendly and cooperative with neighbors and being reasonable rather than excessive in what we do.

Insurance can be used to reduce risks from fire, earthquake, theft, illness, and lawsuits. We should not over-insure but we do need insurance especially from lawsuits. We can reduce our risks by being moderate in our lifestyle and by using good common sense.

Your security depends upon doing a job to the best of your ability. Learn to be motivated. Give yourself something good when you do a real good job and something undesirable when you do a poor job. You are not a rat but he, too, learns to pull the proper lever when he is rewarded with food and he fails to do so when he receives an electric shock. You have a mind and can think so that you can retain good habits after they have been adequately developed.

SINCERITY

Sincere people develop strong friendships and satisfying business relationships. Genuine feelings cannot be faked and insincerity brings disaster and failure to everything that we attempt. Being fair is the only way to win respect of a group or complete a sale. Selling is based on mutual honesty, confidence and respect. People recognize a fair deal and expect to be treated fairly. They cooperate and do business with those who are fair. We tend to forgive errors but we will not forget a "double cross". Sincere, honest people can be trusted to do the right thing at all times. A warm, friendly relationship is possible with a sincere person because such people can be trusted to perform in a manner which is honest and rewarding. They are consistent.

SMILE

You cannot lose when you smile. You can hardly win without a smile. Learn to smile and turn on a valuable asset in personal relations and in business. A smile adds to health and it eases anger and tension. It removes indecision. Cultivate a habit of smiling and watch others follow your lead — a smile is contagious. A smile starts and ends a day properly. A smile establishes harmony and creates interest in the work of the day for all concerned therewith. Everyone likes to do business and be associated with people who smile and are pleasant. People respond to leadership of a genial person who smiles and makes others feel good and glad to be associated with a friend who smiles and is gracious. A smile warms everyone. Days seem shorter and jobs are more interesting in places where people smile and are happy. People like to sense a feeling of cheerfulness and geniality. A smile helps everyone do a better job and gives a feeling that the world is good and life is worth living. Smile often.

TECHNOLOGY

Technology has improved our living standards very substantially but some aspects of technology are not good. We should not be distracted from our goals by either radio or television. Radio has made life more interesting since the

1920's and television entered people's lives during the early 1950's. A pleasant, comfortable and enjoyable life existed in prior years. Social life and basic values probably have declined as we listen to television rather than read good books and listen to good music. A good life become less likely. Relaxation is necessary but even the news is shallow and we fail to understand the needs of ourselves and our neighbors. Our life and its values are less complete if we spend too much time before the tube.

Progress occurs when ideas from one specialty is transferred to another specialty. We need time to keep informed. Without broad knowledge, we simply "reinvent the wheel" and do not recognize what we are doing. Everyone can find a "study" which supports any desired viewpoint and with talk shows, crazy ideas are presented as new inventions. Television and newspapers pick up the "falsehoods" and we have a new "special interest" group which temporarily changes our lives. Always remember that most ideas have been tried before and such ideas have previously been discarded as worthless. New discoveries in "sciences" do occur in fields like computers and genetics but "good thinkers" have also lived in the past and new ideas in older specialties are few. Many ideas in social sciences are devised to make money, win lawsuits and in general are harmful and not in the public good. Increases in our insurance rates in the mid-1980s are an example.

Think and plan. Learn to think and do not be fooled. Beware of advice from groups advocating special ideas. Check several data sources and get a summary from all sides of any social project before reaching your opinion as to worth. Be certain that "studies" have been performed according to rules of statistics. Most "studies" are made to delay needed projects and are biased in favor of the group paying for its costs. Reasonable, sane decisions often are lacking when public decision is needed. Most people do not participate and the advocates control so that their goals are satisfied at public expense and the public is harmed. Most studies are worthless and a little common sense is better.

Schools can help prepare you for living a successful life. They may even promise to teach you truth, character, enlightenment, understanding, justice, liberty, honesty, courage, beauty and develop the whole man, maturity and objective methods of thinking. You need to realize that you attain these desired qualities only if you devote the time and energy required to listen, learn and apply the knowledge of books and the "experienced" to your own living habits. Our individual effort is needed to make it all happen.

TIME MANAGEMENT

Time available for family, friends, work, social activities and recreation always seems to be insufficient.

Time is money and your chances for advancement depend upon using the limited time available effectively. Try to use the following techniques:
1. Establish priorities. List every task into categories such as (1) important and must do myself; (b) important but can be handled by subordinates after making a note instruction; (c) should do sometime so place in hold files for time when subordinate has a little time;

and (d) unimportant and can be thrown in wastebasket immediately.

2. Organize your day by listing tasks to be done each day with time schedule for doing them. Leave some time for surprises and employee interruptions.

3. Head off surprises by anticipating work and performing tasks as they arise. Make decisions immediately and plan ahead so that surprises are few. Do allow some time for surprise in your schedule.

4. Combine and bunch together related problems, errands and meetings so that you prepare only once and spend little time in transportation.

5. Reduce paperwork. Call and voice record for files. Scan mail and delegate most to subordinates. Send to others who should be responsible for decision. Delegate responsibility and authority so that others do their share of work. Have others do research and propose ideas when you must make final decision. Avoid interruptions by going to work early, lunching either early or late, etc.

6. File by categories rather than by detailed sub-groups. You can be too detailed in your thought, ideas, action and files. Learn to think out answers while reading letters and dictate an answer immediately.

7. Learn to say "no". Limit social time at office, chatting with others and coffee breaks. Use discipline at work, at home and in general social activity so that you have time for sleep, work and plan and some time for family. Learn to relax and not get upset.

8. Respect times of others and demand that they do the same with you. Use any excess free time for planning.

9. Control telephone. Have others answer and find out what they want. Make all return calls at one time convenient to you. Be specific in your calls and gracefully terminate conversations after your purpose has been served.

10. Handle decisions by scheduling important work when you are most alert — usually early in the day.

11. Use your time wisely. Control amount of work, handle efficiently and learn to relax. Limit distractions such as radio, television, telephone so that you have time to think, supervise and plan for your future and the future of the company.

We each waste time but we should try to become more efficient at home and at work. Plan ahead and prevent incursions on your time. You must control work habits and your time. There are only 24 hours in a day and each should be used wisely. Keep telephone calls short. Learn to call back at one time. Learn how to close conversations without offense when the call has served its purpose. Have someone else answer the telephone so that you learn the purpose before you call back. Get started on work immediately after each interruption and after completing each task. Handle each problem quickly. Learn self-discipline and limit personal and social activities during work time. Do not waste time out of habits which are detrimental to work. Think ahead and eliminate wasteful motions by review and clear thinking. Do keep concise notes but limit their number. Handle paper and problems only once if possible. Delegate to others the job of accumulating facts and limit your efforts to making decisions. Rank problems and handle related problems at the same time. Plan your day, your week and your year when possible. Learn to delegate daily operations if you are a supervisor so that you have time to plan and think about the operations future. Ask "what is my job?" and arrive at exact answers. Schedule the important meetings and decisions early in the day when you are at peak efficiency. Our grandparents had neither time or money. Our parents had time and little money. Today, the executive finds time very valuable and he orders by mail and telephone and may have others do most of his shopping and other chores.

TACT

Tact is the lubricant in good human relations and is necessary for smooth, efficient production. Its use builds good team interrelations and results in greater efficiency. Do not be blunt but think before speaking or acting. Dealing with people on an individual basis wins each employees full cooperation. Tact builds self-respect in a group and encourages best efforts. Do not speak before thinking and watch your words so that they do not sound harsh. Show goodwill. Explain your reasons and weigh all aspects and angles of a problem before making a decision. Do not make thoughtless remarks, rankle an associate or do anything which will undermine a pleasant relationship. Try to stop problems early before they become important. Never belittle a person in public. Compromise and show a feeling for the person who loses or is out-voted in a meeting. Feel for the other person. A person uses tact when he knows how to say "no" without hurting the other person or disparaging his point of view. You must be able to correct without hurting.

TRUST

Trust is basic to all human relations — both personal and financial-business — and is closely related to basic honesty. Everyone likes to trust others but there is an old rule, "trust once lost is difficult to restore". One can be forgiven for making a mistake one time but misjudging the character a second time is most foolish and few people will give you a second chance if you betray them. Trust can be lost by failure to keep promises, by being dishonest in word and action, by telling lies, by stealing property, by being non-cooperative with others and many other actions. Failure to act may also be a reason for people to lose trust in you. Guilt by association can be very detrimental, particularly when drugs and gangs are involved. Trust of others — by your friends, parents, and business associates — is a most valuable asset. Nurture your trust in others and their trust in you. It is easy to make excuses but they are worthless unless they are saleable to offended parties. Once trust is lost, others simply refuse to believe you. Your words and actions become meaningless to others because they have no confidence in you. Few adults will give you a chance to "double cross" them a second time. If you lie to others, why should they trust or believe you? When you break a contract or promise without the consent of all parties, you take risks of breach of contract lawsuits. Try to be "honest". "I am sorry" is not believed or useable in our adult world. Learn to be consistent so that others know your reactions.

WILLINGNESS

No job is too tough for the willing person but every job is too difficult and monotonous for the unwilling and lazy person. A worker who wants to work and is willing to tackle jobs independently does not make mistakes, does not waste nor increase cost because he likes his work. Learn to be a working leader and set an example but do not be a strong driver. Seek cooperation and inspire a spirit of goodwill through encouragement and appreciation of good performance. Willingness emanates from within and cannot be forced, begrudged or counterfeited. The leader must set an example by good honest work and attitude. Like your work and the quality of the product and service will improve. Otherwise, find other work.

WILLPOWER

We can always find excuses and we often try to escape our responsibilities. It takes willpower to meet our responsibilities and do what is needed correctly and properly.

The old adage which states, "where there is a will or strong desire to accomplish a project, there is a legal way" continues to be acceptable. You can change your life if you really want to do so.

SUMMARY

You alone, by your actions, knowledge, moral character and performance, can control your life and destiny. Your actions, willpower and drive, if used in a consistent, friendly and compassionate manner, are more important than what you know. How you apply yourself, how you use your ability and knowledge and your smile and friendly manner are most important. You can hire knowledge, study books to help you in your work and you must depend upon others often if you are to be successful.

We each must learn the art of compromise so that we live in peace with family members, friends, business asssociates and neighbors. We also must conform with man-made laws and laws of nature if we are to enjoy life and retain physical and mental health so that we live in freedom without fear. Each day must include some gainful work so that we are able to pay for necessities but each day must also find some pleasures and fun so that we remain relaxed, sleep well and continue to be mentally alert and healthy.

Most individuals also require a basic faith in their physical and mental abilities and a belief in a higher authority which may be called "GOD" or "basic nature". Both involve a moral code which controls life and actions. We each need to know the basic laws of nature and how it affects both man and other animals and plants. We also each need to study the lives and ideas of great teachers and ideals of major groups such as Christianity, Judaism, Islamism, Sivaism and Confucianism. Study of other great teachers who did not develop a religious following such as Homer, Plato, Virgil, Aristotle, Socrates, Darwin,

Freud and similar writers also is a basic part of our education and development of our ideals, moral codes and character. We need to acknowledge that these great thinkers lived before the invention of machines which replaced physical manpower so that we live in luxury which could not be imagined. The world has changed as airplanes, cars and trucks replaced the camel, the donkey and the elephant and we must adjust teachings to modern times without distorting the basic concepts expressed by the great teachers.

We have national and state constitutions and a large and massive collection of laws and regulations which we must learn if we are to retain our freedoms. There also are physical laws prescribed by nature, moral codes, customs and fashions which influence our actions. Nature's physical laws include concepts such as gravity, magnetism, electricity, atoms and molecules which control the motion of planets and the parts of our bodies. These place restrictions on our lifestyle and abilities. All may be combined into a concept known as "common sense" or good judgment. We must use this mass of data and basic information to formulate a set of principles which become "guideposts" and control our life, thought and mental reactions to problems as they arise. Most man-made laws and our understanding of the physical laws change with time — often very slowly. We must adapt to the slow changes being made by our society. Even the Constitution of the United States is recognized as a living document which must be interpreted by Congress and the courts to meet conditions in a changing environment. The true need of individuals and society change with time but the problem relates with a determination of "true needs".

Health is a very important asset. Avoid accidents. Doctors are rediscovering the methods used by our great grandfathers. What we eat and drink, how we exercise, worry and how we think do affect our health. Social drugs, including smoking and alcohol, kill us at an earlier age. Drugs in soft drinks and coffee and some foods influence our moods and our behavior. Doctor-prescribed drugs and some "over the counter" drugs create severe side effects, including headaches and depression. Each individual should systematically test food, drinks and each drug as well as exercise and daily life habits for their affect on clarity of mind and thought-processes, physical health and performance ability, mental attitudes and mood changes and headaches, and physical pain using single item at a time methods. Remove one item at a time from your diet for several weeks to a month. You will find that all excessives are harmful.

Our friends, family and business associates have a right to expect us to remain healthy and attractive. They also demand that we be consistent in the use of word, actions and moods. Wide swings in moods can be very disturbing to others. We as individuals should exercise our right to be as healthy as possible by watching what we do and living in moderation so that we enjoy a pleasant and comfortable life.

We must develop our individual character, moral code, beliefs and ideals so that we are not led blindly by others. Some flexibility is necessary but we must change our basic principles only when the evidence of a mistake is sound after careful analysis. We should react and be individuals but we must also be willing to accept the decisions of the majority if they are based on careful analysis and debate by society. We are individuals but we also are part of a whole called society and community. We might remember that we originally belonged to tribes of closely-related people but this organization gradually was replaced by nations and we now face a society which is becoming "one world" in scope. These societies were organized for protection of the individual from physical harm and to improve living standards of members. Easy communication, travel and population growth have all increased the need for international cooperation. We need worldwide cooperation if we are to eat, work and sleep in a peaceful environment and this is possible only if nations recognize their dependence upon a worldwide community.

Our immediate circle of family, friends and business associates demand that we become a pleasant and gracious part of a social unit. They need to like and trust us and we as individuals need their support and help. They and we need to be trustworthy, be loyal to the group, cooperative and consistent in thought, mood and actions. We are permitted to state our views and argue but decisions must be made which affect everyone after adequate deliberation. The will of the majority must prevail in all social groups. That will or decision must always conform with the appropriate legal and moral codes if problems with the "law" are to be avoided. We must obey the nations laws, we must be friendly if we want friends, we must protect ourselves and we must work so that we eat and enjoy life.

You hold the keys to your life and future. Try and make the required effort and use your life to benefit yourself, your family, your fellow man, other animals and plants. Many people have expressed the thought but few have done as effectively as Dr. An Wang who founded Wang Laboratories. "When we enter society at birth, we receive an inheritance from the people who lived before us. It is our responsiblity to augment that inheritance for those who succeed us. I feel that all of us owe the world more than we received when we were born." Try to make your life useful by making a contribution and learn so that you live a moral and useful life which makes you and others proud of accomplishments. Nature gave us many "talents" and we should use them to the best of our ability.

You alone determine your future.

You might wish to keep up to date on new developments in social and medical concepts by subscribing to several good magazines such as Bottom Line Personal and Boardroom Reports; both from Box 1026, Milburn, New Jersey 07041. There are thousands of books and magazines. Read a few of them and try to keep up with changes in the world.

Your Work, Job Or Career

The standard of living and lifestyle which will be enjoyed by your family depends upon your job, your business and the investments which are made while you work.

Your job or your business is usually your largest and most important source of income during early years. These sources of income are basic to your standard of living. Few jobs will make you rich. To become independent, you must have growing investments. All intelligent individuals must make a sincere effort to find work and advance in a chosen work area. A job is a lifetime investment and you should have another job before leaving an existing workplace. Do you really know what your employer expects of you? Please find out immediately.

The average job may look like it is permanent but you should realize that the average job lasts only about five years. Prepare for your next job today and tomorrow. Computers and robots are changing the workplace and will affect your job. Always be prepared to perform the next job.

A satisfying job is the most important investment made by each individual. Some successful individuals do not seek money and comforts but money does ease many problems of life. We can work for others or we can own our own business but we do need to earn a living rather than accept the meager government "doles". We do not eat if we live in a world of fantasy and our dreams. We must cooperate with others and worry less.

Most work is legal and honest and is needed by society. Unlawful "work" should be avoided unless you want to be restricted by a jail cell. Financial rewards differ by type of work, location, supply and demand and what you contribute individually to the owners. Society may reward in a somewhat inefficient way but color, race and sex are rapidly disappearing.

What you know and how you use the knowledge are becoming more important when determining salary and wages. This places you in greater control. Fortunately, we differ as to need for money and we thereby have a strong society with high living standards and are the envy of the world. Most individuals would be on our shores if transportation could be found.

Todays children are taught by using games rather than methods using hard work and basic thought processes. Games may increase interest but they do not teach children the actual practical work world. Life may be a "game" but it is deadly serious and we face life alone. Friends and associates may be helpful but we live with decisions alone which are very important to our future.

WORKPLACE CHARACTERISTICS
The workplace is not a social club, assembly or agency. Business should

show the employee consideration, should allow work with dignity, give the worker a chance to contribute to company profits and reward him accordingly. It should provide advancement by offering training programs and in general, provide opportunity for the willing and energetic worker. An employee should not expect charity and he must perform so that the company makes the money or profit to pay his wages as earned. Company and employees grow together by an overall effort. The bottom line is that the employee must care about the company efforts so that both grow during both good and bad economic times. Job security depends upon sales and profits.

Society demands that people live in peace with their fellow workers, neighbors and children by use of compromise. Arguments must be limited to ideas and personal feuds and disagreements should not continue over long periods. Tempers must be controlled so that discussions are impersonal and friendly and disagreements must be compromised. Our friends and "boss" will not tolerate lengthy disagreements and the number of arguments must be limited. Always use tact and be gracious and do not fight. Be honest with yourself.

Individuals need not always agree but they can often reach compromises which enable the group to work as a team. Everyone must learn to control temper, ego and pride so that they get along with others. It is most difficult to walk away from family members and long time friends. Resigning or being fired from a job can be most costly in money and pride and should not be done unless another job is in your pocket.

Change of job and employer is relatively easy within the same trade or profession. Otherwise change requires study and starting again at the bottom of the job ladder. We compete with others who are entrenched in seniority and know the job when we change to a new field of work. In all cases, we need to study a little each day so that we keep up-to-date in our chosen work endeavors. A change always creates problems and failure is often invited. Nevertheless, chance is frequently necessary if we are to attain our lifeplan. Simply evaluate the risks and benefits carefully and try to have another job in hand before announcing your change.

You cannot expect to find security in life. Partial security and peace can be found in our ability, reputation, financial independence and in good deeds and thoughts. Live the good life by proper mental attitude. Have faith and try.

As we grow older, a degree of financial independence becomes essential to peace of mind and personal comfort because of the greater possibility of loss of job, loss of health and a general loss of drive and energy as we grow older. We each have many freedoms which we inherited from hard work and many battles by our forefathers. We need to be grateful and fight to retain our way of life. We must abide by our laws and accept the restrictions shown by experience to be necessary for peaceful living in a complex society. We, at times, must accept instructions and do the will of others. The orders, in our opinion, may not be the best but they are lawful and we must live with the "boss". We must control our ego and pride and recognize that we, too, may be wrong. Relations with fellow employees and friends must be cordial and involve much understanding and compromise. We must face life in a practical manner and learn how to win friends and influence people and decisions. The stubborn create their own problems. Fighting results in loss of jobs, friends, our pride and income.

Each person must learn how to think. We should think both vertically — logically according to accepted standards — and sidewise — try to rearrange thoughts and facts to find better ways for doing things. The saying "it is not what you know but who you know", in most cases, is not true but it does not hurt to know the influential and successful. Seek their help.

We each must learn that moderation rather than excess is desirable. Excess often associates with poor health and accidents which can change plans and often is rather painful physically. Take care of yourself.

You must decide which type of lifestyle best fits your needs at an early age. You need knowledge in your job field and need to know about computers and robots. You must know how to read rapidly. Available knowledge is increasing very rapidly and you need to be informed — at least in your job field. You also need to know current events so that you can make decisions and vote properly.

Each individual must earn more than he or she spends. Borrowing to increase todays standard of living usually ends in bankruptcy. Your borrowing should be limited to long term investments such as buying a home and possibly to pay for unexpected emergencies. You should quickly create a savings equal to at least six months living expenses to be available in case of sickness and loss of job. Reduce your standard of living a little to accomplish this need. Larger savings are essential as you grow older to cover retirement needs. You also need insurance to reduce risks of life. Establish a credit rating but do not borrow long term to pay for short term need. Pay off your charge accounts each month and do not borrow more than 11% to 15% of take home pay to buy furniture, a car and other items with short life. Use self-control and discipline.

We must direct our continuing education, jobs and business efforts into fields of knowledge which will offer us the money to live the lifestyle chosen. We cannot spend millions if we earn thousands. Sources of information relative to jobs include friends, the successful in your chosen field and books available in stores and libraries. Expect some bias and contact several sources. The tools are available but you alone must make the effort to find information. Learn and develop sound habits. You must have dreams of success but they materialize only if you work with intelligence.

You must locate in an area where work is available and hopefully will be available throughout your lifetime. Everything changes with time and you must constantly be preparing for your next job. The world does not owe us anything — a living or happiness. You make your own success by your efforts. Get your friends and associates to help you when you need help.

The best rewards go to those who have goals, plan and actively work effectively to accomplish their desires. Plan your life and do not spend time with worry, jealousy and petty thoughts. Think and work instead so that you have what you desire. Your desire may be to help others while supporting yourself. Money does give physical comforts and may result in more options but it does not necessarily result in a happy life. Your thoughts, ideals and work habits all make a contribution to your well being. Plan and have it all.

Time can be converted to useful purposes. Budget your time so that it is used for work, exercise, study and play. Possibly to help others and to improve your work.

Individuals and all businesses must be profitable. Business income must exceed all expenses including overhead and taxes. You have no work when the company for which you work does not make a profit. You cut your own throat when you criticize that company in public.

Business relies upon honest, accurate and reliable verbal and written reports. The ability to tell good stories and jokes is an asset since both reduce tensions. Never combine the two in serious conversation or reports without letting everyone know that you do.

Be confident and act accordingly. The "boss", too, puts on his trousers one leg at a time just like you. However, you each must use tact and courtesy, learn the art of compromise, the ability to sell yourselves, and the art of managing other people. You must keep up-to-date by reading and by seeking advice from others. You must constantly grow and advance. You cannot stand at one place very long in this changing world. Make plans and accomplish your goals. The "white lie" might reflect tact and compassion in a social environment but use honesty in business relations. Facts alone should be used in business decisions.

It is very easy to pretend to be working when actually you are hiding behind your fears and not accomplishing anything. Such technique is no solution to problems and is very short term. You must learn to make accomplishments that are real and which are recognized by your superiors or business friends. You gain little from bragging to fellow workers since they quickly realize when you are not performing. Carry your share of the workload and by your actions, create the friendly relations required in the workplace.

Be tolerant and considerate of others. Study the Bible and basis of other religions so that you do not offend others. Also, study history and the sages such as Socrates and Plato. Possibly Thomas Edison, a famous inventor, said it all in "Genius is 1% inspiration and 99% perspiration." Work smarter — not harder.

We need to learn to be creative. Our thinking when we are trying to find new answers and approaches to problems should not use the standard accepted techniques. Instead, our thinking might:

1. Decide that there are no correct answers and explore "grey" areas. Explore all options and do not limit yourself to standard procedures.
2. Recognize that generally accepted ideas may not be the only solution to problems.
3. Decide to break with the basic rules when warranted. Rules are essential in large organizations for uniform control and legal reasons. They must be revised at times to meet existing conditions.
4. Recognize that ideas other than the usual might be workable. Explore.

5. Explore and take risks. Look at all alternate solutions to your problem.

6. Recognize that new ideas often come from other fields of expertise. Have a broad background and read literature of all specialties if possible. Others look at problems differently.

7. Realize that you, too, can be creative and have new "brainstorms". Make the effort to do some thinking rather than always follow others.

The production of food and other products essential to our health, well-being and defense is essential. We should not rely on imports for necessities. We need to read and think soundly so that we are not mislead by special interest groups — some of which place their personal pleasure ahead of your needs and safety. Your forefathers fought long and hard for your freedom and a social system which makes your life a pleasure. You should not surrender these benefits without a fight. Our elders fought for freedom rather than submit to the life of a tortured slave. Defend yourself rather than surrender due to imagined fear. Strive for peace rather than war but death may be favored instead of the life of a slave working for other nations.

Money is not everything but it is one of our driving forces and it does provide food and other necessities together with the many pleasures of life. We must negotiate an initial salary at the time of securing a job. We try to take a vague attitude to money until the employer mentions a value. We talk about our worth to the employer. We negotiate for future security and perks, such as title, car, vacation time, etc., until money is brought into the discussion by the employer. After the employer mentions a figure, we earnestly negotiate for the best possible salary and future additions.

Most employers consider merit raises as your ability to make money for the company increases. In times of inflation, general, accross-the-board raises may be substituted. We probably need to pressure the "boss" for raises in a courteous and tactful manner and ask for raises. We do not apologize and we talk in terms of our added value and contribution to the company. We show in dollars what we believe to be our contribution and ask for a portion of that amount. Many recent union contracts use this method. At the end of our verbal request and discussion, we leave a written memo which explains how our responsibilities have increased, how we help the company by increasing income and reducing costs. We justify our raise in writing.

All of life is filled with risk. We try to keep them small and manageable but we do take risks for the company and for our well-being. You take a risk when you get out of bed and there is no way to avoid risks and mistakes. We can strive to keep both at a minimum, to keep them small in cost, and we make certain that we do not make the same mistake a second time.

CAREER SELECTION

You must allocate time so that you continue your formal education each year.

Jobs available change quickly and often. You never can feel secure in any job since companies go broke, are required to change their objectives and must keep changing to operate successfuly in an ever-changing business environment. Selecting your career involves an analysis of your interests rather than your abilities since working in a field of interest relates with happiness. Consultant groups have developed questionnaires which include as many as 325 items. The questions often include the broad fields of interest such as:

Conventional traits or an interest in economics, making statistical charts, desire for regular hours of work, an interest in developing business systems and a habit of being thrifty. People with these traits often are accountants, dental assistants, proofreaders, secretaries and statisticians. They work in fields which require attention to details and accuracy. They probably work for large corporations in subordinate roles. They are not leaders.

Social traits or an interest in working with people, solving problems by discussing feelings and interaction with others. They like to share responsibilities but want to be the center of attention. They are elementary school teachers, licensed practical nurses and playground directors, etc. They are interested in sociology, like to go to church and meetings, often lead scout troops, like babies and work with charities and other groups.

Artistic traits or a need for self-expression and an appreciation of aesthetic ideas. These people are interested in dramatics, art galleries, poetry, art and music. They possibly should be art museum directors, authors, dancers, artists, reporters, librarians and photographers.

Enterprising traits or an interest in leadership and power. They enjoy working with others toward organizational goals and economic success. They take financial and personal risks and like competitive activities, always want to challenge others. They easily start conversations with strangers, they like to swap and bargain. They like to shop. They like aggressive people and people who are leaders in business and society. They might be a beautician, elected public official, agent, personnel director, restaurant manager. They often are leaders in business and society.

Investigative traits or interest in scientific activities, gathering information, analyzing data, discovering new theories. They are self-reliant at work and play. They like calculus, chemistry, physical and natural sciences, play chess and do research work. They might be biologists, geographers, researchers, mathematicians, researchers, engineers, etc.

Realistic traits. People who like action rather than thought, concrete problems rather than the abstract. They like nature, the mechanical, construction, repair and military activities. They like agriculture, read Popular Mechanics. They make cabinets, like to operate machinery and dream about being a forest ranger. They work as carpenters, cartographers and ranchers.

Most people have interest in two or three fields as described above. As examples, the lawyer often has artistic and investigative interests and the computer programmer has interests in investigative, realistic and conventional areas. Continue your formal education each year. You need drive, ambition, common sense, education and ability.

JOB EVALUATION

Society has developed and uses many criteria and standards in the workplace. Throughout our history, the workplace has changed from hunting, farming, manufacturing to a relatively service-type environment. In the 1980s, dependence upon others is very substantial and we must cooperate and work together if we are to eat, have housing, and live a secure, peaceful life. You must learn to trust yourself and be independent while fully cooperating with others.

The future earning lifetime of an individual at age 25 years should be about 40 years if age 65 is an acceptable retirement age. Earnings during this time should be about as follows:

Average yearly earnings	Lifetime Earnings	Today's value discounted @ 5%
$10,000	$ 400,000	$175,000
20,000	600,000	263,000
30,000	800,000	351,000
40,000	1,200,000	527,000
50,000	2,000,000	879,000

The values shown should be after tax. Also, inflation will affect values and probably increase them. You probably expect yearly increases in salary and you can construct tables including such variables as increasing wages, taxes and inflation to meet your expectations.

Real after tax and inflation wages were almost constant during the 1970s but have again increased during 1983. You can also determine values if you are now over age 25 or if you expect early retirement.

You should learn how to find and protect your job or business.

Your living habits will control the amount of income needed to support your lifestyle. High living and waste create a higher need for money. Excesses in all forms such as drink, sex, and excitement all have their price and future costs in money and health.

Reading, studying and managing your assets can be more fun than a dull party or movie. Learn to use and enjoy your private hours. Data from the Commerce Department show that education is worthwhile. For heads of family over 25 years of age, yearly salaries are in range during 1986:

One or more years of graduate school	$49,000
Bachelor's degree	42,000
Some college	31,000
High school diploma	27,000
High school dropout	18,000
Grade school graduate	15,000
Grade school dropout	12,000

A large difference in lifetime earnings results from what each person knows and how he or she makes use of that knowledge. The world favors those who try and work to the best of their ability. Much knowledge can be learned in the workplace and life depends upon learning at all ages throughout life from books and experience.

A study of MONEY Magazine in 1986 indicates that the best paid employees in 160 major corporations earn following salaries plus bonus. These salaries often are increased by perks which often approach 35% of salary. These may include social security contributions, cars, insurance, tax benefits, medical benefits.

Occupation	Beginners	Veterans	Exceptional Maximum
Accountant	$24,000	$ 32,000	$ 90,000
Actor	12,000	12,000	12 million
Advertising executive	14,000	55,000	742,000
Airline pilot	55,000	110,000	161,000
Chef	18,000	45,000	105,000
Chemist	40,000	57,000	85,000
Commercial Banker	29,000	55,000	575,000
Computer Programmer	21,000	33,000	50,000
Dentist	55,000	91,000	300,000
Diplomat	25,000	60,000	75,000
Electrician Unionized	15,000	40,000	43,000
Elementary teacher	17,000	31,000	42,000
Executive recruiter	70,000	150,000	300,000
Geologist	27,000	80,000	148,000
Investment Banker	98,000	250,000	1,500,000
Lawyer	48,000	225,000	1,200,000
Librarian	18,000	31,000	58,000
Insurance agent	16,000	53,000	300,000
Mail carrier	20,000	27,000	68,000
Model	60,000	175,000	400,000
Fund manager	50,000	250,000	692,000
Newspaper reporter	19,000	30,000	47,000
Paralegal	16,000	35,000	50,000
Photographer	17,000	29,000	53,000
Physician	79,000	129,000	350,000
Professor	27,000	45,000	67,000
Nurse	20,000	25,000	44,000
Social worker	18,000	24,000	26,000
Stockbroker	36,000	80,000	2,000,000

Individuals and companies often do not discuss salary. Information is available free from:

Administrative Management Society, 2360 Maryland Road, Willow Grove, Pennsylvania 19090; Bureau of Labor Statistics, U. S. Government Printing Office, Washington, DC 20402; Various trade associations, professional societies, labor unions, associations, etc. often collect such information. For lists of organizations, contact Encyclopedia of Associations, Gale Research Company, which is available in libraries.

There are many sources of information and some may disagree with the above values. You need to analyze before making decisions which may control your life during many years.

JOBS AVAILABLE

Our earning ability must be greater than our spending habits if we are to avoid bankruptcy. Education is the learning of the experiences and ideas of others and education does increase earning ability. The stubborn and those who refuse to study and accept advice must learn by their experiences and failures and their life usually is more difficult than necessary. Education and experience is a key which opens to opportunities. Those who adapt and have the discipline to acquire and apply existing knowledge usually have the ambition, drive and tact to perform in a superior manner by relating with others so that earning power is increased.

In the 1980s, many books are available which describe in detail the characteristics of various jobs, the expected pay and possibly the future of such jobs. Not all forecasts are reliable and you should read many of such texts before deciding your life's work. The world is changing rapidly and the computer and robot may displace your job every five years. However, the past experience may be useful in new work.

Competition for job opportunities requires that we select a job field at the earliest age. Thereafter, we should direct our life and education in a manner which will enable us to be successful — emotionally, physically, mentally and financially — in our chosen area of work. Our work should be reasonably enjoyable and a change should be made immediately if your first choice proves in error. We must work to eat and we should do so with gusto. Our desires for a "good life" will not materialize unless we individually make the required effort. We cannot attain success by dreams and wishes. Work is required together with sound and cooperative relations with fellow workers to create our luck. We can sell our services or products only if someone is willing to buy at an acceptable profit. You become a supervisor with higher pay if you convince others to work with you — not against you.

Write to National Association of Trade and Technical Schools for a 50-page guidebook, "Trade and Technical Careers and Training", Box 10429, Department US, Rockville, Maryland 20850.

Estimates of jobs available vary with time and place and persons involved. The following jobs are expected to have prospects for above average growth:

	Jobs in 1995	Change From 1982
Accountants, auditors	1,200,000	40%
Actors, actresses	49,000	43%
Aerospace engineers	62,000	41%
Architects	117,000	40%
Auto mechanics	1,168,000	38%
Bank officers, managers	617,000	45%
Biological scientists	71,000	36%
Cashiers	2,314,000	47%
Cement masons	136,000	43%
Civil engineers	228,000	47%
Clinical-lab technicians	292,000	40%

	Jobs in 1995	Change From 1982
Computer programmers	471,000	77%
Computer-service technicians	108,000	97%
Computer-systems analysts	471,000	85%
Construction-machine operators	291,000	44%
Corrections officers	147,000	33%
Dancers	11,000	43%
Dental assistants	217,000	42%
Dental hygienists	99,000	43%
Designers	253,000	41%
Dietitians	62,000	40%
Electrical engineers	529,000	65%
Electronics technicians	588,000	61%
Grade, preschool teachers	1,877,000	37%
Guards	937,000	47%
Health-service administrators	478,000	58%
Ironworkers	129,000	39%
Legal assistants	88,000	94%
Licensed practical nurses	814,000	37%
Mechanical engineers	318,000	52%
Medical assistants	104,800	47%
Nursing aides, orderlies	1,641,000	35%
Occupational therapists	40,000	60%
Office-machine repairers	96,000	72%
Physical therapists	68,000	58%
Physicists	25,900	37%
Podiatrists	19,700	52%
Receptionists	861,000	45%
Registered nurses	1,954,000	49%
Respiratory therapists	67,000	45%
Securities-sales workers	106,000	36%
Surgical technicians	49,000	40%
Surveyors	63,000	43%
Tool programmers	21,700	78%
Travel agents	88,000	43%
Writers, editors	162,000	35%
X-ray technologists	157,000	43%

Always remember that forecasts are a guess and may be wrong. Trends change and the forecaster may not be competent. Use only as very general guides. Review data from several sources before making your decisions.

JOB LOCATION

For names of companies, names of executives, products made, etc., consult:

Polk City Directory
McRae's City Directories
Standard and Poors Register
Value Line Reports

State and federal governments have agencies which help the job seeker. Books also are available which describe the location of jobs, areas of probable growth and make forecasts as to the probable existence of work of different types during the future. The work world is changing rapidly as new ideas and inventions displace older job opportunities. As an example, blowing glass jars by mouth disappeared many years ago; the tractor replaced the mule, etc. Current changes are much more rapid.

Individuals who have spent a lifetime tracking such changes suggest that:

1. The western world is rapidly changing from an industrial environment to an information-service-based society. Computers and robots are replacing many people in the assembly-line while creating jobs repairing the robots. Computers and robots work cheaper than man and do the job more accurately. Population growth, the number of people in each age group, the desires of people as to location and type of work all influence availability of jobs and demand versus supply determines pay scales. Defense and a desire to retain control over local consumption will influence imports although labor is cheaper in some undeveloped countries and they are developing necessary skills. Industrial nations must retain the power to defend themselves and we as a nation must again realize that allies are undependable and the meek, weak and defenseless — those who lack desire and will — always have been slaves — at least poor — throughout history. We must be prepared to defend our nation and its lifestyle. You should not be mislead by false leaders, special interest groups, false statistics and non-sound thinking. Learn to read history, study statistics and think for yourself rather than being lead as a horse by others.

2. The workplace is changing rapidly and you should be preparing for your next job, hopefully it also will be an advancement. The use of technology in medicine and industry is questioned by the uninformed. High technology has given us a superior standard of living but it can be over-used and be detrimental to our society. In some cases it can prove too expensive. An example is the cost of keeping terminally ill people on machines for another 30 days of misery which might be questioned. Our natural resources are declining and cost/benefit studies are becoming popular.

3. The economy of the western nations is becoming dependent upon each other and upon the material and labor resources of undeveloped nations. Isolation and self-sufficiency of nations is disappearing as worldwide trade increases. Actions in one country influence all other nations.

4. Managers consider the worldwide environment. They also are be-

ginning to think long term rather than profits today. The history of their company and its long term future are more important than its profitability during tenure of todays manager. You need employment over years.

5. Centralized structures are crumbling. Our government and many company managements are decentralizing and growing stronger from the bottom up. Top management is not giving all orders. The worker's rights are greater as he becomes more involved.

6. We, as individuals, are reverting back to the self-reliance of our fathers. We look for less help from institutions and government and rely more on ourselves. IRA's encourage personal savings.

7. Citizens, workers and consumers are demanding and getting a greater voice in government, business and the marketplace. Lawsuits are beginning to make others responsive and in the extreme, are keeping useful products from the marketplace, which is not in the public interest when carried to extremes.

8. The nation is moving toward a "net-work" organization. This is a three-way communications structure in which the constantly changing participants treat each other as peers. The computer and telephone lines, including cable TV, are connecting homes and offices so that people can see each other and communicate without traveling for meetings. Work in home is easier and may change the office workplace of the future. People at many locations can be connected easily for conferences and meetings. Business often locates close to major universities so that superior minds are available for consultation in their research and business practices.

9. The population center of the United States is shifting toward the south and west. Population is moving to jobs and better climates and environments.

10. People are getting a wide variety of choices. There is now part-time work, flex-time, work in home, shared work and temporary work. The marketplace, too, is changing.

Students of change suggest that the fastest growing areas include Texas, Colorado, Utah, New Mexico, Arizona, California and Florida. The relative rate of change also changes between surveys, and books such as Megatrands by Naisbitt may not be entirely correct in their forecasts. Trends do change at times.

It is obvious that we as individuals are rather insignificant when population is in the billions. We cannot exist without the help and cooperation with others who supply us with food, housing and other essentials. Most of us eventually must realize that we will not be important nor influential. We learn that we can be happy and comfortable in a lesser niche in society. We work as part of the team rather than as the chief executive who gives orders and possibly leadership. We, too, can be important at a lower level.

We should have high ambitions but we also should be realistic and be happy with the attainable after doing our best with what we have to offer.

JOB SEARCHING

Employment agencies have found that:

1. Many large, mature companies tend to promote from within. Thus, management and supervisors are selected from company employees and few outside people are hired except at starting or entry positions.
2. Managers and supervisors should be looking for employment with smaller companies. They may be growing.
3. Well written letters often replace resumes when applying for management jobs. Resumes are often sent to personnel offices and often do not reach the present managers who make the selections.
4. After age 45, you should never leave existing employment before getting another job unless you are financially secure and widely known. This advice is good at any age. Finding work is harder as age increases.
5. Do not send your letters to top managers of very large companies. Instead find the name of the manager who needs help. Top management will probably send your letter to personnel where it may become lost. A mail or letter campaign may be necessary if you are not employed. Employment ads may be useful but they are rather broad in scope and may not be read by busy people.
6. Mail campaigns should be comprehensive unless you already know of a job opening. 500 to 1000 letters may be appropriate. Careful selection of names may reduce number of letters.
7. Quality of your letter is of vital importance. Give your letters your best effort.
8. Entry at lower levels in administration, retail sales, and other work is controlled by the personnel department. Such jobs may be filled at recruitment centers and by walk-in at job locations — usually the personnel office.
9. Companies with less than 5000 people are good job prospects. They may be growing faster and they often receive fewer resumes.
10. Large, diversified companies are good prospects if they circulate resumes among their offices and groups.
11. Fast growth companies are good prospects since they often need employees at all levels.
12. Small and stable industries are not growing and job prospects and advancement may not exist. Rapid growth relates with advancement. Determine whether the company is expanding research.
13. Develop a habit of thinking about yourself and your job on a regular basis. Review your accomplishments and keep a continuing record of your progress in writing. Are you satisfied? If your abilities are not being used and developed, you may want to do something about the situation before you become discouraged and angry.

You increase your income by doing your home chores yourself rather than having others do them. Also, no tax is paid when you do the work but tax is paid on all income earned if paid by cash or barter.

14. Plan in detail the steps required to remove yourself from any job in which you are stymied through no fault of your own if you are truly qualified for greater opportunity. Be certain that you have the ability and drive and really want to make the change. Then start the process either within the company transfer system or with a new employer.

15. Most jobs are never advertised. You can only find out about them by sending resumes or letters, visits to offices, and referrals. You must make yourself available by letting others know that you want to make a change and are looking for other employment. You probably do not want your present employer to know and this creates some problems.

16. The lower the level within the company of the sought after job, the easier it is to get a job. There are many more low level jobs than top supervisor jobs. "Manual labor" types are being replaced by machines.

17. Many people find jobs by being at the right place at the right time, by references of friends and by having made themselves known to be available.

18. There is always insecurity in all jobs. You should think about the possibility of your job disappearing due to technical advance, lack of demand for the product, etc. Also, your boss may be replaced by someone who has a friend. Being fired today is more difficult than during the past, but your job is not secure unless you make it so. Always study and prepare for advancement and other work. Be prepared to make a change even when no change is deemed to be necessary. Computers and robots are changing the workplace in both plant and factory/stores. Learn to adapt to change and be prepared to move if necessary. The task is both physical and mental. Educate yourself.

19. A year or more may be required to find a new job. Finding jobs in management and when no education is required are most difficult. Study daily.

20. You can at times create a new job by convincing an employer that you can fill his needs. He may not recognize the need. You must have the ability.

21. Marketable skill is to be found in your accomplishments. You have to be certain that you have and can suitably identify tangible and important accomplishments before offering yourself to others. You can offer your services if you strongly believe that you can make a major contribution to an employer and that you have the drive to accomplish your promise and sales proposal. You are selling yourself and your ideas and thereafter you must perform.

22. Most jobs are offered by employers with less than five employees. Such employment often is short term and benefits may be limited. If they are successful, however, the overall package could be most

worthwhile and offer great potential.

You might consult with employment agencies and firms which offer job interview services. They can give data on job availability and types of interviews. Ask for instructions regarding preparation for interview.

EMPLOYMENT PLANNING

Study the company annual reports, S&P reports, Value Line data of the company where you plan to apply for a job. Try to get a job offer.

Think about the interview after you have received an appointment. Do use the following rules when you rehearse for the interview:

Do not tell a prospective employer how to run his business.

Do not criticize previous employer.

Do not volunteer your shortcomings and deficiencies.

Do not emphasize salary, fringes, etc. during first interview.

Do not ask too many questions.

Do not arrive late for appointments.

Dress properly. Do not wear casual clothes.

Be pleasant and courteous. Use tact but do "blow your own horn".

Let others know your qualifications — technically, morally and personally.

Show that you know how to handle people by convincing employer of your merits.

Even when you are under no economic pressure to find employment quickly, starting your search promptly is a smart idea. Delays may hurt your chances of finding the job you want. After you start, keep looking. Job searching can be discouraging at times but sustained effort is essential for morale and usually is successful. Some useful tips follow:

1. Plan and start your search as soon as you know that you need to make a job move. You should have been preparing daily during employment period.

2. Make your job hunt a full-time job. You previously worked forty or more hours and you should work no less for yourself when you need a job. Again, always realize that there is no job security and that you should be prepared to seek new work at all times. Constantly study and be prepared educationally, mentally and emotionally for another job.

3. Once you start your search, do not allow yourself little vacations. Really try.

4. If possible, start your search before leaving other work. Have a job in your pocket before leaving.

5. Apply and start your interviews early in the day so that you have time for multiple interviews, examinations and other procedures used by employers.

6. Always be on time for appointments. Go early and wait on the street if necessary but do not be late.

7. Find out the best time of day and week to apply for a job and

interview before approaching employer. If necessary, ask when making appointments. Read books regarding the employer and industry before contacting employer.

8. Let friends and acquaintances know that you are looking. Advertise widely so that you have many people helping you locate possible job openings.

9. Follow up leads immediately. If you learn of a job possibility late in the day, call immediately and try for an early appointment during the following morning.

10. Write a letter stating what you know and what you have done. Leave a copy at the interview.

Write for "Occupational Outlook Handbook", Superintendent of Documents, Washington, D.C. 20402.

JOB RESUME

Your future is for sale when you look for work. Any resume that ties you down to the past hurts your prospects. Do not use the usual resume which dates past job experience and is really an obituary. Instead of discussing the companies that were in your past, show your real talents. Know the prospective company before you apply and send a letter showing how you can fit into the new company; how you can contribute and help it make money and grow. List your contributions. Show that you have been developing and advancing your ability and knowledge during each past job and that this all fits into your work in the prospective new job. Finding a job which you like, which you will enjoy, and in which you can make a contribution by hard work with enthusiasm is very important to you and your employer. Please study a text by Half, published in 1982, under the title, *How To Get Hired in Todays Job Market*. Learn to sell yourself -- your knowledge, ability, energy and effort. Develop a sales package and ability to sell yourself to others.

JOB INTERVIEW

Make each job interview a learning experience. After it is over, ask yourself:

1. How did the interview go?

2. What points did I make that seemed to interest the prospective employer? Was my salary and job description the best attainable? Did I present my qualifications well? What pertinent facts did I overlook? Will the prospective employer call back? When should I again call him?

3. Did I show how I can help make money for him? What did I overlook that was important?

4. Did I pass up clues and methods as to the best way to sell myself? What was missing?

5. Did I learn all that I needed to know about the job? Did I ask the proper questions? Did I do my best?

6. Did I talk too much or too little? Was I too aggressive or not aggres-

sive enough? What went good and what went wrong?

7.   How can the next interview be improved? How can I do better the next time, possibly with the next company?

The job interview is a selling job and it is very important because you are selling yourself. You need work to live so give interviews your all. Study the techniques used by successful salesmen. Many such books are available in the library and bookstores. They differ somewhat by industry. Be confident. Use a strong handshake, good eye contact, sit straight in your chair, be enthusiastic, neat, friendly. You now have employment. Now work to keep it and plan for your advancements. You might improve your understanding of the following business related concepts.

IMPROVING JOB PERFORMANCE

You might review the following concepts to see if your job performance can be improved.

ABSENTEEISM

The absence of an employee affects the productivity of the entire operation. When an individual feels that his attendance record is important, he will not make a habit of being absent without real cause. Like your work and there is no excuse for playing sick. The leader should sell his workers on the importance of each job, appeal to the employees loyalty, to his sense of fairness and each worker's responsibility to the group or team. Many people can be kidded into proper behavior but the leader should not bully. Workers and leaders should be firm with those who break the rules of the workplace and not allow bad habits to develop. Many people do not realize that their absence upsets schedules and operations of the group because they do not understand the entire operation. Show them how their cooperation is essential to overall performance. Explain the work of the group and the individual contributions of each member of the team. Create in each employee a feeling of respect and confidence in you as a supervisor. Mutual respect between each worker and the supervisor is essential. Sick days are for emergencies and sickness and should not be vacations unless such use is in written company policy. The worker who takes them for amusement is dishonest and the practice should be nipped when it occurs. The supervisors should tell each employee when he starts work and show them repeatedly how their work is very important to the performance of the team. Create a feeling of responsibility in each individual for contributing to the overall effort. Create a feeling of need, of being wanted and responsibility for contributing to the effort of the group. All workers and supervisors should work together when someone violates the rules. Each person should realize that all wages are affected adversely when the group does not perform efficiently as a group. Each individual must carry his share of the workload.

Keeping people working to the end of each day is a year round problem similar to getting people to start on time. It, too, can become a habit. Too little discipline and lack of interest on the part of all employees causes resentment and deliberate "goldbricking". Good judgment and finesse in supervision is a key. Deal on an individual basis but do be certain that each worker is doing his share and performing efficiently. Some people can be influenced by reason, others require firmness. Instruct each new person as to the rules in utmost detail and insist that he perform. Show the group the actual figures as to performance and set an example as leader. The average person will give a square deal when the leader has confidence and when all within the group are treated equally and fairly so that no one gets by at the cost of others. Learn to use preventative techniques rather than corrective measures. Be sure that everyone knows and follows the rules. The group should use "peer pressure" to force everyone to make the necessary effort in the team activity.

COMMUNICATION

You cannot expect to hold down a job nor find advancement unless you are able to read instructions. You also need to listen and be able to talk with others in a friendly and tactful manner. To work, you simply must accept and follow instructions from others.

Safety considerations often require that people converse with each other. Life is more enjoyable when we talk to and get along with our fellow workers. Exchange of information is essential in the workplace.

We also should observe and know that bright people talk about ideas and issues, mediocre people talk about things, and small people talk about other people — they gossip. Read and study so that your conversations are respected and help you in your work. Try to get along with and impress superiors of your ability and other favorable characteristics.

Good conversation should be articulate, clear, understandable, honest and welcomed by others. Try to develop a pleasant voice, facial expressions and actions which express friendship.

Instructions to others and social conversation should be pleasant, tactful and considerate of the beliefs and feelings of others. The haughty and stubborn are not liked. Try to be friendly.

Good communication requires that:

1. We do not interrupt others while they talk. We should not rush their thoughts and words.
2. We listen to what others say and honestly consider their viewpoint.
3. We use valuable tools such as paraphrasing or summarizing the thoughts of others so that we do not fail to understand. Others are also impressed with our ability and sincere desire to gain insights into their thoughts.
4. We do not allow our mind to wander nor show boredom. Do not ask others to repeat their words. We must listen intently instead.
5. We should not interrupt with questions which make us appear pushy or demanding. Always be tolerant. Ask questions which clarify and increase mutual respect and understanding.
6. Control level of voice and emotions.
7. Do not give quick or cliche-ridden answers. Really take the time to listen and understand the problems and ideas of others.

8. We should not be the expert. Do not interrupt but use tact and understanding, particularly when there is a misunderstanding. Learn to use compliments.

9. We should not hide our true personal feelings when talking with the boss. We should honestly discuss our differences and seek acceptable, true, meaningful compromise of differences. We must learn to be honest and truthful so that we obtain the respect of friends, supervisors and family. Get to the problem without giving excessive irrelevant detail. Respect the decisions after compromise has been reached. Keep your promises.

10. We should not bore people with minor details nor embarrass them with too much talk about personal matters.

11. We should stop the conversation at intervals to comment on how the conversation is going. Such effort can repair broken messages and bring openness to the dialogue. Learn to summarize the conversation and reach agreement – close the sale.

12. We should never agree with misstatements of fact and obviously wrong conclusions. Bad advice and errors of thought are corrected if they are stated as truth by the other party. Errors are always challenged. Error in view and thinking should be shown to be in error and unacceptable. This is particularly true when company policy is involved.

13. Good conversation requires fairness, honest respect of another's viewpoints, truthfulness, courtesy, tact, a feeling and consideration of others, and patience. Remember that the other viewpoint may be as reasonable as the one which you advance. Argument and correction is necessary only when rules are broken or when ideas have rather universal acceptance. As an example, the earth has been proven to be round, not square.

Have respect for yourself and others. The honest advocate of sound ideas gets attention when he is forceful. Decency, courtesy and tact are necessary when relating with people. You can cause change if you really try.

Learn how to organize your thoughts, place them into a draft letter and then take time to polish the work. Frequent use of "I" in communications often is associated with an in-fighter who has not learned how to cooperate. Failing to work the allocated hours, excessive talking on the job and excessive use of the toilet often are associated with a slacker and inefficient worker.

Your bookstore and library contain many good books which will help you speak to audiences and help you write good letters and reports. Some even contain form letters which you may place in your computer so that you can use appropriate letters and paragraphs. You may also join study groups and classes.

Most supervisors have accomplished the art of speaking and writing. They are also fast readers. Today, everyone is exposed to large amounts of paper as required to keep up to date at work and know facts about the rapidly changing world. A good citizen must read trade journals, papers and study economics. We can be trained to read 200 to 600 words per minute with complete comprehension/meaning. Schools are available to teach individuals to read faster. See your phone book.

Each speaker encounters some emotional disturbance before giving a talk before a large group. Experience reduces our fears. Join a speakers club. You also must speak and think clearly before small groups in the workplace. Instructions and ideas must be exchanged. We must each learn to listen and ask questions when we do not clearly understand another's statements.

We must also be able to write clearly and concisely. Speaking usually comes naturally after we have learned to collect our thoughts and express them in an understandable manner in writing.

The usual letter and report are composed of three parts. These are: (1) an opening statement which often gives the purpose, (2) the body which explains basic facts, and (3) the closing which gives recommendations and conclusions, requests action, etc.

The opening should be very short but it should get favorable attention of the reader so that he continues to read. It might:

1. Give the purpose of the letter or report, possibly listing the major subjects or ideas to be discussed.
2. Ask questions requiring action by reader.
3. Show appreciation and thanks to reader for past favors or actions.
4. Accentuate the possitive by admitting an error in the past, announcing a solution to a mutual problem, authorize an action or a favor to the reader, etc.
5. Introduce a new contact known to both parties.

The opening should not include:

1. A participle or trite expression such as reference to a recent memorandum, refer to matter previously discussed, etc.
2. An acknowledgement of receipt of letter or other document.
3. A review of a prior letter. Do not use "in which you state." Instead, use the opening to orient your reader to your present subject.

The body of any letter or report should support and cause the reader to reach the conclusions desired by you as stated in the last section of your letter. The body should clearly and concisely explain your reasons why the reader should reach a desired action or conclusion. Clarity of thought, reasoning and expression are all important. Arrange your thoughts in proper order so that the reader is lead to understand and react favorably to your recommendations or request. The need is no different than that required before discussing a problem over the phone or in private. In all cases, you must have a well thought out proposition.

You might ask yourself as you think about a letter:

1. What does the reader need to know? Limit your discussion but do be honest and do not omit any important thoughts or negative aspects of basic information.
2. What do I want to tell him? Read above again?
3. What is the purpose of the document?

4. How will the reader use the material? How will he react? Am I misleading the reader by including many details or by omitting details of importance to a decision?

5. How shall you as writer organize and arrange the material? Use good logic and lead the reader to conclusions desired by writer in a sound, honest manner.

6. What do you, as the writer, want reader to do?

7. How will reader feel and react after reading?

8. How would you, the writer, react if you received the letter or report? The reader may have a similar reaction. Again, you need the long term "goodwill" of the reader and you must be sincere and honest in giving him all pertinent facts so that he can make a logical decision.

The body of the letter or report should include:

1. Proper organization of thought and factual data. Ask yourself the questions using "what", "why", "where", "when", and "how". Many reports in the opening section give conclusions reached by the writer and the body supports such recommendations in a concise, practical and logical manner. Letters are shorter but may use the same technique.

2. Simple words — words which have a well understood, single meaning. State exactly what you intend to say. Use simple, short sentences and paragraphs. Some variations in length may be desired but no sentence should exceed 20 to 30 words.

3. Paragraphs should discuss a single idea. Separate the various parts of your argument by the use of paragraphs.

4. Be concise and do not use unneeded words. Make every word carry its own weight. Do not use junk words such as "you know", "uh" in either speech or writing. Instead, pause, collect your thoughts and then continue.

5. Use active words when possible. Use words which tell who does what. Give specific thoughts and action.

6. Write as though you are having a private talk with the reader. Use short sentences — 30 words or less.

7. Always write and talk to express logical thought. Do not try to impress others since they judge you by your past and present actions and ideas and not by your words. Always remember that "little men" use big words, long sentences, etc., but they do not impress a reader or listener who is looking for sound thoughts and ideas. You want the reader to accept your ideas and recommendations and you should not actively try to make a good impression by being obnoxious. The smart leader looks for leadership and is favorably impressed by ideas, dress and actions. He does not want to waste time with long words and long discussions. He has other work.

The closing of your letter should be original and to the point. Stress action on the part of the reader. Your closing should contain very few specific recommendations and should concentrate on them in a manner which will leave the reader with only the choice of accepting your plan and recommendation. You may wish to ask yourself the following when thinking about your closing.

1. Have I properly used "how", "where", etc.? Have I requested the desired action and approval by a date which is reasonable?
2. Have I stated the facts properly and strongly? Should I give a promise, an authorization for action, give an order or command, etc.?
3. Should I request specific action, ask for specific advice or information, request a study?
4. Should I express a courtesy, say "thank you", ask for help?

You might give some thought to the use of tactful and courteous expressions. Say what you mean in a clear, concise manner which cannot be misunderstood but say it with tact. The idea may be conveyed but remember that phases such as the following are useable. "It was nice of you to invite me and I would be happy to be your guest but, unfortunately, I will be out of town on the date of your meeting." "It will be a pleasure to _____ and I look forward to a pleasant association with you." "We suggest that you favorably consider _____" What is your opinion regarding _____?" "Please complete the attached form and return it by _____" There are many ways to use tact and courtesy without the loss of accuracy and intent. Be kind to others.

You might study:

The Elements of Style by Strunk and White
On Writing Well by Zinsser
How to Write by Meyers

EDUCATION

Programming the computer, operating the device and related robots probably is important as part of many job fields. These instruments also need repair and determining what is wrong may be useful employment for those who prefer to work with their hands rather than with their minds. Work you must if you want to eat. The writer has often been told by supervisors, "If you do not use your head, you must use your hands." New ideas often are very valuable. Learn to think for pay and to avoid accidents. Know some history, study nature and learn to handle people. Insist on basics — not views and beliefs of the teacher.

In public schools, students learn when parents, teachers and students accept firm discipline, have clear expectations, consistent leadership and strong commitment by parents and teachers. Help in job finding also is desired.

Education is a process by which the experiences of others and knowledge accepted by past generations is passed along quickly to future generations. You do have to learn from your own mistakes if you don't read and study. As individuals, we each must keep up to date in our job field and in current events taking place around us. We then may perform our job properly and we may have the knowledge to vote and help form public opinion intelligently.

The work environment today is changing very rapidly. Experts believe that large numbers of us will change work every five years. Communication and computational skills, a broad knowledge of today and history and cooperation with our fellow man are all essential. Each person must adapt to new habits and develop new ideas which are necessary for success. Always be ready for your next job whether it be advancement or replacement.

You and your children should make school count. As an adult, you should make an effort to learn quickly. As a parent, you should urge your children to take advantage of education. The following tips seem worthwhile.

1. Class participation is essential. Sit close to the front of the classroom. Join in class discussions and ask questions. If you are in doubt, others, too, will need to know the answers. Do not hesitate but do not be a showoff. Take the hard courses needed for jobs.

2. Keep up with your homework and class assignments. Ask for help from the teacher and friends when you start falling behind. Most people want to be helpful. Try to find a quiet place to study, preferably at home and spend the time necessary to learn assignments.

    Practice and look for ways to sharpen your basic skill in each class. You can practice your reading skill in mathematics, your writing skill in history and your algebra skill in science. Learn to reason and think.

3. Develop your skill in typing and with a computer. Take complete class notes so that you remember what was said in addition to what was in the book. Good notes can be used as a lifetime reference in your work.

4. Practice correcting and rewriting your work. Help friends to gain experience and be subject to their correction. You learn to communicate and you thereby correct your errors in understanding. Learn human relations.

5. Learn — do extra reading. Get in the habit of reading books, a newspaper and several magazines. Talk with family and friends about what you read and the ideas which you develop while reading. Look up words in the dictionary for meaning and spelling. Learn to educate yourself without the help of others. You need to read and think in many jobs, particularly in management.

There are many jobs. Pay in service jobs usually is lowest and managers usually receive the highest pay. Your job field should have a long life expectancy.

Contact a college admissions office or a college financial aid office if money is needed.

DELEGATION

You cannot do everything. Time is lacking. Part of the job of every supervisor is to delegate and assign work to others. He also is responsible for the work performed and supervises other employees working with him or her. Failure to properly delegate both workload and authority to make related decisions is a major cause for failure of the supervisor to advance and often such failure retards the growth of the company. You are not delegating properly if (1) you have to let one important job slip in order to take care of another; (2) you are unable to find time to plan ahead; (3) you are unable to find a subordinate who can relieve you when you are under pressure; (4) you miss deadlines frequently and consistently; (5) you have a waiting list of subordinates wishing to discuss their projects with you; (6) you prepared letters and reports yourself when the subject should be handled by others; (7) you take work home or work overtime regularly; (8) you fail to find time for public relations and professional functions; (9) you feel tired and overworked. You may fail to delegate because you are fearful of not maintaining control of work performed by others, you believe that you can do the work better and faster than others, you do not realize the need to train others, you do not arrange time for training, you do not realize the help that you can get from others, you fail to trust those working for you, you do not know how to train others, you do not wish to show your ignorance, your superior does not allow you to delegate, you fear that others will take advantage and reduce your chances for advancement, you do not want to give up responsibility, etc. Usually you will not advance until you have trained your replacement. Select good subordinates and train them so that you have time to plan for the company and your own future. Delegation does not imply abdication of responsibility or your need for supervision. You continue to be accountable for the work of subordinates and their work usually continues to require your approval. They should do basic work but you must check often so that they comply with your views. You reserve for yourself the responsibility to read the reports and letters of your subordinates, you probably will sign the more important documents and depending upon the wishes of your supervisors, you may sign all documents. You remain in control. You must be certain that you set policy and that it is followed by everyone. You should (1) maintain frequent contact with subordinates, (2) know what they are doing, (3) check their work frequently, (4) make key decisions, and (5) make long range plans. You must always check and supervise so that important decisions which affect the company —determine progress or failure — are under your control at all times. You, as supervisor, must retain control but you should use others to do the basic work and possibly make decisions involving daily operations. If you cannot delegate these functions to others, you do not have time to do your job. If subordinates do not have the ability to share the workload, they should not be on your payroll. Others need some responsibility to maintain the drive desired by you.

FAVORITISM

Do not show special attention or favors to people that you like in the workplace. Watch that you do not favor those who have interests similar to yours. Maintain a friendly and impartial attitude. Treat all employees fairly — as you want to be treated. Recognize ability and willingness to cooperate and get a job done — favor merit and not personalities. Every decision should be based on merit, ability and performance rather than on instinctive reaction to personalities. Naturally, a friendly, willing attitude is part of merit and ability to get along with fellow workers. Also, you must trust others. Promotions should be fair so that they are approved by fellow workers. Promotions should be based on merit.

Favoritism in raising children can leave lifetime scars. Treat children as individuals, reduce competition between siblings and treat all fairly but not equally. They have different interests and needs which should be respected by parents and among the children.

LOST MOTION

Rushing around, accomplishing little is a fault of most people. Plan so that tasks are assigned specifically to individuals. Make motion studies and improve efficiency in factory and office. Analyze each step in an operation and change procedures and correct bad work habits. Figure out a method for doing each job in shorter time without loss of quality to improve efficiency and company profits. Establish rest periods as needed. Require work rather than conversation. Limit time away from work station. Figure out ways for doing the job with ease and safety. Have suggestion boxes and reward for work improvement. Create alertness and a willingness to change work methods for greater profits and wages. Feather-bedding and long-standing work rules damage competition within one world environment. You must compete both as a company and as individuals in the marketplace which is the entire world. It is easy to worry and put off doing a chore for weeks. Your health and job are better served if you get the job completed — you can probably do it in an hour or two and there is no excuse to worry about it for weeks.

Plan your chores at home for efficiency.

MOTIVATION

A strong leader has the ability to motivate people. He takes charge and he is confident, has a good, strong self-image. He reacts supportively with customers, employees and colleagues. He encourages others to take risks and he supports others. He has the talent to be both a thinker and a doer who has the confidence and support of staff. He is motivated to do the best possible job and obtain cooperation of others.

During the past years, the comparable concepts were drive and ambition. Studies show that we will not change our habits or performance until we individually decide that a change will result in a reward or benefit which is in our own self-interest. A few people might increase their performance for public good and possibly for family interests. The benefit may have monetary value. At times we react favorably to simple words such as "that was a good job" and possibly a simple "thank you". We like to know that our efforts are appreciated by others even when we do only a satisfactory job. The words of encouragement may come from the "Boss" or fellow workers. We each need to know from others "how we are doing" and we like words which encourage.

Rewards usually go to those who perform above average in a superior and possibly unexpected manner. As an individual worker, we must always try to please both the "Boss" and our fellow workers. If we are to accomplish our goals, their help is needed. They should recognize that superior performance of one helps the entire team effort. Everyone on the team must agree that any reward or benefit to an individual is justly earned and is not granted because of favoritism. Always remember that the "Boss", the janitor and most people in between must remain friendly and appreciate our efforts. The skills related to handling people are very important in all business, community and social activities. Learn to eliminate the lazy, unsafe and inefficient habits so that the overall team effort is improved.

We must motivate ourselves with possible aid and encouragement from family and friends. You must develop an "I can do" rather than an "I don't care" attitude. We need a plan which we recognize to be attainable and which will satisfy our emotional, physical, intellectual and financial needs for the short and long timeframes. Learn to give yourself special favors when you accomplish something but do remember that we must spend less than we earn. Relaxing, reading, listening to music, enjoying family and friends may serve as rewards for a successful effort.

We need to recognize that others, too, have needs and desires. Learn to compliment and say "thank you" to fellow workers, family and friends. Give them a helping hand when possible. Life is a "two-way street" and we must live with others. People often do not forgive those who "doublecross" and fail to keep promises. Give credit to others and do not be haughty or greedy. Learn to be considerate of others and try to help those around you while also helping yourself. Being firm is often very helpful.

The successful leader and manager knows how to give rewards of many types to those who work with him. He rewards for superior service and he encourages the average worker to do a better job for the benefit of the team effort. He helps everyone.

Success goes to people who really try. Plan soundly and "give your best" to make your dreams come true. Honestly try. Sit down with a pencil and paper and decide, "What do I want from life?" Then decide which paths and tools you need to get from "Where I am to where I want to go". Study as needed and really try to accomplish. You will probably succeed if you give the needed effort.

ORDERS

Issue clear orders. Elimination of confusion and misunderstanding in orders and instructions for the workplace results in fewer errors, improves safety and production. The leaders must think about their orders so that they are very concise, clear and complete. Instructions should be in writing and explanations given verbally should be clear and specific. Fellow workers often hesitate to ask questions designed to clarify. Clear instructions which are easy to remember and use are essential. Encourage others to ask questions by stopping and asking whether your words are understood. Give copies of instructions to those who use them so that they can be consulted from time to time. Always be definite and specific in your instructions and discussions with others. Do not assume that others will interpret as you do. Put yourself in the other person's shoes and try to think as he does. People cannot read your mind so do not leave anything to chance. Say what you intend to say very exactly. Be specific and clear in your conversations and in your writing. Spend the time necessary to edit and be certain that others clearly understand your words.

We all must accept orders and follow instructions.

OVERHEAD

Overhead, which includes items such as rentals, taxes, insurance, etc., must be controlled by good judgment. In good times, companies tend to establish added layers of management. New people are hired at all levels of employment. People get lazy and many reduce overall efficiency. Often people interfere with the work of others by extra handling of paper, extra meetings, unneeded planning, unnecessary requests for studies and detail, delay of decisions because of confused thinking and general duplication of work. The result is needless waste of time and materials, carelessness, reduced morale and general loss of efficiency. People and costs at all levels must always be controlled. No company ever needs non-workers. Everyone must contribute to production, research and sales. People always must have pride in their work, fellow workers and company so that their contribution is always at maximum level. Some overheads are difficult to control because the company needs electricity, heat and many other items if it is to operate. Overhead is a necessary cost but it should be kept at minimum levels. It is controlled when everyone does useful work with minimum waste in the shortest possible time. Americans must work and produce products of quality very efficiently, possibly at lower cost, if products are to be marketed in worldwide competition. America is running out of some raw materials and costly work habits are making products costly because of inefficiencies which they create. We need to change.

PAPER MANAGEMENT

Time managers all say, "Handle each piece of paper that crosses your desk no more than twice." Try to handle only once. The first time, get the paper off your desk. Dictate a letter, mark it for file, initial it and send it to a subordinate for handling, act or throw it away. Never allow paper to accumulate on your desk. Use the help available unless the subject is very important and requires your decision. Then have a subordinate do research, prepare a draft so that you only have to sign a letter.

If the subject is confidential and requires your personal work, put it into a pending file and start getting the necessary facts for a decision. Reach a decision as soon as possible and get the subject out of your mind. Possibly make a note for future review after your recommendation has been implemented for sufficient time to warrant review as to how it is working in practice. Do not procrastinate so that your productivity and efficiency are lowered. Be a manager. It is easy to postpone decisions and worry about a problem for days but this is detrimental to your efficiency and your health. Why worry when you can handle a problem within a few minutes or possibly hours?

Tackle important problems when you are most alert. Handle each days most important problem first and then work down your list of problems after giving each an order of importance. Set aside some time so that you are not interrupted. Work behind a closed door part of each day. Some open door time may be necessary to make it possible for others to see you but you also need private time to think and handle problems which cannot be planned or handled by others.

You also must take time to review work of subordinates. You must catch mistakes before they damage your business or career. Be trusting but do check others. Always control yourself the items which can make or quickly bankrupt your business. Finances, bidding and purchasing may be examples. Watch sales and cash flow.

Quickly recognizing the important messages is the key to success. Know what you should be seeking.

Read "Cutting Paperwork in Corporate Culture" by Dianna Booher.

PEOPLE MANAGEMENT

United Technologies, a major U.S.company, recently distributed the following advice in newspaper ads:

"There is nothing more awkward than a misunderstanding — nothing more unnecessary.

It leads to strain, tension, invectiveness and an atmosphere leading to open hostility.

Why risk losing a friend, a colleague or a customer?

If you have a misunderstanding that is a tempest in a teapot, do not allow it to blow into a hurricane. Get it solved.

Take the initiative.

Pick up a phone.

Pick yourself up and march right now to the other's office and clear the air and find a solution.

How we perform individually also determines how we perform as a company and as a nation."

We also need to react as normal human beings. Keep your voice low and soothing. Do not wrinkle your forehead. Relax eyebrows and mouth, uncross arms and legs and open hands. Be calm and relaxed.

You need to develop certain characteristics if you are to get along in the world. You should:

1. Be intelligent, educated, scholarly and look good.
2. Have common sense and see the broad scope of operations in the corporation and the world. Plan your life.
3. Be accurate and reliable — be honest.
4. Be objective and realize that decisions involve many facets of business and politics.
5. Be loyal, cooperative, industrious and sincere. Recognize that decisions are based on much information including experience and that your own views may not always be the best.
6. Be resourceful and recognize that new ideas may be more important than basic knowledge.
7. Be energetic in mind and body; stamina and sweat are required in

addition to brains.

8. Have a high tolerance to pressure created by work and relations with others.
9. Know law, business, human relations, sales and other technical fields as well as your specialty.
10. Get the facts, be honest, ambitious and do your best at all times. Cooperation is essential.
11. Get a job done. This requires energy and tact so that you get help from others.
12. Learn to acknowledge another's anger quickly. Make it plain that you are concerned. Listen until others have run down. Keep calm and find out what is really bothering others and really is wrong. Compromise and strive for a solution using a specified timeframe. Always keep your promises.
13. Be human and solve problems with new and old ideas. Strive to make the operation grow so that your wages grow. Get along with your fellow workers.

PLACEMENT

Finding the willing, capable and honest person for each job is essential in all business. To reduce turnover, people should be in jobs which meet their desires, aptitude and capability. Bored employees lack interest which is reflected in accidents, waste and morale problems. Place each person in a job which he can handle, where they find interest and where they contribute to performance effectively. Most people do not want to be drones — they want work which they like. Some people have high expectations above their capability. It is also not possible to advance everyone in accord with their expectations. Explain the company must make a profit to pay wages and such profits are shared with investors and workers on the basis of contribution to the company profits in a manner which is fair. Also, work at times is boring and unpleasant. Life does have its unpleasant times and we need to accept the good and the bad.

PLANNING

Long range objectives and short term detailed plans must be established and reviewed as necessary. Plan the work of each individual so that he makes a real contribution to company income. Research to find and develop new products to keep ahead of the competition in a rapidly changing world is essential. New ideas are necessary. Make plans and decide what is wanted today and during future years. Also, plan to get from here to there. Show the blueprint to employees, ask for suggestions and get their help in making it work. Organize and coordinate the efforts of each employee to get work done efficiently and on time as scheduled. Make critical path diagrams and move along as quickly as possible. Make every worker a partner in the project and inspire them to get it completed with a quality product on schedule or sooner. Failure to meet schedules can be very costly since time costs money in manufacture, in lost sales and in lost customer goodwill. Every supervisor should make a plan, fill in the general plan with all details, assign people with skills and desire to do quality work. The plan should be based on past experience. We each seem to underestimate time to do a job. Without the guide of experience, estimates may be only half the time actually required. This relates with disaster if prices quoted to customers are based on the unrealistic time estimates. Time is money and your estimates will kill you when wrong in bids and product prices.

It is difficult to maintain employee morale when employees do not believe that their efforts are making a contribution to company success. Individuals want a challenge but they also want to believe that the project on which they work will be successful. The following diagram depicts the degree of subordinates motivation.

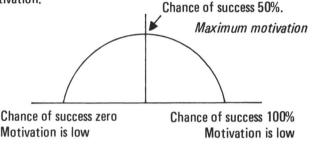

Chance of success 50%.

Maximum motivation

Chance of success zero
Motivation is low

Chance of success 100%
Motivation is low

PROFITS

You live in a country which allows you many freedoms and its business methods enable you to enjoy one of the best living standards in the world. Be thankful to your forefathers and work to keep our country free and productive. The entire world envy us and would like to join us — often wish to take what we have and make us work as slaves for other countries. Study and do not allow special interest groups to deprive you of your heritage. Political policy affects you personally. Vote with intelligence.

Every business is composed of three elements — workers, capital and management. All must work together as a team and each must share in the profits or earnings of the effort. The capital is money supplied for use in the business by owner, investors and lenders who demand dividends and interest. Management directs the operation and serves a very useful purpose. You, as a worker, expect to be paid fairly for your work efforts and the investors also must be assured of a reasonable return. Management usually is paid a higher return for the longer hours devoted to the operation. If you want higher wages, work to become part of management. Insufficient capital limits company growth and job opportunities. Insufficient capital can cause loss of jobs and can bankrupt a company. During many years, capital has cost about 12% of invested capital. Lenders during 1984 demanded ever higher interest for borrowed money but in the past, long term interest rates have been much lower. Interest rates depend on taxes and are strongly influenced by inflation rate. Profits contribute to available cash and reduce need for outside money. Profits are essential since there are no jobs if a company fails. You, as an employee, must recognize the need for company profits if you want work. Your advancement, equipment to improve your work efficiency, materials purchased for use in manufacture, needed research to develop new products, advertising and product promotion and your wages all are dependent upon your working so that the company makes a profit. You must learn basic economics and recognize the need for profits for your security and well-being. Today the competition is worldwide and jobs will not be available in the United States unless we each work effectively. You are hired to make profits for the company — you should be discharged when you do not make the required contribution. Theft of tools, small items and merchandise and time wasted by you are all severe drains on company efforts. You prosper when you find ways to make a company more profitable.

PROMOTIONS
The steps which often result in advancement include:
1. Specify your objectives and desires precisely.
2. Envision your goal and define means of achievement.
3. Put the 80/20 rule to work. Spend at least 80% of your time on solid work — not 80% on unnecessary detail.
4. Heighten your visibility as a star performer.
5. Take chances and responsibility. Accept important jobs and make decisions.
6. Broaden your business vision beyond your specialized area of work.
7. Never risk your credibility with inaccurate, incomplete or outdated information.
8. Be the first to spot trends that affect you and your organization.
9. Study and learn from success and failures of others. Learn to solve your problems quickly. When there can be no answer, reach a decision or decide to take no action. Forget the past when it has no use in the future. Do not get moody and do not retain a grudge. Be pleasant and remove unpleasant thoughts from your mind and try to never recall them. Work is discipline, sacrifice, competition, endurance, repetition, concentration, dedication and principle. Work is not always fun, relevant or meaningful. It is doing a job that needs to be done. The person who has the willpower to accomplish will get advancement if tact and goodwill are used in relations with others.

Excessive greed and ambition can be very harmful. Associates must like you and want to work with you.

PROBLEM SOLVING
Life often involves the solution of problems of living. Problem-solving is the heart of jobs and business. The approaches to problem-solving can be reduced to the following:
1. Define the problem or project being reviewed very exactly. Determine the objectives of the proposed study. First observe the forest and thereafter study the tree. Ask whether the study is worth the time and costs — does study meet cost/benefit requirements.
2. Obtain and organize properly all facts and ideas related to the

project. Review so that none are overlooked which would influence decisions. Review existing reports and books related to the subject. Determine the relative importance and accuracy of the assembled information. Outline and plan the study in detail. Develop a plan for solving the problem and reaching conclusions in the shortest possible time. Ask the pertinent questions — insist on true, honest, reliable answers. Remember that "garbage in" results in "garbage out". Be practical, mature and use common sense in both action and thought.

Construct flow and "minimum path diagrams" which relate the study and actual implementation of the project with time. This places your plans on paper and organizes your thinking.

Upgrade the basic data using statistics, experience, analogy, computers, equations, and literature. Be sure that you have considered and properly weighted all information. Do not be proud or stubborn but do consult with the knowledgeable and successful as needed. Think and use common sense.

3. Evaluate, think and apply judgment in a professional and unbiased manner. Check conclusions using equations and analogy — past experience. Plot both input and output data so that you can make comparisons. Obtain an overall solution which fits all facts in the best possible manner.

4. Make a sound, reliable and unbiased final decision. Reduce the decision and supporting facts to a very brief written report. Sell your decision to management and obtain approvals to spend money or take other necessary action. Also, sell to public officials to avoid political complications.

5. Act, implement the decision and make the necessary changes or construct the facility. Supervise carefully to be certain that your decision is implemented in detail. Constantly review the project.

6. Later review results. Change your plan or the construction when an error has been made.

Books are available which detail "How To Do" most tasks. Also, advice of the successful and experts can be obtained, often without cost. Always seek and use advice.

The reliability of any work or study depends upon spending energy, time, effort and money wisely. Sound decisions based upon accurate data are essential. The study must be made by people who are able to think with intelligence, have ability and integrity — use reliable, unbiased, professional judgment. The lazy, the "showoff", the person who is deficient and covers up and the dishonest are not helpful or needed. Studies by experts serving government agencies are often biased and serve no useful purpose except to advance the ideas of the group belonging to their biased organization. Use a little common sense and experience instead and save the public money in addition to arriving at the best decision. Critical path and decision tree are two useful techniques.

TWO METHODS FOR SCHEDULING WORK
The Critical Path Techniques
TIME IN DAYS

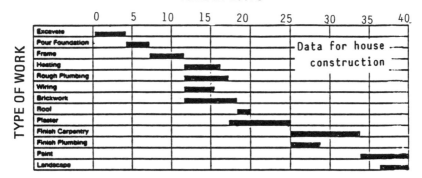

You save time and money when you schedule both your work and your projects.

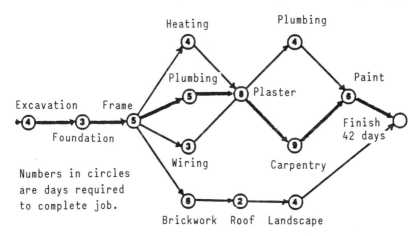

TIME IN DAYS

The method has many uses. All projects such as construction, studies and reviews should be diagrammed so that you understand the needed work and time before starting work. You also clarify your thinking and properly schedule manpower and work.

There are many types of problems and effective solution is not limited to one decision method. In all cases, the problem needs to be analyzed using approaches such as previously detailed. The basic premises and facts must be true and sound. We need the skills in science, mathematics, language, grammar and logic to analyze. The decision may be influenced by our intuition and past experience and may need to imagine the resulting effects on company and environment, etc. Ethics and standards must always be considered since basic rules and concepts found reliable in the past are seldom wrong. We cannot violate the laws of man or nature. We should make decisions after discussing with others whom we trust to give sound, unbiased advice. We need to ask whether the decision meets people's needs and the needs of the community. We need to look at the decision from many directions. We should be aware of cultural effects such as customs and local religion. We should learn to transfer ideas from other sciences and cultures so that new ideas and techniques are incorporated in decisions and company operations.

QUALITY

The consumer demands a good product which will perform as advertised and will last a reasonable time. The manufacturer may hope that the product will wear out or become outdated so that he can sell a replacement. Due to foreign competition, quality is improving. Specifications, rules in the workplace and quality checks can account for only part of the quality — the balance must be contributed by the spirit and cooperation of employees who are inspired by sound management. Each individual, by doing his job properly, makes a contribution to the final product. Employees must feel enthusiastically that they are part of a team so that personal pride of accomplishment causes them to make quality products for the marketplace. Employees must want to do a good job — doing it better than anyone else. This beats the competition and develops and maintains a worldwide consumer base.

SAFETY

Most accidents occur in the car and near the home. Accidents, especially at the workplace, are a serious drain on finances because of lost time, insurance and lawsuits. Safety is the mark of an efficient operation. Safety results partly from awareness of hazards on the part of each individual. Safety requires more than posters and meetings. High morale is needed and each employee must cooperate. Guards and safety devices on equipment are necessary. Everyone must be safety-conscious. Good housekeeping, orderly thinking and cleanliness are important. Workers cannot be careless nor consider work to be mechanical. We each must constantly recognize possible danger. Work with confidence, be alert, do not participate in horseplay, and do not take anything for granted. Drive your car carefully and work while thinking about safety at home and on the job — act defensively.

Over 45,000 deaths a year are caused by car accidents and accidents in homes cause over 12,000 deaths. With government paying for most health costs, we might ask whether our priorities need to be revised.

Send for the "Home Safety Kit", AARP Fulfillment, 1909 K Street, N.W., Washington, D.C. 20049.

RESPECT

You often become successful by properly handling people. We always need to consider the true needs of our nation, the company for which we work, and the individuals involved in our life. Individuals control our governments and business in the world. Individuals at all levels of an organization desire attention, support, encouragement and need self-esteem. Feedback in both directions is needed to obtain maximum flow of new ideas and to avoid major mistakes. Everyone must make decisions but the leader must establish overall policy for guidance. The leader and everyone working with him must accept responsibility. All individuals need to read very rapidly, be given equal opportunity to succeed, to think, and know how to assemble and analyze fact so that sound decisions are made. We simply must help each other — in schools, in social contacts and in the workplace. Learn to say "thank you" and give honest compliments. We should feel confident and comfortable. We should not feel guilty nor apologize when making reasonable requests to friends and fellow workers. We should be firm when making demands and when giving instructions to others. Errors and mistakes should be admitted with friendliness when they affect others. Offering excuses rather than contructive alternates is poor strategy. Bad habits in communication and relations with others are reduced when we (1) are direct and detailed in stating our expectations and giving instructions, (2) confront problems immediately as they occur, (3) think things through — consider the alternatives before speaking and acting, (4) choose subjects for argument or confrontation carefully and make only those which are very important, (5) separate anger from assertiveness, (6) avoid threats which cannot be enforced, (7) use our own turf or office for discussions, and (8) use silence so others can talk rather than repeat our previously stated positions. You might consider the above guidelines when dealing with the "boss", subordinates, your friends and your children. Each of us likes to be shown respect and dignity as well as "goodwill".

SPOILAGE
Control of product and labor waste makes the difference between a successful company and one that becomes bankrupt with loss of jobs. Everyone in an operation should reduce waste by calling wasteful operations to the attention of supervisors and supervisors should carefully investigate all suggested improvements. Get the team to look for waste. Use suggestion boxes with a reward for savings made. Supervisors and management must want to improve the operation and so should employees. Jobs are at stake. The leaders and employees who refuse to improve the profitability of an operation should be replaced. Past work rules, which increase costs, cannot be supported by todays worker because his job is being lost to the competition. Spoilage and improper use of materials should not be tolerated. Careful inspection, control of operations and review of procedures should reduce waste to a minimum. Also, time motion studies can reduce waste of time which, too, is a form of spoilage in the workplace. Small items, when wasted, become very large when multiplied by the occurrence in many series of operations and combined to obtain companywide loss.

SUCCESS
Success has many definitions. You are successful if you are at peace with yourself. Others want money and fame.
Believe that you have in your mind or that you can quickly acquire all

of the resources that you will ever need to solve your problems. Know sources of information and where to get help quickly.

Build up your resource base and thought inventory by both faith and "know how". Learn from your experiences, read and study daily.

Remember that spiritual forces activate your potential use of both mind and spirit. Use your mind and willpower. You are as good as your fellow man if you only try and work.

We each need faith in something higher than ourself. Religions have served this purpose in many societies and have helped many people in times of severe stress such as death, loss of a job and emotional difficulty.

Never minimize your ability to think and work through any situation. "I can do it" should always be your motto. You can if you really try.

Have faith in your ability and thoughts. If your thought-process is dull at any time, find out what is offering a potential block and remove it immediately. You may be worrying, be jealous, etc.

Keep alert for flashes of insight which come when you are really feeling good. Thoughts usually occur when you are trying to solve a problem but sometime solutions appear unsolicited.

Consult books and other literature to obtain necessary facts and possible solutions to your problems. Also, study life of the successful and consult with them when possible.

Skip thoughts involving "if only I had", but do think in terms of "next time". Keep searching, studying and working so that the next time occurs and you then handle it so that sound solutions are found. Ask yourself, "Do I really want to succeed."

Expect success and victory and never bog down in thoughts of defeat. Think and plan for success. You must really want to do the job at hand today.

Be bold and the correct powers and thoughts will come to your aid. Learn to accept a few risks.

The tests of life are not to break you but they should make you stronger and give you the experience so that you can handle harder problems the next time. You must live your life yourself and solve your problems, possibly with the help of professionals, book knowledge, associates and friends. Learn to be practical and live in the real world.

The competition is always advancing and life and success will bypass the lazy, the ignorant and those who do not apply themselves. Again, "you can do it if you really try" is sound advice. Be diplomatic and show advantages of proposed alternatives rather than argue against proposals made by others.

Learn the rules and motivate yourself if you want money.

WINNERS VERSUS LOSERS

A winner smiles and works to improve the world around him. The loser is unhappy and is usually unfriendly because he is insecure and not sincere with others. A winner rebukes when wronged and thereafter forgives while a loser is too timid to rebuke and does not try to correct an unpleasant situation. The loser is too petty to forgive. Winners ask for and seek help while the loser is too proud to do so. The winner makes commitments but the loser makes only unkept promises. A winner, when wrong, shows that he is sorry by making up for his errors while the loser may say that he is sorry but repeats the same mistakes. Losers are insincere and lie. A winner listens, thinks, and accepts criticism while the loser only waits for his turn to talk and to again pull another "double cross". A winner admits his mistakes while a loser blames others. A winner knows that others are usually kind if given a chance. A loser believes that others will always be unkind and that they will take advantage. A winner is cautious but wants to trust others when trust is earned. A winner is strong enough to be gentle and considerate. A loser does not accept others and is petty or weak in his relations with others. A winner really likes others while a loser only pretends and puts on a false front. A winner is friendly while a loser is often angry. A winner likes to be helpful while a loser feels hurt when he gives more than he receives. A winner respects superiors while a loser resents authority. A winner is always learning from others while a loser is chatting about insignificance and bragging. A winner seeks facts, reasons and acts while a loser hesitates because he does not wish to make decisions. A winner becomes part of the company and neighborhood teams while the loser never fits anywhere. A winner is secure, sincere, cooperative, helpful and others like him and his performance. The loser has not become an adult and has not developed these character traits. A winner is strong, secure and feels good about himself. A loser is afraid and has never learned to take care of himself emotionally, morally or financially.

Surveys show that companies rank the worst traits as follows:
1. Dishonesty and "goofing off".
2. Arrogance and egotism.
3. Disregarding instructions and ignoring company policy. Theft means jail.
4. Whining and complaining attitude toward job and company.
5. Absence of commitment, concern or dedication.
6. Lack of motivation and enthusiasm.

You can always make the changes necessary to become a winner rather than a loser. Please try to be a winner. You will be a better person. Study "Business Confidential" by Boardroom Books, 330 West 42nd Street, New York, New York 10036.

UNDERSTUDIES

The supervisor's advancement and vacation requires that another person perform his duties. Each supervisor must select and train an understudy. Training a capable successor is required to maintain production when others are absent due to illness and other reasons. Talking about the job is not training. The understudy must be taught, shown, encouraged step-by-step so that confidence is established. Proper training of all employees involves a partial understanding of other duties within the group. Building confidence in others relates with greater appreciation for the leadership ability of the supervisors. Higher management recognizes the capabilities of supervisors who train those working in the workplace. Proper training is basic to advancement from within the ranks.

114

Develop people and delegate responsibility and authority without losing control and supervision. Develop a smooth operating organization of capable, honest employees.

The supervisor must be responsible and he must know "what is going on". He delegates work and authority but he remains in control. He is informed about details and knows that his policy is being implemented.

SUMMARY — BE A PROFESSIONAL

Most organizations have a code of ethics for guidance of members. You should avoid business deals with those who violate such codes. Likewise, you should try to avoid business and social relations with those who violate the basic laws and rules of society so that you are not thought to be one of the violators. Those who violate codes, laws and rules and those who lie, cheat and are dishonest as well as individuals who are incapable of planning and performing reliable work on time should not be among your close associates. Such relationships usually are harmful to your reputation and if the relation involves legal factors, you make yourself liable to censure of professional organizations, guilt by association and possibly lawsuits from government regulators and disgruntled customers. Lawsuits are very expensive and can cause bankruptcy. We can each find good qualities in every individual and we can be friendly at professional meetings with all present. Unless the violations are very substantial, we might even be kind socially and on the golf course, but we do not become friends with those who violate common decency. By being socially acceptable and decent in public, we tend to remove negative emotions of jealousy and hate and replace such emotions with positive emotions of friendliness and cooperation. In rare cases, the offenders may even see their errors and change for the benefit of all. In the adult world, we must be mature and gracious but we also need to protect ourselves. Offenders need to learn to accept and welcome friendly, constructive and helpful ideas expressed by speakers at meetings and in private discussion with law officers and club members authorized and charged with the job of enforcing membership codes.

Society, during thousands of years, has developed a system of laws which governs legal and social relationship between organizations and individuals. Most people learn to accept such principles by age 20 years. Such rules change very slowly and they will not change to accommodate your "whims".

You should learn to treat the honest janitor and boss alike — both as you want to be treated. It is easy to be sincere and honest and at the same time be courteous, friendly and diplomatic. It is also necessary to keep the dishonest at a distance and do no business with them to avoid loss.

The professional is a good, sincere, friendly, sensitive communicator. Throughout life he keeps learning and growing mentally, emotionally, socially, recreationally and professionally. He also learns to relax — both on and off the job. He relaxes as needed — usually a few minutes each hour or two — by (1) assuming a comfortable position in a quiet environment, (2) closing eyes and consciously relaxing muscles, (3) breathing slowly and naturally while repeating silently a simple, positive word with personal meaning with each exhaling of breath when outside thoughts disturb his mind. No outside, worrysome thoughts are allowed to interfere with the relaxing process. After a short period, he returns to work with renewed zeal and energy. He again tackles work physically and mentally refreshed. The technique can be used to control sleep, reduce pain and generally improve health. The benefits are greater if you have faith in yourself, your friends, your doctor, your medical treatments and your religion.

The PROFESSIONAL does not "reinvent the wheel". He knows that over 90% of "new ideas" are actually ideas which have been previously discarded because they were proven worthless. Know the past from study of history and experience of yourself and others. He studies and reads in many fields of interest.

BE A LEADER AND CONVINCE OTHERS TO HELP YOU ATTAIN YOUR IDEALS, WISHES AND GOALS.

Read IRS Publication No. 17. Contact The American Management Association, 135 West 50th Street, New York, New York 10020 for a list of their courses taught by correspondence. Take Boardroom Reports by contacting Box 1026, Millburn, New Jersey 07041 for a subscription.

Managing Your Business

Workers and consumers need to know principles of business in order to work and purchase items properly. We each would benefit if we read summaries of books which are published by Soundview Executive Books Summaries, 5 Main Street, Bristol, Vermont 05443.

You must have the cash or liquid assets to support your business venture during its startup phase when expenses normally would not be expected to be completely offset by income. You and your business must be able to pay all expenses regardless of income and you are bankrupt when you cannot borrow to meet all obligations in a timely manner.

A business during startup requires detailed attention to all of its aspects and you need experience in the technical aspects of what you are doing plus a knowledge of how to choose associates and handle people. The tasks are very different from the simple techniques for working at a single job for others. You do not have the responsibilities when you work for others. When you own your business, you are involved with the daily operations as well as finance and longer range planning. You must be informed as to various business and tax forms, permits and other business criteria such as income statement, balance sheet, profit, percent profit, payout time, cost of capital or interest effects on borrowed money, average annual earning power.

No business can be successful without capable people. The owner of a business must know how to find individuals who are honest, ambitious, capable and willing to work to make the business successful. Someone in the organization must keep records, must make bids, must buy materials in proper quantity, must run the operation each day, must solicit work or sales, and negotiate contracts. You also must plan for the future, secure finances and perform many others chores.

Hopefully, the owner can delegate to trusted employees the daily operating decisions. However, he must give overall supervision and watch purchases and inventory so that the business operates at a profit. The owner also must plan for the future, develop people as the business expands, watch cash flow and finances.

Most business operations fail because the owner does not find time to handle his chores and watch his business. Watching details is boring and there are other aspects that are more interesting to most people. There is also a tendency to forget hidden costs such as taxes, insurance, rents — what have you. The owner or someone he trusts must find time to give overall management — must follow the business so that there are no surprises. The daily strengths and weaknesses of the business must be reviewed so that future cash flow exceeds future expenses and that the company grows as desired by the owner. Finding good, honest, hard-working employees and keeping them is a test of good management. So is watching trends in costs and sales so that changes are recognized in time to avoid loss.

The business world is complex and usually experience plus book learning is desired. The owner of a business must produce — make or buy a product, be a salesman — sell his products to consumers and he also must be a planner and financial officer — keep control of inventory and keep income above costs. The hours may be long and the detail may be boring but the chores must get done. Owning your business when it is successful can make you rich and wealthy.

Many of us have dreamed about being our own boss. Also, most individuals would like more income. Owning a businss is one alternative. The other is to have a job which puts food on the table and shelter overhead. Part of the worker's income is invested which, too, is a form of owning your own business. Investment management will be discussed in a later section and this section will be limited to a very short discussion of business. Before you start a business, go to your library and study books about the proposed specialty — know the job and risks involved. You also need to know a little about business principles if you are to make investments.. Study of this section, therefore, is useful to a worker, a businessman and an investor. The entrepreneur takes risks and fails three or more times before success. Study "Is Your Business All It Could Be", Mathais Hoffman Publishers, Box 2776, Reston, Virginia 22090.

BUSINESS PLAN

You cannot live your life successfully without a plan. Likewise, you cannot start or operate a business without a plan. Most business ventures become failures because they were not properly planned, the financial backing was not sufficient and the people did not have proper qualifications. You will need a plan before you go to your banker or invest your own funds. You cannot get money or operate a business without a detailed plan. The plan also needs to be revised at times.

Historically, very few business ventures are successful — maybe about 20%. Startup money is difficult to obtain and business operations are undertaken with inadequate financing. Owners often are not qualified. A banker, the Small Business Administration and venture capital groups are possible sources of money and advice. Books also can give good advice.

Your business plan should be well thought out for both startup and continued operation. The plan should be in writing and the first paragraph should give information about type of operation. What do you intend to do? Be very specific and detailed. You must define your operation so that you and those reading your plan know exactly what you will be doing.

The second paragraph should show how your proposed business can be successful. How will it meet the competition successfully? Are all of your costs, expenses, income and customers realistic estimates? Your banker can be helpful since he reviews many plans and has more experience than you. Also, see your lawyer and accountant.

The third paragraph of your plan should detail how you propose to handle the key elements of your proposed business. If success depends upon sales, how do you propose to sell your product? What personnel do you need? What physical facilities? Where will you buy your material? You need to show projections as to how your company will grow. Show size of industry market, trends in the market; talk about the competition, how you will beat the competition. Include pricing, sales, tactics, number and type of sales organization, warranties, service facilities, advertising, public relations. Many business failures relate with a lack of planning — often related to sales. If success depends upon manufacturing, you should show how you plan to make your product, and how you plan to sell it. Items to be considered might include source of supplies, your plant, your storage, proposed inventory, and all other details.

You also need a paragraph related to management team. Also, who are owners, etc. Details regarding management staffs and organization are desired. You should construct a PERT diagram which shows what needs to be done, who will do each detail, when each job will be completed, etc. This is similar to the critical path diagrams shown previously.

A section showing and justifying in great detail your estimated cash flow is needed. If cash flow is negative for a day or a week, you must have cash on hand to pay the bills as they become due. You must obtain financing to cover all cumulative negative cash flows before you start. It is difficult to estimate the startup of a new business so you must arrange for lines of credit to cover maximum emergency. When you cannot borrow to pay your bills, you are out of business. After your business has started, you will need to keep records. Read books before you start. "Up Front Financing" by David Silver, Ronald Press, is an example.

The final section should include a section giving any other information of importance to your operation. Be prepared to answer all questions asked by the banker, accountant, lawyer, etc. You also must know what you want from each of them.

You will find that your business includes close supervision of costs, manpower, inventory and income. Many wearisome details are constantly involved and you must learn to find many details interesting so that you handle each in a timely manner. If handling detail is boring, you should not start a business. Thousands of nagging details are part of all business. Starting and operating a small business is hard work and involves long hours with little time off.

Your business must be run properly. Accounting should quickly indicate changes in trends or ratios so that adjustments can be made early so that damage can be minimized. A business should be abandoned or it should be revised as necessary.

Expenditures should be limited to essentials. Unnecessary telephone calls and trips in a car cost money and can destroy a small business. All purchases must be limited to essentials — no extras. Although risks are high, return from a business can be great. Do try a business or alternately make investments and manage them as your investment business. Use time to accomplish.

You should always be in control of your life, your business and your investments.

Is your accounting system adequate? Does it alert for a change in trends at an early time?

BUSINESS ORGANIZATION TYPES

The individual who works for a company must know its organizational structure so that he knows who can give him orders, to whom he reports, etc. The business owner must have an organization to run his company. Usually, one of three types will be used.

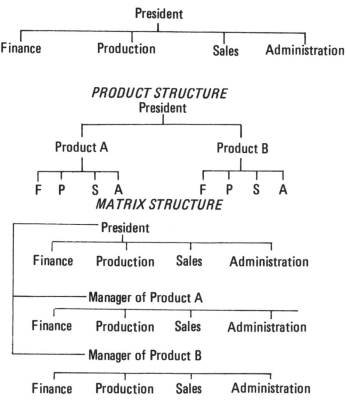

Note: The staff working directly for the President freely makes contact with the staffs of the managers of the various product managers. Orders are given only through management channel — president to managers to staffs.

If the market in which you operate is stable and predictable — change is slow — the functional structure is more appropriate.

A product structure is more appropriate when competition is volatile — difficult to forecast and decisions must be made quickly at a decentralized location. To overcome the expense of product structure and still retain control of certain important products at top level of management, the matrix structure may be used. Here a manager is assigned to coordinate a particular product. Such manager reports directly to the head office top management. The computer in 1984 offers possibility of handling much information and facilitates communication so that the head office might retain control without intermediate management. The many layers of management complicates operations and often causes paper handling problems so that no one accepts responsibility. Unnecessary levels of management are expensive in salary, rentals, etc. Management should be as direct as possible and job descriptions and responsibility authorizations should be in writing.

In a very small business, the owner may be the only employee and he must then be familiar with the duties of all phases of the company in utmost detail.

Some large companies are rewarding those who win and those "who try". Future success is dependent upon those willing to dream, to reach and to dare — develop new ideas.

SUCCESSFUL BUSINESS CHARACTERISTICS

A successful businessman must watch all income and expenses. Excessive management can paralyze. Cash flow must always be positive. Accounts receivable should be small. The accounting system must be able to control costs, inventory, fixed assets, intangibles and a host of other details so that all are consistent with the needs of the business. It also must be timely in making payments to tax collectors — federal and state income and city, etc., pay payrolls and keep records required by governments.

A few important rules follow:
1. Always have too few people. Never have an excess.
2. Judge people carefully and watch for changes in their performance. If you choose carefully and well, everything becomes easier.
3. Seek changes in business — look for trends and do not just accept change. Be ahead of the crowd.
4. Decision-making should be at the point of action.
5. Organization follows ability and need. Do not place too much time on organization — rather get the job done and make a profit so that you stay in business.
6. Fit your organization to your people. Plans should adjust to people available to do the job.
7. Learn from the past experiences of yourself and others but plan and invest for the future.
8. Usurp responsibility — do not just accept it when offered. Try for leadership.
9. Demand excellence in yourself and others. Plans are accomplished by effort — not by dreams.
10. Develop a vision of what is to occur in the future. Good plans and implementation are your insurance of success over the long term.
11. The owner or manager has the skill, determination, ability, willingness to sacrifice and knows how to select and manage people. The management as a team knows all facets of the business and they

have faith and a sense of humor.

BUSINESS FAILURES CHARACTERISTICS

The businessman who does not believe that he has problems has a big, hidden problem. All organizations constantly must solve problems. The businessman and the investor seems to be able to talk about his winners, but his ability to recall and talk about losers often is near zero. A new company's ability to succeed is inversely proportional to the amount of publicity received prior to its manufacture of its first product. Bragging often is a sign of weakness. A positive cash flow is essential and it solves most business problems. Excessive office space and plant is a sign of a potential failure. Entrepreneurs who pick up the check at lunch discussions often are losers. A long investment plan is often a sign of a potential failure. There is no such thing as an under-financed company. Managers who worry too much about voting control usually have no assets worth controlling. There is no limit on what a man can do or when and where he can go if he doesn't worry about "who gets credit".

NECESSARY ACTIONS BEFORE SEEKING MONEY

You should have a number of answers before seeking credit from banks and investors. Examples are:

1. Have a product or service with a competitive edge in a field with recognizable opportunity for growth.
2. Develop a plan — business and profit — that includes an analysis of your market, an evaluation of competition, a list of possible problems, how problems will be solved, realistic estimates of capital requirements, cash flow and expenses, and a clear summary as to how you intend to make the plan work.
3. Have a management team who individually have a demonstrated ability to perform and make a contribution to the project's success. Experience is important.
4. Admit past mistakes of the team but show that a lesson has been learned so that future mistakes are very uniikely. Get to details. Do not explain by cover-up because of growth.
5. Have a clear and concise plan. Emphasize key factors and support your plan with hard substantiated facts. Do not use wild estimates and general sales pitches. Be realistic.
6. Prove that you are completely committed to success of your operation; that you are willing to devote long hours of work and back up your project with substantial use of your own money.
7. Show that you know what you are doing. Read good books and seek advice from others. As a start, you might study "Starting and Managing a Small Business," Mathias Hoffman Publishing, Box 3094, Annapolis, Maryland 21403.

BUSINESS CRITERIA

Return on investment is frequently used by investors to screen investment opportunities. A business which does not return at least 12% on its invested capital — exclusive of borrowed money — will find capital hard to obtain. It will not long succeed. Return on investment and cost of capital are closely related and often are the same. Cost of capital may be computed as given by the following equations:

CALCULATING COST OF CAPITAL
FINANCIAL METHOD FOR RETURN ON INVESTMENT

Static condition:

$$\text{Cost of capital} = \frac{\text{Earnings}}{\text{Market value of asset}}$$

Simple growth

$$\text{Cost of capital} = \frac{\text{Dividend}}{\text{Market value}}$$
$$+ \frac{(\text{Money reinvested})\left[\dfrac{\text{Return on reinvestment}}{\text{Cost of capital}}\right]}{\text{Market value}}$$

Dynamic growth

$$\text{Cost of capital} = \frac{\text{Dividend}}{\text{Market value}} + \left[\begin{array}{c}\text{Growth rate}\\ \text{as a decimal}\end{array}\right]$$

Your business must show an overall profit if it is to survive. Profit may be defined as:

$$\text{Profit} = (\text{unit sales})(\text{Unit price} - \text{unit costs})$$

You must be careful to include all costs. Overheads including loss and taxes, etc. must be included.

For a sales oriented business, the diagram on page 124 should be useful.

The rules of accounting can be complicated and must legally be followed when corporations are public. If you are owner or an investor, some of these rules may not be realistic for use by you. Know accounting.

Your choice when selecting possible capital investments and when available capital is limited might involve the following criteria.

Dollar profit discounted at the firm's cost of capital and discounted cash flow rate of return are the two predominant profitability criteria. Older criteria included payout time, profit; both before and after tax, inflation and discounted for interest on money.

Three methods are used to determine value of physical property such as your home.

1. Market value or sales price obtained from recent sales of comparable property between informed and unrelated sellers and buyers in an open market. Use care when values are changing rapidly.
2. Replacement cost of the property, possibly adjusted for use, depreciation, obsolescence and inflation.
3. Present day value of the income stream generated by the highest and best use of the property.

Values may be adjusted for present value — interest on money, inflation,

ACCOUNTING METHOD FOR RETURN ON INVESTMENT

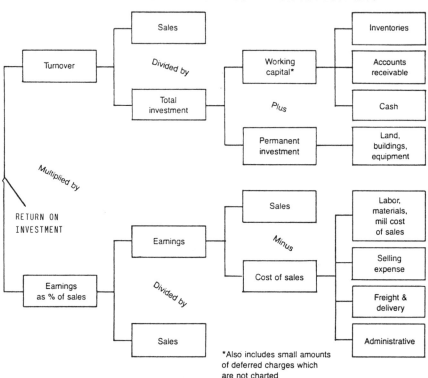

*Also includes small amounts
of deferred charges which
are not charted

taxes and other items involved in the sale and disposal of property. The evaluation also may be adjusted for time lag of income and expenditures and the risks involved in sale and operation.

The risk element usually can be handled by past experience and a simple correction factor. However, the more complex, important, unfamiliar and uncertain ventures such as the drilling of a wildcat oil well involve some form of risk analysis using a computer and probabilistically-generated data — the Monte Carlo system of gambling.

PAYOUT TIME

This is the time required for the income stream to return all costs expended to date. Values may be expressed with and before application of interest on the money used to construct the project, taxes, inflation, etc.

PROFIT

Values may be expressed in dollars and as a percent of the capital used. Values often include cost of the interest on borrowed money and the money cost of the delay in receiving the income stream.

PROFIT DISCOUNTED AT COST OF MONEY TO COMPANY

Management can usually determine its average cost of capital. When various types of money are available, some type of average should be used. It is easy to apply this value for cost of capital to the stream of income to be derived from the project and the capital costs for its installation. The difference between the two values is the anticipated profit. Risks, taxes and other variables can be included in the calculations when necessary.

When capital required for a single project is large compared with overall money available for investment, capital investment must be spread over a number of projects to prevent a single failure to bankrupt the company. Possibly partners, etc., are then desired. You want to stay in business.

CALCULATION OF AVERAGE ANNUAL EARNING POWER (AAEP)

This method works well when only a single option is possible. When two or more options are possible, two points of intersection are found and selection of the correct AAEP is not possible. Then the profit discounted at the company cost of capital is possibly more indicative of the proper procedure to be used. If you are responsible for evaluating projects, you should be thoroughly familiar with all of the above evaluation methods. Values should be calculated for inflation, taxes and risks. Make calculations in as many ways as appropriate.

The average annual earning power or AAEP is understood by analyzing the following example. A capital investment of $10,000 is expected to be returned at a uniform daily rate so that $5,000 is returned during each of ten years. See the following table. The AAEP is the effective interest rate (d) that makes the present value of the income stream equal to the present value of the capital expenditure. The capital and income are multiplied by deferment factors for a series of interest rates and the results are plotted. A computer program also can determine the point of interesection of the two data sets.

Year	Undeferred	PDV(d = 20%) DF	$	PDV(d = 40%) DF	$	PDV(d = 60%) DF	$
1	I_1 = $ 5.000	0.914	$ 4,570	0.849	$ 4.245	0.798	$ 3,990
2	I_2 = 5,000	0.762	3,810	0.607	3.035	0.499	2,595
3	I_3 = 5,000	0.635	3,175	0.433	2,165	0.312	1,560
4	I_4 = 5,000	0.529	2,645	0.309	1,545	0.195	975
5	I_5 = 5,000	0.441	2,205	0.221	1,105	0.122	610
6	I_6 = 5,000	0.367	1,835	0.158	790	0.076	380
7	I_7 = 5,000	0.306	1,530	0,113	565	0.048	240
8	I_8 = 5,000	0.255	1,275	0.081	405	0.030	150
9	I_9 = 5,000	0.213	1,065	0.058	290	0.019	95
10	I_{10} = 5,000	0.177	885	0.041	205	0.012	60
	I = $50,000		$22.995		$14.350		$10,655

Note: See section dealing with investments for graphs giving values for deferment factors, or page 192.

The calculated present day values for income and capital costs are plotted as shown on page 126.

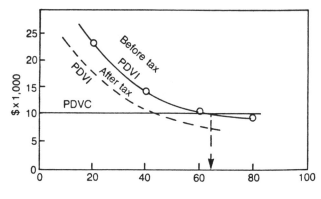

AVERAGE ANNUAL EARNING POWER

The point of intersection of income and capital lines is the desired value for AAEP.

AAPEP is related to (1) the amount of capital, (2) when the capital is invested, (3) the amount of income, and (4) the manner in which incremental amounts of income are received as a function of time. With this information and appropriate tables of deferment factors, AAPEP can be computed.

Caution: The slope of the present-day value-of-income curve and the slope of the present-day value-of-cost curve often are almost parallel at the point at which they cross the value chosen for average annual earning power. Small changes in basic values chosen can make substantial changes in the value for AAEP. If the computer is used to calculate AAEP without plotting the curve, the sensitivity often is not appreciated.

The rate of return, etc., can be rapidly obtained by plotting information on a graph. The slope of the plotted data is adjusted to the same slope on the graph originally and the value so read is the growth rate of the item of interest to you as plotted. The method is detailed under investments analysis, page 193.

CHARACTERISTICS OF AN ENTREPRENEUR

Are you an entrepreneur? They often have had the following background and characteristics. Their father or a close relative was in business for himself and the person grew up around the operation, thereby gaining experience necessary to operate a small business. They also probably worked for a small firm — had close contact and learned from the owner. Their schooling and their experience included a variety of functional areas, such as marketing, finance and production. They have learned to select and associate with reliable hard workers. They are independent and their ideas probably have been rejected by their superiors. They do not like to work for others but they do work hard and have new ideas. Entrepreneurs have worked in several cities and jobs. They have strong support from family and friends in their ventures and they are leaders — they influence their lives and do not drift, depend on chance or luck. They are willing to work hard at half the wages paid by others so that they can be independent by owning their own business. They are capable of solving problems and handling their affairs. They know business. They have always had a strong desire to accomplish firm goals — they worked as a paper boy, sold lemonade, etc. Subordinates respect the entrepreneurs and are willing to help them. They have the respect of others.

The owner of a small business must have energy, drive, goals and know what he is doing to be successful. He must be able to select proper consultants, lawyers, accountants and capable fellow workers. He must obtain information necessary to comply with laws and make his business grow. He must keep informed. Further details may be found in books such as "Starting and Managing a Small Business", Superintendent of Documents, Government Printing Office, Washington, D.C. 20402 and other books, some of which are listed herein under references.

FORMS USED BY CORPORATIONS

Corporations — both ordinary and S-corporations — offer advantages since legal obligations can be reduced and at times tax advantages are available. Corporations exist only on paper through their charter, by-laws, stock certificates, and minutes. Complete compliance with the applicable laws is essential. Many of these forms have been assembled in a text by Ted Nichols, Enterprise Publishing Company, 725 Market Street, Wilmington, Delaware 19801. Study of such forms should help you when discussing problems with your lawyer. Some of the forms may not be applicable because state law differs between states. The forms include items such as minutes of meetings, changes in by-laws and form of corporation, major business actions, dividends, compensation, fringe benefits, employee benefit plans, etc.

BUSINESS PRINCIPLES — COMMON SENSE PROCEDURES

Studies have shown that:

1. Doing the right thing is more important than doing it well. Good management alone, although very important, can rarely overcome flawed choice of business, operation in wrong location, choice of poor industry or selection of wrong products.
2. Timing is important. The same venture may be very profitable today and be a complete failure at another time.
3. A business which requires large amounts of capital usually is less profitable than one which needs little capital for start-up and operation. Large interest payments often hurt.
4. A business which is in trouble should not seek diversification until its trouble is solved. Poor management must be changed before adding new problems.
5. Business that produces a high added value per employee or unit of capital — sales per employee is high — usually is more profitable.
6. A high quality product as evaluated by the consumer enhances profit potential.
7. A larger share of the market relative to that of the three largest competitors improves profit and cash flow if the industry is profitable.

8. Consumers trust a company which is already producing high quality products. Consumers associate a new product with previous experience.

9. A strong market position often produces a good financial effect from new product introductions, added R&E and increased marketing efforts.

10. If the business and industry is mature and the market is stable so that it can be accurately forecast, consider vertical integration — making more of what you sell rather than buying parts from others.

11. Growth, either from industry expansion or from increase in company share of market, tends to help company profits but it also tends to reduce net cash flow. Thus, growth can be rapid and profitable while being ruinous unless there is a steady and available access to new capital to finance the growth. Most fast-track companies must learn to temper growth so that it does not outpace capital availability and internal management and other people-type expertise. Fast growth companies should market aggressively while continuing high research into the next generation of products. They do not build monolithic headquarters or other buildings nor accumulate cumbersome staffs or buy other business types to diversify until capital problems are solved.

12. Two companies making entirely different products while having the same investment intensity, productivity, market share position, etc., usually show similar financial results. Ability rather than product is often important.

13. A proposed strategy change should be evaluated using cost/benefit projections and should be undertaken only if supported by fact and an indication of very strong, favorable results. For a new venture to be successful, the future projection should be very favorable and robust. Weak projections do not justify any change, a new investment, or any other move. The analysis must be unbiased, sound, detailed, honest, and should include all risks.

14. The time, energy and money spent on a project are wasted when the project is unsuccessful and does not make money. The cause of failure should be investigated for salvage purposes — determine what went wrong so that the mistake is not repeated — but the project should be abandoned immediately when it is shown to be unprofitable. If others are involved, the project possibly must be completed to protect "goodwill". Never spend money unless a profit potential is strongly indicated.

15. Improper planning — failure to test market, to obtain all pertinent facts, to honestly analyze and evaluate data — often is the cause for failure. The probability of success should be strong before a proposal is given a test in the marketplace. Constantly look at the probable profitability as your study proceeds and stop whenever you have information that the chance of success is not extremely

strong. Increase research — find other ventures.

METHODS FOR PRICING PRODUCTS

Over the lifetime of a product, the cost of production drops about 25% every time that the volume doubles. Most managers do not reduce price as cost declines. Competition is able to make an early profit at lower price and they force prices down and may even take over the entire market if they compete effectively at a leader type loss. Lowering prices as market volume increased may have limited the competition. Managers must decide whether short-term high profits are preferable to competition and chances of competition when prices are lower but profitable and reasonable.

Pricing methods are important and the following discussion is desired:

1. The "skim the cream by high short-term profits" might be used. You simply determine the preliminary customer reaction to price in a limited short-term market and use the price at which the product sells today. The method can be used when no comparable competitive products are available, when the number of buyers are large and when the danger from competition in short-term market is small. Also, when the life cycle of a product is short, when demand is inelastic and when costs of production are uncertain. High prices cushion against cost overruns, reduce investment risks, provide funds rapidly, limit demand until production is adequate, emphasize value to a select group of cusomters and provide for a test of a larger market. Limitations include the possibility that adequate market is available at the price selected, that customers will not react unfavorably in case the price is reduced later, that competition will not undercut long-term market share, and that long options will be available when the need arises.

2. The second method depends upon a reduction in price as the market expands and product becomes available. Here you take advantage of scarce availability short-term and allow price to decline with time to hopefully forestall competition as costs decline. In time, you establish a large market share at an affordable price and reasonable profit and hopefully keep competition at a disadvantage. This method is used by established companies when launching innovations such as durable goods, when products have a medium lifespan and when competition is expected immediately if price remains high. Price is based on value and sales rather than costs. The initial high price favors early return of investment which offers protection from errors in estimating sales and costs while the lowering of price handicaps the competition. A broad knowledge of competitors ability is required to stay ahead of them and the possibility of some customer ill-will should be anticipated as early purchasers see price decline on the product bought.

3. You might decide to compete initially at the final market price to encourage high overall demand. Competition will operate under a

handicap. Advertising probably will be required to create demand. If others do compete, they will share advertising costs and all may prosper as market overall expands rapidly. This pricing method is used when comparable products are available to customers, when the overall market is expected to expand rapidly, when product life is medium to long and production costs are accurately known. Fewer market studies are required since market is known, promotion costs are shared, and ill will of customers should be small. The approach offers only limited flexibility, cushion for error is very small. The investment is recovered very slowly and selling tools may become complicated.

4. Initially, use a low price to increase market penetration in an existing competitive market where new product already has competition. You hope for a larger industry overall market and an increase of market share as the product is introduced at a low price. The product life should be long, a mass market is available, costs of entering the market are small, production costs are small and an elite market is not available. Penetration of the market must be rapid and you hope that competitors will not reduce their prices. You might hope that a price war can be avoided and that you will be able to raise prices to the level of competition after the desired market penetration has been achieved. At some time, prices must adjust so that profit in the mass market is acceptable to all. You must have a capital base to operate during a "price war" which might be anticipated when competition already exists. This method is risky particularly for a company with a small capital base and income levels. There can be cash flow problems if the time required to establish the desired market share is long.

5. Pre-emptive pricing may be used. This often is risky since very low prices usually attempt to gain market share or keep competitors out of the market. Your profit margins are very low and small errors in sales and operating costs can cause negative cash flows. Other products probably must sustain the company until the market is established to absorb sales costs. Payback period can be long and the method may not be useful to a small company.

Your pricing policy is very important since volume multiplied by market price per unit determines the income of your operation. Your operation must be or soon must become profitable if you are to remain in business.

CONTROL OF ACCOUNTS RECEIVABLE

Unpaid accounts of customers are costly since you do not earn interest on money owed from most customer accounts. They may also not ever pay so that the total owed is lost. You must make a profit — your income must exceed your costs each day and month — if you are to stay in business over the longer term. You simply must take the time to perform the unpleasant tasks of making collection of accounts receivable from customers. Pay your bills, pay taxes and permit fees and keep records demanded by the government. You must know your business.

Some lag in accounts receivable is inherent in all business unless you sell only "for cash". Most products are shipped to buyers and they pay at a date later than the date of the receipt of the materials. This lag can be tracked by use of the formula:

$$\text{"Time lag"} = \left[\frac{\text{Average Accounts Receivable}}{\text{Average Sales Level}}\right] \quad \begin{array}{c}\text{Time Interval used for}\\ \text{data in Days}\end{array}$$

Some time lag is inherent in any business but collection time should be kept at minimum levels. Interest income is lost when you lend money at no charge to others. The above formula shows average days before collection of accounts and it should be kept at a minimum.

You should also remember that:

1. New customers may be coming to you because they have credit difficulties with other people.
2. A sale is not completed until the payment is in your account at a bank.
3. Loss from a bad debt goes immediately to the bottom line. As examples:

Your profit margin on sales	Added sales required to offset $100 bad debt
5%	$2000
10%	1000
15%	500

You simply must investigate the credit reliability of all new customers. Check with past suppliers and bank references and monitor your accounts. Also, check with credit reporting agencies. Know your customers.

You should also use a collection procedure for all accounts receivable. Remember that a past due debt is a possible potential for stolen merchandise. You should:

1. Mail invoices the same day that merchandise is shipped. Include on the invoice the date shipped, the date the customer ordered, name of the person who ordered, a description of the shipped merchandise, unit price of shipped articles, the total amount owed by the customer. The discount, if any, should be underlined and the net payment should be circled in red. Enclose a return envelope. The bill also should include your address, your telephone number and the name of your bookkeeper who can discuss the bill in case of an error. Make it easy for customers to pay and stress on your invoice severe penalty for late payments such as late charges, etc.
2. Monitor the account by keeping a detailed record on customer's file, possibly on your copy of the invoice. Be consistent in your collection practices. Send a "memory jogger" on the tenth day after mailing the original bill. If a customer calls, handle any problems immediately. At 20 days, request immediate payment by phone call. Get promise of an immediate date for payment from

the customer. If payment is not received on the date promised, call again. Tell the customer that his credit has been suspended but will be reinstated after his payment has cleared the bank. Confirm all conversations in writing and advise that collection will be turned over to a collection agency within a stated time. Turn account over to such an agency as stated. Do not violate state and federal laws relative to harassment.

3. You may improve collections by:
   a. Charging interest at a high rate 5 to 10 days after shipment.
   b. Using installment payments with highest interest rate permitted by law.
   c. Varying people who make calls.
   d. Taking back unused merchandise.
4. Arrange your records so that you know the past payment record of each client.

Do not allow collection problems to ruin your business.

PRODUCT LIABILITY

The manufacturer and seller of merchandise face the possibility of lawsuits relative to product reliability and safety and may be held responsible for injury caused by goods sold as well as quality of goods. Some liabilities are included in state and federal statutes, laws and regulations. Other responsibilities relate to negligence in design, inspection, testing, failing to disclose possible problems, inadequate instructions and anything else that a good lawyer might convince a jury as a cause of accident or defect. Misrepresentation in advertising and selling are also not permitted. Class action lawsuits are particularly troublesome. Various implied and assumed warranties must be strictly observed. Expressed warranties are oral and written parts of sales procedures. Implied warranties may, in part, be imposed by "Uniform Commercial Codes". Most products are assumed to be of reasonable quality and are useable for the general and specific purposes relied on by customers. Often you must disclose to the consumer all warranty rights as specified by law. You must be absolutely certain that your operation (1) conforms with all trade and legal standards, (2) potentially dangerous products are tested by an independent agency, (3) all dangerous parts are identified and labeled, (4) all instructions, manuals, sales procedures, literature is absolutely clear and detailed, and (5) do not include any unintended warranties by implication in literature or sales talks. You should consider warranty and liability insurance. Also, contact a good lawyer and U. S. Consumer Product Safety Commission, Washington, D.C. 20207.

FINANCING YOUR BUSINESS

Equity funds and borrowed money are usually used. You may sell stock of various types and you may borrow from a bank or others using security of various types. Interest must be paid on borrowed funds and the owners of stocks expect a return as dividends and capital appreciation with time. Borrowed money must be repaid on dates specified on the loan agreements or the accounts must be refinanced at such times. Tax considerations are somewhat different to both lender and borrower. The lender pays income tax at regular rates on both interest and dividends. The tax position of borrower is illustrated by the following example:

	Debt	Equity
Present earnings before interest and taxes	$530,000	$530,000
Less: Present interest expense	50,000	50,000
Less: New interest on $200,000 @ 20%	40,000	--
Earnings before taxes	440,000	480,000
Less: Taxes @ 46%	202,400	220,800
Profits after tax	$237,600	$259,200
Common shares outstanding	100,000	104,000
Earnings-per-share (EPS)	$2.38	$2.49

The above calculations are based on need of $200,000 additional financing.

Your decision as to alternate financing methods should include risk — ability to repay loan on due date; flexibility — what are restrictive terms of various agreements; and control — stock sale often dilutes ownership while a loan might result in bankruptcy if terms are not met. Also, credit may be limited by risk of your venture, high cost of money and, during recessions, money of any type may simply not be available regardless of credit rating.

SELECTION OF DISTRIBUTION METHOD

You must get your product into the hands of customers. You might use direct sales — sales by your staff or by direct mail; you might use manufacturers agents and you might use distributors. When selling to many customers, you may sell direct, you might use a wholesaler and you might sell to a retailer. Someone must finance inventory, provide for storage of goods and make contact with final customers. These all cost money. The method selected provides a service which is needed by you and the ultimate buyer. There is no "free way" and the middleman between manufacturer and final user serves a useful service for which he deserves to earn a reward. Business cannot exist without a distribution system in our complicated society and the book economist is wrong in trying to eliminate the middleman. There is no way to do so.

The method to be used should be different when selling to industry and when selling to a person in a store. The method used by a lawyer is different than that of a large manufacturer. You must use experience and possibly market surveys before reaching a decision as to the best method for your particular product.

You may wish to have your product in every store on the street and this intensive distribution is required when the product is low priced, when the use is widespread and the necessary volume is large. If the customer will go out of his way to find and buy your product, you may use fewer outlets and be somewhat selective in outlets used. Exclusive distribution, using very few first class outlets, may be desired when your product is unique, rare, expensive. Pianos and imported crystal are examples.

The advantages and disadvantages of each distribution method is illustrated below:

Advantages | **Disadvantages**

Direct Sales

Advantages	Disadvantages
Good control of prices.	Combine with existing sales force and thereby reduce costs.
Only your product is sold by your salesmen.	Increased effort required to expand sales into new areas.
Easy to adjust prices.	Do not need additional service organization, delivery facilities and management.
Superior feedback from buyers.	
You control services.	

Manufacturers Agents

Advantages	Disadvantages
You retain good cost control and do not need a sales force	Less control over sales and over actions of sales force.
You may control prices.	Little feedback from buyers.
The sales force has contacts from previous sales of other products	Salesman may also sell products of your competitors.
Less need for training, supervision and other services.	Your organization has less contact with purchasers.

Distributors

Advantages	Disadvantages
Already has established sales staff who know local market.	Less control over operations, including prices, advertising and services.
Little front end costs since distributor handles sales, warehouse and distribution.	Distributor may not have enthusiasm to sell your product instead of those of other firms.
Local warehousing of stock.	Distributor may demand special discounts.
Distributor handles complains unless you are asked to help.	You may be insulated from customers and end users which makes planning difficult. May not know problems.

Distribution agreements can be very complex and they should define territorial rights, the specific obligations of each party, terms of sales, the price and discount structure, etc. The selection of your distribution techniques determines your success. Be careful.

COST CONTROL

Many costs are associated with a business. Failure to consider all costs when determining prices and making bids can ruin your business efforts. Usually, cost estimates made by the inexperienced are very low — often about 50% of true costs. Individuals who have not worked on a similar project or business always believe that they can accomplish the impossible. In life there are always problems such as failure of suppliers, weather variations, breakdowns. These all increase costs. Find advice based on actual experience before making a bid or determining a price. Also, read a book which outlines cost of insurance, bad debts, permits, what have you.

Cost broadly can be divided into fixed costs and costs which vary with sales or production volumes. Fixed costs include cost of money, interest, capital amortization, minimum administration, overhead, property taxes, other taxes, utilities, minimum required space rental. Variable costs include cost of materials, labor costs, social security and "pensions" which may amount to over 35% of labor costs, sales costs, commissions, shipping and transportation costs, cost of lost, stolen and damaged goods, cost of uncollected receivables, any cost which varies with units produced, and other losses, etc. Carefully obtain a list of costs associated with your specific business and determine all costs so that none are overlooked. Check routinely with suppliers to be aware of price changes before they occur. If you make bids, have suppliers and sub-contractors confirm your estimates or give you firm bids. Have an accounting system which monitors costs and income weekly on each project or category. A large organization may have capital resources to absorb loss created by mistakes but mistakes often force a small business into bankruptcy. Try to reduce costs by improving efficiency, improving productivity, lowering cost of materials by buying in quantity, etc.

Often costs can be lowered by greater supervision and control. The following two methods illustrated by an example using inventory control are often used.

ECONOMIC ORDER QUANTITY ANALYSIS OR "EOQ"

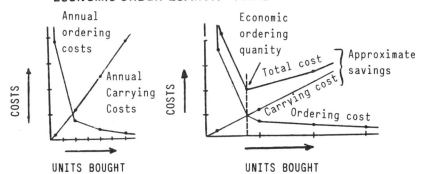

The above chart combines carrying costs and ordering costs to obtain "EOQ". Inventories are required to fill finished product orders from customers quickly and to maintain the raw materials for use in manufacture.

THE ABC SYSTEM

The "EOQ" and "THE ABC SYSTEM" should be combined for best results. The "ABC SYSTEM" splits inventory into the following three groups.
1. The few very expensive items — this group includes only 10% of total items but its value is 60%, more or less, of total cost on inventory. Group A.
2. A group B consisting of about 30% of dollar investment and about 20% of physical stock.
3. A group C consisting of remaining items. Their low cost does not justify supervision and large stocks are kept to assure supply. Group

C includes 70% of stock but only 10-20% of value.

You achieve the smallest stock level in dollars by:

1. Watching group A. Reduce their inventory to a minimum, check this stock often, order when necessary and demand fast delivery from suppliers.
2. Give attention to group B but supervise much less than group A inventory.
3. Order group C in large quantities to obtain discounts at infrequent intervals.

Use todays computers to control individual items in all groups. Demand "on time delivery" from suppliers. Work closely with plant supervisors and insist that they enter withdrawals of stock into records so inventory controls are always accurate and inventory is sufficient to prevent delay in manufacture. Take inventory to assure accuracy of computer records, to check on possible theft, etc. You want lowest possible inventory but you cannot allow lack of inventory to stop operations. You do need to reduce interest on capital, reduce cost of placing and controlling orders and you should get discounts and lowest prices by using a plan. Keep controls and make them work. The key, again, is capable, willing and honest help. No shortcuts.

DETERMINING BREAKEVEN POINT – CAPITAL ANALYSIS

Your operation must make a profit or your income must always exceed your payments. You make a profit when sales income exceeds all costs and you have a loss when sales income is less than costs. The point at which you start to make a profit is your "breakeven point". A breakeven point can be lowered by an increase in sales income and by a reduction in costs. Both must be carefully controlled. The technique can be understood by constructing a chart similar to that shown below for your operation.

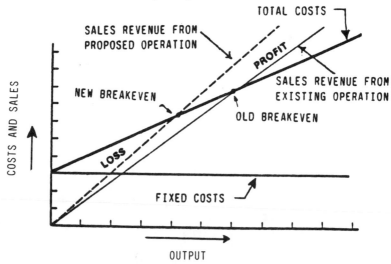

DETERMINING BREAKEVEN POINT

The above example illustrates an increase in sales but the method is equally useful when costs are reduced. Variable costs may not be entirely dependent on output so variations of the method are necessary. In the 1980s, the "Visicalc" computer may be used or accounting may relate with large computer programs. You should always plot some of the results to check for reliability and to aid in your interpretation of the data.

You should use breakeven graphs to analyze:
1. Relations between volume, price and expenses.
2. Analyze alternate management and economic assumptions.
3. Control costs – use with budget techniques.
4. Relate impact of price changes on profit.
5. Analyze plant expansions and capital expenditures.
6. The method can reflect errors in simple mathematical and computer analysis by comparing results of various studies and placing results at one place.

Characteristics of the perfect business:
1. Mass acceptance by consumers.
2. Already in place, proven and with excellent return.
3. Is free from franchise fees and royalties.
4. Is exciting and in early stages of high growth.
5. Is completely turnkey and payments are all cash.
6. Is easy to operate either full-time or part-time.
7. Can be a family venture and others can operate when owner absent.
8. Business has mail order potential or multi-store possibility.

ANALYSIS OF CAPITAL EXPENDITURES
EXAMPLE ANALYSIS OF PURCHASE OF NEW MACHINE

New Cash Outlays – Cost of new machine		$10,000
Savings from investment		(666)
Installation Charge		2,000
Sales of old equipment		(2,500)
NET INVESTMENT		$ 8,834
Savings @ $1500/Year:		
Year 1 $1500 x 0.870	$1,305	
Year 2 1500 x 0.756	1,134	
Year 3 1500 x 0.658	987	
Year 4 1500 x 0.572	858	
Year 5 1500 x 0.497	746	
TOTAL	$5,030	
Sale after 5 years	1,000	
Present Value Cash Flows	$6,030	$ 6,030
Inflows minus outflows in todays dollars		($ 2,804)

The proposed purchase shows a dollar loss. The new machine should not be bought.

Additional analysis techniques were discussed earlier.

Capital expenditures often involve a determination of alternate project profitability. As examples, you might refurbish old equipment, you might buy new equipment or you might continue using present facilities. Always analyze carefully and compare financial results after taxes and inflation using your current cost of capital for delayed items. Carefully and realistically evaluate costs and income streams resulting from the alternate possible plans of action. Again, honesty and accuracy are important and human desires should be eliminated from consideration. Think, analyze and discount your emotions. New, shiny equipment, too, becomes old-looking.

S-CORPORATIONS AND OWNERSHIP TYPES

Your attorney and accountant should be consulted before you decide upon a form of ownership for your proposed operation. Options include individual ownership, partnerships using general partners and possibly limited partners, S-Corporations and regular corporations. Each offers advantages and disadvantages depending upon size, probable growth and your needs. Personal ownership and partnerships increase your personal responsibility and each has its own tax considerations. Formation of an S-corporation involves strict Federal tax laws as to number of owners, etc. In general, all of your assets are liable when ownership is private or in a partnership, while liabilities may be limited to the assets of only the corporation. Corporations of the regular type pay "double taxes" since the corporation pays tax on earnings and the owner pays tax on dividends. All aspects are complicated and you need expert advice when selecting type of ownership.

Obtain from the IRS the material necessary to understand tax laws and go to the library and ask for a book on legal responsibilities. Thereafter, see your experts for final advice after you know enough to carry on a logical conversation. Do not blindly trust the advice of a tax accountant or lawyer. They, too, may not be entirely informed and they do not have the time — you will not pay them for it — to really study your situation in the detail necessary.

SUCCESSFUL MANAGEMENT

Management is the most important aspect of your business. You must learn to manage your life, your business and your time. Learn to ask: Where am I? Where am I going? Where do I want to go and be? How do I get from here to there? How do I wish to live my life? What is the plan for my business and my investments? All are very important.

You should consider trends but recognize that they can change quickly. Focus on the future as well as the present. Do not worry about the past except to avoid future mistakes of a similar nature. The past is gone forever. Consider your objectives and prepare to meet them during a time period which is realistic. Consider trends, laws, environmental concepts, governmental restrictions, your people, your approach to life and the nature of your business. Think and plan your work, business, investments and your private life so that it is possible to reach your goals.

The most important asset of any business is its management and its supervisors. You need good, honest and capable people who know what they are doing. You should, as owner or top executive, supervise them carefully while giving them freedom to make decisions. You should react quickly when mistakes are made and when character changes are noted on and off the job so that their actions do not kill your operation. You need to trust but make sure that trust is warranted at all times.

Management must have and use practical common sense and intelligence, basic knowledge of all facets of the business and lead by exhibiting motivation and leadership ability to develop a team effort. Managers must constantly probe for weakness as well as strengths of the business. The manager or owner must know his capabilities and know his limits. He must hire capable people to fill in at his weak points but he must make certain that he is not mislead. The manager must act and make the hard decisions immediately as they arise. He even must be able to fire his friends when essential for the good of the business. All managers must recognize the strengths and weaknesses of staff and create an overall efficient working team. The manager should handle problems immediately by (1) assembling all facts pertinent to making a decision, (2) analyzing the facts, thinking, reasoning and making a decision, (3) acting and implementing the decision and (4) constantly reviewing results so that revisions are made when necessary in a timely fashion.

The manager must delegate authority and decision-making, particularly the daily operation. The owner should know the business in detail to be certain that employees are performing properly. The manager faces the difficult task of giving others authority and responsibility while at the same time making sure that his business is operating efficiently. He studies financial records daily to track performance and know that his company is on the right track and profitable. As his company grows, he also must devote more time to approving and planning long range policy. The failure of many growing companies relates with inadequate controls of financial records and supervision of operations. The owner who does not realize his own limitations is also a cause of failure. Few managers have the expertise, ability and drive to be the financial expert, overall planner, the sales manager and the operations manager. Select your help with care.

The owner—president—chairman of the board does have to know his operation although details have been delegated to others. You must know that information furnished by subordinates is reliable. His staff may deceive him — may be "yes" people — in an effort to obtain favors and advancement. The owner needs to use outside audits and consultants. He also should inspect operations frequently and ask pertinent questions. The successful manager uses many sources of information and knows the daily operation — controls his business — but he also retains the respect of those working for him. He insists on honesty, accurate reports, accurate information as to the progress in operations. He manages people rather than allowing others to manipulate him. He spends the time and energy required to really be a manager who knows his business. He runs the organization by using people hired to perform assigned chores — by insisting that they honestly perform in a capable and efficient manner. He has a check and balance system which controls but is not offensive to those working for him. He is always correctly informed and knows his business and what to do when things go wrong. He is friendly and also capable. His employees like him and willingly give their all because he is fair.

The successful manager knows his employees and makes suggestions which improve operations while at the same time inspecting the operations. The employee feels that he is being helped and the manager gains information which helps him in his control.

In a very small business, you initially will be doing selling, buying, billing, paying bills, writing letters, typing labels, handling publicity, advertising, etc. The job is difficult, the hours are long and you cannot be an expert in all of these fields. Recognize this as a passing phase and do not allow the workload to become a habit. After the business becomes profitable, hire needed professionals. Before starting, contact a lawyer and an accountant to help you know the laws and regulations and basic accounting. You always need to have an understanding, preferably in writing, as to who makes basic decisions. The rules of the workplace and necessary work relationships must be understood by everyone so that everyone knows his responsibilities and remains friendly and cooperative so that the overall operation is a team effort.

The small businessman also needs to have basic knowledge in many fields of expertise. Experience is the best teacher but books can substitute.

Ask your library for:

1. The American Management Association Handbook.
2. The Practice of Management by Peter Drucker.
3. Business Reference Sources by Lorna Daniels.
4. Handbook of Modern Personnel Administration by Joseph Famularo, editor.
5. Personnel: The Human Problems of Management by George Strauss and Leonard Sayes.
6. Statistical Abstract of the United States. U. S. Census Bureau.
7. Census Statistics by U. S. Census Bureau.
8. Books and magazines published by Trade Associations.
9. National Trade Associations and Professional Association of United States and Canada by Columbia Books, Inc.
10. Standard Periodical Directory by Oxbridge Publishing Company.
11. A Guide to Consumer Marketing by U. S. Conference Board.
12. Survey of Current Business by U. S. Department of Commerce — monthly.
13. Market Guide by Editor and Publisher Company.
14. Guide to American Directories by Bernard Klein & Company.
15. Million Dollar Directory by Dun and Bradstreet.
16. Poors Register of Corporations, Directors and Executives by Standard and Poors.
17. Thomas Register of American Manufacturers.
18. Guide to Venture Capital Sources by Standley Rubel.

Your library and bookstore can find many additional references. They both are most helpful. You also should look for free advice. Learn to use what is available at no or small cost. Many professionals such as lawyers and accountants as well as publicity people at newspapers, artists, consultants will lend a helping hand to those who are starting a new business. New business generates additional work for them when successful. College and high school instructors can be helpful. Seek advice — the worst that you will hear is "no".

CORPORATE TAXES, PERMITS, ETC.

Business is harmed by many local, state and federal laws, regulations, permits and taxes. These can be handled by a competent lawyer and accountant. Always comply so that your business is not shut down. You also should contact the government agencies yourself and ask their experts for advice so that you can ask your experts the proper questions. They never will know your business like you do and they, too, make mistakes. You alone are responsible for violations so do be careful.

The federal tax laws change on short notice. Your tax expert should constantly advise you of changes.

At some point, speculation may cause your assets to have a value far in excess of true value. As an example, it is not too unusual for a property or stock to have a market value of say $25.00 per share which later declines to below $2.00 per share. Watch for these speculations. If you decide to sell, recognize that tax considerations of buyer and seller may vary widely. A good, capable lawyer and accountant are essential.

Business partnerships and S-Corporations pay no federal income tax but the income and liabilities are passed each year to the owners who pay taxes.

AVERAGE VALUES FOR BUSINESS INDEXES

Your business competes with others for sales and capital. The following overall criteria might be useful when defining your goals.

AVERAGES FOR YEARS 1920 TO 1981 INCLUSIVE
DOW JONES INDUSTRIALS
(Some data exclude years 1921, 31 and 33.)

Price/Earnings ratio	13.7%	Range since 1950	7 to 22	
Price/Dividend ratio	22.5		13	30
Earned on Book Value	11.3		8	13
Earnings Yield	7.7		5	15
Dividend Yield	4.7		3	6
Earnings Growth Rate	5.5			
Dividend Growth Rate	4.4			
Book Value Growth Rate	5.2	Lows occur at bottom of		
Earnings Yield + Earnings Growth	13.2	business cycle and highs		
Dividend Yield + Dividend Growth	9.1	at crests.		
Moodys Aaa Bond Yield	5.0			
Inflation — CPI	2.5			

AVERAGES FOR 950 COMPANIES
(Assumes operation as one company) (Value Line)

Year	1978	1979	1980	1981	1982
Average Price/Earnings (primary)	7.93	6.61	8.13	8.91	10.98
Average Price/Sales	0.38	0.36	0.39	0.39	0.36
Dividend Yield – percent	4.7	4.9	4.5	4.4	5.0
Inflation Rate – CPI – percent	7.7	11.3	13.5	10.4	6.1
P/E plus inflation	15.6	17.9	21.6	19.3	17.0
Gross Margin	26.9	26.6	25.6	25.1	25.4
Depreciation rate	5.8	6.0	6.0	6.1	6.3
Pretax margin	9.6	10.4	9.3	8.3	6.6
Income tax rate	48.2	45.4	46.6	44.5	46.2
Net Income Margin	4.9	5.5	4.9	4.6	3.4
Cash Flow Payout	23.0	21.0	22.2	22.8	26.0
Working Capital/Sales	14.8	13.7	12.6	11.8	11.4
Cash/Current Liability	30.5	26.3	25.0	22.5	24.2
Current Ratio	173.0	166.1	161.9	158.5	155.7
Inventory/Sales	13.9	13.9	13.4	13.1	12.6
Accounts Receivable/Sales	13.2	13.3	12.7	12.4	12.1
Working Capital/Sales	14.8	13.7	12.6	11.8	11.4
Gross Plant/Sales	52.4	52.1	51.9	54.2	60.3
Total Capital/Sales	47.6	45.4	44.8	46.2	49.4
Long Term Debt/Capital	28.6	28.1	28.0	29.2	29.9
Common Equity/Capital	69.0	69.6	69.8	68.6	67.6
Equity/Capital	71.4	71.9	72.0	70.8	70.1
Earned on Total Capital	11.3	13.3	12.0	11.0	8.3
Earned on Equity	14.3	16.8	14.9	13.6	9.6
Earned on Net Plant	15.4	17.7	15.2	13.2	8.9

SOURCES OF INFORMATION

"The Instant MBA", G. G. Putnam & Sons.

Write to Executive Director, Institute of Management Consultants, 19 West 44th Street, New York, New York 10022 for possible advice.

Write for Franchise Opportunities Handbook, Superintendent of Documents, U. S. Printing Office, Washing, D.C. 20402.

You can get help in locating specific information by writing National Referral Center, Library of Congress, Washington, D.C. Also write to your congressman. Phone 202-287-5670.

When you need to sell your handicrafts, contact, before sending samples, either New York Exchange for Womens Work, 660 Madison Avenue, New York, New York 10021, or The Elder Craftsman of New York, 851 Lexington Avenue, New York, New York 10021.

Inventions must be evaluated and many patent attorneys are frauds. Learn to do the paperwork necessary to prove date of invention, etc.

Check with the following: Professor Richard Buskirk, Director of the Entrepreneur Program, The University of Southern California, Los Angeles,

California 90007; Edison E. Easton, Professor of Management, Oregon State University, Corvallis, Oregon 97331; Professor Donald Sexton, Caruth Professor of Entrepreneurship, Baylor University, Waco, Taxas 76706.

For free information on job sharing, write to the Association of Part-Time Professionals, 7655 Old Springhouse Road, McLean, Virginia 20102, or New Ways to Work, 149 Ninth Street, San Francisco, California 94103.

For marketing advice, write to Direct Marketing Association, 6 East 43rd Street, New York, New York 10017, or to Direct Marketing News, 19 West 21st Street, New York, New York 10010, or to Direct Marketing Magazine, 224 7th Street, Garden City, New York 11530.

When you need to investigate an industry, go to your local library and check the Business Section of Standard Rate and Data, a 1500 page book listing all industries and their trade journals.

Service Corps. of Retired Executives or SCORE offers free help. Call the U. S. Small Business Office for the address in your city. Use your telephone book.

Active Corps of Retired Executives or ACE offers help. Again call the Small Business Office.

U. S. Small Business Administration offers many publications and conferences. Write to Small Business Administration, Office of Publications, Room 100, Washington, D.C. 20416, Phone 800-368-5855.

The Superintendent of Documents, Government Printing Office, Washington, D.C. 20402 offers many publications related to business.

Also, check with the Consumer Information Center, Pueblo, Colorado 81009.

Write the Minority Business Development Agency, U. S. Department of Commerce, Washington, D.C. 20230 for information.

For 4-8 page summaries of current textbooks, write Soundview Executive Books Summaries, 5 Main Street, Bristol, Vermont 05443.

SUMMARY

You own a business to make money. Always protect a portion of your assets by removing money from the business. At the start, decide how much you can afford to lose and this is the only loss which you should accept. If a going business is losing money, either fix it quickly or get out. Never spend the money required to protect the living standards of your family and always retain enough money to get started again in a job or other venture. Never bet your entire future because of pride. Make sure that you can survive.

Also, please study the section on "Investments", particularly the part dealing with ratios.

Directors, and probably officers, are expected by the courts to behave like fiduciaries. They should act prudently, follow basic guidelines and have good, well-documented reasons for decisions.

BUSINESS LIBRARY

Every business should have in its possession for ready reference the informational statistics which affect its operations. Sources of such information can be determined by consulting the Business Information Sources by Lorna M. Daniels, Head of the Reference Department of the Harvard Business School's Baker Library, Other similar information is available in Business Reference Sources by Lorna M. Daniels. Federal agencies such as the Commerce Department, Labor Department and Census Bureau are good sources of information and their offices in your area or in Washington should be contacted for recommendations. Directories include (1) Guide to American Directories by Bernard Klein & Co., (2) Million Dollar Directory by Dun and Bradstreet, (3) Poors Directory of Corporations, Directors and Executives by Standard and Poors, (4) Thomas Register of American Manufacturers, and (5) Guide to Venture Capital Sources by Standley Rubel. These are probably available in your library.

Many sources are available for information on market research. Please contact the Conference Board for its annual Guide to Consumer Markets. The U. S. Commerce Department monthly publishes Survey of Current Business. An annual compendium of marketing information is available in the Market Guide by Editor and Publisher Co., Inc. The Sales and Marketing Magazine publishes a Survey of Buying Power.

Your organization might also consider (1) Statistical Abstract of the United States by U. S. Census Bureau, (2) Census Statistics, and (3) Monthly Periodicals published by President's Council of Economic Advisors. The Federal Reserve Regional Office also publishes useful information. Write the U. S. Government Printing Office, Washington, D.C. for other sources of information published by government agencies.

Trade Associations often publish results affecting their readers and many of these are available in public libraries. Consult (1) National Trade and Professional Associations of the United States and Canada by Columbia Books for lists of organizations, (2) F&S Index of Corporations and Industries by Predicasts, Inc., and (3) Standard Periodical Directory by Oxbridge Publishing Co.

There are many books on Personal Management, Sales Manager and General Management which are must reading for students in business studies. Your librarian can help you make a selection for your personal references. Also, Boardroom Reports, 330 West 42nd Street, New York, New York 10036 often includes very short reviews of new books. Soundview Executive Book Summaries, 100 Heights Road, Darien, Connecticut 06820 publishes six page summaries of new books related to business problems and solutions. These and trade magazines allow one to keep current.

You also need a good dictionary, atlas, zip code directory, telephone directory, hotel directory with 800 numbers and magazines covering your business, known as trade magazines.

Meet the librarian who handles the business section at your local public library. This person can be most helpful by referring you to sources of information related to the problems faced by your organization. Today, "How-To-Do" books are available which may offer solutions or suggestions useful to you when deciding courses of action. Help is available but you must seek solutions and you, alone, are responsible for your actions. Learn to also contact local Chambers of Commerce, planning groups, tax authorities and other groups who control your activities.

"Getting Started in Federal Contracting" is used by contractors.

Management Of Personal Finances

Do you wish to be one of the 75% of all Americans who are dependent upon charity and friends when you are old? If you do not, read the following and be one of the few who are financially independent instead. You can experience the joys and benefits of independence if you plan your work, investments and play. You can plan your life and you might start today. It is your decision.

If you like your lifestyle and want something better for your children, accept your responsibilities today and help make democracy and the American free enterprise system work. Vote with intelligence after careful study of the issues and the candidates. Defend our society and business methods which make it all possible. Learn to contact the politicians to obtain your objectives.

Travel to a poor, developing country if you need to see an alternative to our system of free enterprise.

BLUNDERS

Do you have a plan for your life? Do you live your plan? Do you have a financial plan? If you do not, you are not alone. About 80% of all successful people do not take the time and make this blunder. They claim to be too busy. Actually, they are simply lazy. They allow distractions such as television and the lack of willpower to keep them from doing the most important thing in their life. It is easy to become so involved in making a living that you do not plan and thereby reduce your ability to live a complete and successful life. Your financial plan is most important.

Not having a comprehensive plan to deal with taxes, inflation, family protection through insurance, retirement and the other challenges which you face, both today and tomorrow, can ruin you. It is sad but true — most successful people are so busy making money that they devote little if any time learning how to manage their assets. They simply drift without direction. Usually, your job supports necessities but management and a few savings create your future higher living standards, the education of your children, home ownership, etc. If you do not plan, you financial affairs, and possibly your life, is in a chronic state of confusion and disarray. You have no idea of your goals — what you want out of your single stay on the planet earth. You are probably overpaying your taxes, your investments, if any, are not properly balanced, your wages and other income are much less than possible and you spend it foolishly. It pays to plan and think a little.

The consequences of not having a plan can be severe in case of accident or death. In todays rapidly changing world, minor disturbances in your health, your emotions, your job or your financial arrangements can be catastrophic.

Even under the best of luck and circumstances, inflation and taxes are wrecking havoc with both your earnings and other assets.

The first step in making a financial plan is to make an inventory of net worth using forms presented on the following pages. Thereafter, you must learn to manage time and assets. Your assets should grow at a rate consistent with your willingness to accept risk. When assets are small, risks also should be small. Investments should be spread over several investment types to avoid complete loss in case of error in judgment. At first you might use a mutual fund as discussed in later sections of this text. Many books are available which discuss various types of investments — how to find and manage them. Most discuss only one type of medium and you will possibly be confused. Likewise, your broker, real estate agent, your banker and accountant will, too, have special interests and may not be reliable. You, alone, must reach decisions and you should be knowledgeable.

If your investment program is successful, you also need to pass your assets to your children for education, for starting life and finally for inheritance. You also may wish to make gifts to church, school, etc. The problem is largely tax avoidance. The techniques used depend upon the age of the children, their interests and their ability. You need to consult with one of the few good estate planning advisors who is aware of details of tax law and state laws applicable to gifts and inheritance. You must choose wisely.

You must know tax and state law yourself so that you can evaluate the advice of your tax attorney. You probably cannot pay him for the time required to think of the many details involved in your plans.

Congress has been revising the tax laws each year in a manner which makes it easier for you to save without paying taxes and for you to make gifts. In 1984, you can give to your spouse, without taxes, even at the time of death. You and your wife can each give $10,000 to as many people as you desire without paying transfer taxes. The gifts can be made each year. You can also make a major gift to children with the tax free amount changing with the whims of Congress. However, giving may not be desirable until children have learned to manage money. Trusts may be useful. The law is rather complicated but you will understand if you only take the time to read the documents available from the Internal Revenue Service. Why delay? Give it a try. Thereafter, you should become familiar with state laws.

In most case, you cannot retain any control over trusts after the children reach age 21 years. You can allow management by others in whom you have confidence. Property which is increasing in value often makes the best gifts since both income and inheritance taxes are thereby reduced. Inheritance taxes are very high and you are urged to understand tax laws, starting today.

You and your children should study current tax law — read IRS Publication 463 dealing with estate and gift taxes and Publication 17 dealing with yearly income taxes. You should consult with a good tax attorney and possibly with a financial consultant before making a plan for giving money to children, etc.

Children must learn to manage money. They must grow up and know the

rules of business and management. They must know tax, business and investment rules. They must know rules and the requirements of life in our society
before you can allow them to handle your assets. You worked hard to save and
pass to them savings made by grandparents and these savings should not be spent
foolishly — at least not while you can have fun with it. It may hurt deeply when
you deny your children but your money does not help others when they have
not grown to accept the related responsibility.

Most children, by age 18 years, have developed the intelligence to recognize that their life will not be long enough to learn how society works without
learning from the experiences of those who have lived during earlier times. They
also realize that they must accept instructions or orders from others — at least
during their learning years. Children learn to accept and seek knowledge, the
rules and regulations required for a successful financial, mental and physical life.
They seek out books, magazines, newspapers, radio, television and teachers who
can help them in daily living. They also begin to realize that advice given them
by parents was not all bad. They start to become adults. Children who do not
react so that they learn from their elders usually do not convert their rebellion
into useful drives and by their failures may become misfits in society. Independence is necessary but when carried to an extreme it can be a lifelong handicap. We all must join the society in which we will live. We work for change
using existing laws as a base.

Parents do find it hard to recognize that they cannot help children who do
not want help. Studies show that giving extra money only compounds the problems of these children and assures eventual failure. Parents should demand that
gifts be managed and invested wisely and that income derived from gifts be spent
in an accepted, prudent manner before giving large gifts to their children.

Sound management of assets requires that you:

1. Be informed. You must spend time collecting and studying basic
    relevant information.
2. Seek sound advice from experts but use your own judgment during
    evaluation.
3. Learn and use the techniques required to properly evaluate avail-
    able data. Learn to be a manager.
4. Spend time necessary to evaluate advice and data.
5. Act based on your best judgment and analysis.
6. Constantly review results and change when necessary.

If you do not want to do the necessary work, you might invest in money
market funds and mutual funds. You must continue to supervise but the job is
easier. Most of the work required to manage your investments is necessary if
you want to perform properly when you work for others or when you run your
business. After you start and learn a little, you will find that management of
your investments is fun and adds to your joy.

A few words regarding sources of income are desired while you are working and need to plan for your retirement. Discussion at this time will be brief
since later sections are devoted to your management of investments.

1. Salary and/or business income results from a service rendered by

you to others. During younger years, salary often increases with experience so that living standards improve during a period of increasing responsibilities.

2. Investment income results from a return or interest received on capital invested. The money you invest is your capital. In addition to interest or dividends, an astute investor may earn an appreciation or increase in value for his assets. A company may retain and invest part of its earnings for the benefit of the investor. An investor may also benefit from superior judgment and poor investment habits of other investors as to both value and timing of purchases and sales of investments. You may also take advantage of tax laws and inflation by sound adjustment or revisions in your investments. You may also borrow from others and earn a return above the costs of borrowing. American industry has always used a large amount of borrowed money and so can you. When borrowing, you must always be able to repay debts when due. Do not borrow long term and use for short term. This always is a road to disaster.

3. Insurance is used for protection of remote hazards which often never occur to you individually. Insurance spreads risk over many and thereby is able to protect you at small cost. Insurance is designed to give survivors a reasonable lifestyle in case of death or accident. Insurance also is used to protect from fire and other casualty. Insurance also may be used to protect the family from business debts, pay off the home mortgage in case of death. Liability insurance also is essential. Insurance is very useful but it is not an investment. You should not overinsure but should invest in higher return areas instead. As an example, term life insurance often is more rewarding than 20 year paid-up insurance.

Sources of information include:

1. Bests Insurance Reports, A.M. Best Co., Oldwick, New Jersey.
2. The Insurance Forum (newsletter), Joseph Belth, Indiana University Press, Tenth & Morton Streets, Bollmington, Indiana 47705.
3. "Junk Mail" can be reduced. Write to Mail Preference Service, Direct Marketing Associates, 6 E. 43rd Street, New York 10017.
4. Investment Company Institute, Box 86140, Washington, D.C. 20035 offers guides to mutual funds, etc.
5. For information regarding bank interest rates, write to "100 Highest Yields", North Palm Beach, Florida.
6. For aid in finding a financial planner, write to the International Association of Financial Planning, 2 Concourse Parkway, Suite 800, Atlanta, Georgia 30328.
7. For aid in finding investment clubs, write to National Association of Investment Clubs, 1515 East Eleven Mile Road, Royal Oak, Michigan 48067.
8. For a list of mutual funds, contact your broker or write to: No-Load Mutual Fund Association, Box 2004, New York 10116.

COMPUTERS

Machines can make life easier if used with common sense. Some better personal finance programs follow:

MANAGING YOUR MONEY, Micro Education Corporation of America, 185 Riverside Avenue, Westport, Connecticut 06880.

DOLLARS AND SENSE, Monogram, 8295 S. La Cienega Boulevard, Inglewood, California 90301. Good for family or small business use.

FINANCIER II, Financial Software, 3 Kane Industrial Drive, Hudson, Massachusetts 01749.

HOME ACCOUNTANT and HOME ACCOUNTANT PLUS, Continental Software, 6711 Valjean Avenue, Van Nuys, California 91406. These run on more different computers than any other home finance program.

PERSONAL ACCOUNTING, BPI Systems, 3001 Bee Cave Road, Austin, Texas 78746. A good choice for those with complicated finances.

ASSET RECORDS

TABLE SUMMARIZING CASH FLOW

You need to calculate your cash flow to know how well you have done. Combine the results from your job, business and investment efforts using the following form. Your income tax return should show comparable results.

THE MOST IMPORTANT TOOL YOU CAN USE TO CONTROL YOUR LIFE AND YOUR ASSETS IS "KNOW YOUR CASH FLOW". You and your business should check your cash flow and the present value of your assets at least once each month.

BUDGET FOR MONTH _____ *YEAR* _____

	Yourself	*Spouse*	*Combined*
Salary	$____	$____	$_____
Bonus			
Social Security			
Pension plan			
Profit sharing			
IRA/Keogh			
Private annuity			
Savings bank interest			
Bond interest			
Stock dividends			
Rental income			
Other			
TOTAL INCOME			
YOUR SAVINGS -- a payment to yourself			
SPENDABLE INCOME			
Food			
Transportation			

continued on page 152

152

Clothing ....

Home maintenance & improvement ....

Utilities ....

Mortgage interest ....

Real estate taxes ....

Contributions ....

Entertainment ....

Interest expense ....

Medical (unreimbursed) ....

Insurance premiums ....

Personal ....

Other ....

    TOTAL EXPENSES ....

Bank debt ....

Mortgage principal ....

Installment debt ....

Other ....

    TOTAL DEBT AMORTIZATION ....

Federal income tax ....

State and city income tax ....

Social Security tax ....

    TOTAL TAXES ....

    TOTAL EXPENSES AND DISBURSEMENTS ....

NET CASH FLOW (income minus disbursements) ....

TABLE SUMMARIZING YOUR NET WORTH

NAME_____ DATE_____

ASSETS:	VALUE:
Cash	....
Stocks	....
Bonds	....
Real Estate	....
Loans to others	....
Business Interests	....
Vested Retirement	....
IRA's	....
Keogh Plan	....
Other Assets	....
TOTAL	....
Insurance and Social Security (convert to present value)	....
GRAND TOTAL	....

continued on page 153

LIABILITIES:
    Mortgages to be paid   _____
    Loans with brokers   _____
    Loans with banks, etc.   _____
    Other loans   _____
    Charge accounts   _____
    Income tax liability   _____
    Other taxes due   _____
    Other liabilities   _____
        TOTAL   _____

NET WORTH (Assets minus liabilities)   _____
ESTIMATED INHERITANCE TAX   _____

    Include all assets such as cars, jewelry, art. Use following pages to detail all categories.

WORK SHEET FOR LISTING ASSETS AND LIABILITIES

CASH:
    Institution   _____   _____
    Type of Account   _____   _____
    Account Number   _____   _____
    Balance   _____   _____
        TOTAL   _____
STOCKS:
    Name   _____   _____
    Shares   _____   _____
    Tax Basis   _____   _____
    Market Value   _____   _____
        TOTAL   _____
BONDS:
    Issuer   _____   _____
    Face value   _____   _____
    Tax Basis   _____   _____
    Market Value   _____   _____
        TOTAL   _____
REAL ESTATE:
    Location   _____   _____
    Tax Basis   _____   _____
    Market Value   _____   _____
    Mortgages   _____   _____
    Tax owed   _____   _____
    Net Value   _____   _____
        TOTAL   _____

continued on page 154

INSURANCE:
    Policy
    Insured
    Owner
    Beneficiary
    Face Value
    Cash Value
        TOTAL

OTHER ASSETS:
    Cars
    Jewels
    Furniture
    Art
        TOTAL

MONEY BORROWED -- LIABILITIES
    Lender
    Due Dates
    Interest rates
    Balance due
    Other terms
        TOTAL

OTHER LIABILITIES:
    Tax owed
    Charge Accounts
        TOTAL

FINANCIAL CHECKLIST

The advice presented on the previous pages may be summarized by asking yourself the following questions:

1.   Money Management.

Do you have savings equal to about six months expenses? Place savings in a separate account to make highest safe return on investment.

Do you borrow money for investments? Borrowed money should earn more than the cost of borrowing so that you make a profit on its use.

Do you owe too much? Short term credit should be paid off rapidly — less than one year. Debt for living purposes other than for shelter and car should not exceed 15% of take home pay. Always strive to keep debt for living expenses near zero but do borrow for your investments if risk is low and return is high.

Do you reconcile bank statements with your own records? Bank computer operators also make mistakes.

Do you run all receipts and expenses through a checking account? You do need a permanent record and this method causes you to review your expenditures.

Do you perform chores such as painting your house yourself? This increases your income by saving actual cost and tax benefits. Know tax laws.

Do you pay debts including mortgages when due? Payments when due preserve your credit rating.

2. Insurance.

Are possessions insured for todays replacement costs? Inflation increases replacement costs. Review limits on policies. Do they cover you for possible liability? Are silver, furs, coins and other items covered by the policy? Should they be included?

Are your possessions appraised? Can you prove your ownership. Have pictures and appraisals in your file.

Is your insurance proper? Do you have proper distribution of life, property, liability for your needs?

Do you have liability insurance to protect from lawsuits? Do you have accident and health insurance? You can recover from financial adversity if you are able to work.

Do you have major medical insurance? You may want a lifetime limit of about $1,000,000.

Are you overinsured? The first $200 on home and car are expensive. Likewise, 20 year life versus term. Insurance is not an investment but it is protection from risks.

3. Taxes.

Do you use tax shelters such as IRA and Keogh? Do you own your home which can shelter taxes, etc.?

Do you take tax deductions available by law? Do not be lazy. Instead, know tax law and seek advice when your assets are complicated taxwise.

Do you adjust withholding of taxes to a minimum? You should not pay taxes early. Earn interest instead.

Do you know and use your marginal tax bracket in all decisions? What is the highest tax bracket applicable to your income? You should always calculate and think in terms of income and costs after considering taxes, interest rates, inflation effects.

Do you really manage your assets? Do you buy tax free bonds? Do you take advantage of tax shelters which are relatively free of added risks, etc.

4. Investments.

Are your investments prudently diversified — are they spread over equities, bonds, others?

Do you have an investment plan? Do you supervise? Do you know what you want out of life?

Do you appreciate the value of safety — know risk in your investment techniques? Income return increases with risk. Investments which suggest a return in excess of the normal relative to risks usually are a fraud and an invitation for total loss. Investigate before you invest. Trust few people and then only after they have proven to be honest and have shown a good track record in handling investments. Most salesmen are looking for their commissions – not your best interests.

Do you recognize the need for a balance in your life and in your investments? Excesses cause trouble.

Do you know that Treasury Bills can be bought from Federal Reserve Banks? Do you buy mutual funds without paying front end sales commissions? Buy no-load funds since some of these have good records. Do you buy stocks from discount brokers or from the companies directly using reinvestment plans?

Do you really manage your assets? Do you find and study books and papers giving useful advice? Your broker and banker may be biased and you should always know how to evaluate their advice.

Do you have the discipline which enables you to save, manage your investments and life. You need to study, evaluate, decide and act.

5.   Estate Planning.

Do you and other adults have wills? Are trusts in place for children? Do you make tax free gifts and use trusts ?

Are your wills useable in the state where you now live?

Are important papers in a safe place? Does your executor know where they are? Do you use a bank vault?

Do you review your plans? State and tax laws change frequently.

6.   Retirement.

Are you providing for your retirement? Inflation is eroding values and must be overcome by sound management.

Have you learned to save and manage savings? Will you be able to manage your retirement funds? How much do you need in later years? Are necessary funds being saved and managed so that they grow to meet need?

What will you do with money received upon retirement? Learn to manage today. If you have no funds, select an imaginary group of investments and watch and manage so that you learn without actually taking risks. After you feel confident, replace with actual money as it can be saved. Have you learned to take care of car, home, tools?

You must protect what you have. Maintain your home, your tools and your car, etc. so that they have a long, useful life. Learn to compare costs in relation to benefits adjusting both for taxes and inflation.

We can enjoy today and be reasonably certain of a pleasant future if we plan and save a little today. Savings naturally must be properly supervised and invested. We develop an interest in life as we learn to manage our savings and life. "The Book of Inside Information" and a monthly newsletter, "Bottom Line", both by Boardroom Books, 500 Fifth Avenue, New York 10110 are recommended.

INFLATION

Inflation is in part compensated by increased wages so that the working people find that their living standards are relatively unaffected. The retired without social security are affected since social security has been indexed by the government so that this pension increases with inflation. All investments are affected by inflation as discussed under the section dealing with investments.

The affects of inflation vary by industry, location and many other factors. The increase in prices of products which we buy is also variable as shown below:

INCREASE IN KEY CONSUMER COSTS 1967 TO 1983

Television	00.1%	ALL GOODS AND SERVICES	200.3
Whiskey	51.6	Home purchases	204.1
Woman's dress	71.4	Cigarettes	206.1
Telephone service	73.9	Food away from home	221.0
Men's and boy's apparel	88.3	Postage	237.5
Refrigerator	91.4	Electricity	240.7
Bicycle	99.9	Train fare	264.5
New car	102.1	Hotel, motel room	278.4
Shoes	105.7	Airline fare	320.7
Furniture	117.2	Gasoline	289.5
Property taxes	137.1	Fuel oil	526.5
Residential rent	138.2	Hospital room	527.6
Ground beef	156.5		
Food at home	182.5	Increase in Minimum Wage	239.0

The increase since 1983 has been relatively small — averages 1-4% annually.

PRICE CHANGES OVER THE PAST
(1986 is base year)

	Month	Year	5 Years	10 Years	20 Years	30 Years
Milk	0.0%	−0.4%	3.0%	42%	130%	170%
Hamburger	1.5%	0.7%	−8.0%	52%	149%	267%
Single Family Home	−3.5%	9.7%	25.9%	107%	342%	N/A
Television Set	−0.4%	−4.8%	−21.2%	−19%	−19%	−30%
Woman's Dress	4.1%	2.0%	3.2%	15%	86%	110%
New Car	0.0%	4.7%	17.1%	67%	130%	147%
Gasoline	−5.2%	−30.5%	−35.6%	46%	171%	200%
Newspaper	0.1%	4.1%	28.7%	87%	253%	442%

Source: U. S. Department of Labor; Commerce Department

The minimum wage increased at a rate greater than the average rate of inflation. Hospital, health care and fuel increased very rapidly.

INSURANCE

Insurance is not an investment but is needed to reduce risks to an individual. Insurance spreads risks over a group rather than a single individual. It is difficult to insure against all risks but with todays "take you to court" legal system and liberal jury awards, insurance is a most important tool for protecting your assets and income. General guidelines might include some of the following concepts.

You need to spend time to select the correct insurance agent. Insurance agents are selling you a product and they, too, want to make money necessary to live the "good life". You should ask whether the agent is overlooking some important facts. Does he provide you with correct information? Does he explain terms and give you choices?

Does he represent the correct company or group of companies? Does the company offer security at a competitive price? Does the agent know of the policies offered by alternate companies and select what is right for your needs?

Do you have the correct policy for your needs? Does the policy adequately cover your needs at a fair price? You must individually determine your needs with possible help from that agent and you should read the "fine print of the policies". Does your policy contain premiums for overlapping coverage? The policy must clearly state what is covered or you face expensive lawsuits and delays. Are you paying for the "name" rather than the insurance? Large companies often have poor records and rely upon their name and prestige rather than on service. "You do not always get what you pay for".

The insurance industry is changing rapidly by offering new policies. Also, the financial condition of the companies and ability to pay claims changes with time. Your agent must keep up-to-date and keep you informed so that you can change policies as necessary to obtain the protection needed by you. You must also keep the agent informed as to your changing needs as you change assets and responsibilities.

Inflation has increased property values and courts have increased the need for higher liability protection. Set aside some time to think about your insurance needs so that you avoid disaster when insurance coverage is inadequate.

Explore the advantages of taking the small risks yourself. Can you afford to pay the first few hundred dollars of damage to reduce insurance costs. Many policies carry high premiums for small amounts because of operating and coverage costs. Those with high risk do not "self insure".

LEGAL TECHNIQUES

You and everyone else in the United States needs to use financial planning today because of inflation and the progressive income tax system. You must structure your investment and financial affairs with these objectives:

1. Legally reducing estate taxes to near zero with cooperation of your children, charities, etc.
2. Rearranging your investment income and holdings so that income tax is reduced to low values.
3. Increasing the size of your estate without a corresponding increase in taxes.

You must learn to make sound and money-making investments in jobs, business, real estate, stocks, bonds, and other assets. Gifts and inheritances should be saved and not spent on "whims" and "toys" which bring only fleeting satisfaction. Plan a little.

The first step in any plan is to list the assets which you now have and which is your base. The second step is to determine your objectives. What do you want for yourself, your wife and children? The information should be analyzed by you and a plan for the future should be made. Then you contact an attorney and other consultants to have your plan placed in legal context. Advisors should be competent and have a good knowledge of investments and tax and state laws. He will recommend:

1. A will and other necessary legal documents for each party.
2. A Marital Deduction Trust if both husband and spouse are alive.
3. Government savings bonds may help defer taxes.
4. A defined Benefits Pension Trust or IRA and Keogh saving technique to save taxes from wages.
5. A Charitable Remainder Trust to cover your desire to help church, colleges and charities.

YOU SHOULD ALWAYS CAREFULLY INVESTIGATE BEFORE GIVING OR INVESTING. Everyone is willing to take your money. The advice of many professional advisors often is poor. They misinterpret the future and are reluctant to part from the crowd of their peers. If you want a good investment advisor, consult with your friends, lawyer, banker and accountant for recommendations. Thereafter, slowly allow the professional to convince you of his ability by reviewing his performance. Evaluate through a business cycle before really trusting him. You should also learn the art of investing. The basic rule, "Buy when prices are low and sell when prices are high" should guide you. You may also use an averaging technique which usually favors long term investors. Also, use "stop order" techniques to protect on declines. Any investment which looks too good to be true usually is a fraud and you will lose your savings when you try to make a return above the norm for the risk involved. There is no "free lunch" but you can make money if your investments anticipate future movement in business. As an example, buying real estate in an area where trends indicate future growth might be worthwhile as a long term investment. You must plan, study and think before acting and spending money. Additional information regarding estate planning is available from books such as "Estate Planning" by Holzman from Boardroom Books.

An accepted rule in estate planning states that the children should not be given money until they mature and in most cases maturity occurs before age 30 years. The opinions of parents and children often converge during this process. Most individuals are forced to learn money management as part of the experience of daily living in an adult world. Unfortunately, history shows the savings of one generation is often lost after several later generations because of taxes and by "show-off" living habits of children and grandchildren.

Credit cards create obligations as well as benefits. Cardholder negligence doesn't relieve the bank of its legal obligations. But your bank may balk at replacing funds if it thinks you're at fault. You can seek relief from one of several federal agencies. If the bank is nationally chartered, write the Controller of the Currency, Washington, D.C. 20219. For state-chartered banks, write the Federal Reserve Board, Washington, D.C. 20551. If your bank is state chartered but not a Fed member, write the Federal Deposit Insurance Corporation, 550 17th Street, N.W., Washington, D.C. 20429. For savings and loan associations, write the Federal Home Loan Bank Board, 1700 G Street, N.W., Washington, D.C. 20552. The agencies should make a decision within four weeks.

A CHECKLIST TO BE LEFT FOR YOUR EXECUTOR

Your executor should be left with a summary of your operations and assets. Leave a financial statement. He needs a detailed statement of financial assets and your relationships with others in business with you. The list should include:

1. Bank accounts.
2. Safe deposit boxes and private safes.
3. Partnerships and contractual relationships.
4. Trust agreements.
5. Brokerage accounts.
6. Retirement and other benefit plans.
7. Tax cost basis of stocks, bonds, other assets.
8. Tax cost basis of home and real estate, etc.
9. Names of professional advisors such as lawyer, accountants, insurance agents, bankers, stock brokers, etc.
10. Location of documents such as wills, deeds, insruance policies, leases, credit cards, legal papers, birth certificates, marriage license.
11. Income and gift tax returns for three years.
12. Passports and naturalization papers.

Have your lawyer explain the advantages of a living will. The revocable trust — one of the two major kinds of living trusts — offers several advantages for an individual with substantial investments.

PURCHASING HABITS

We must make purchases if we are to eat and dress ourselves. The purpose of advertising is to sell us products which we do not need. The money you earn should be spent and saved wisely. Always have a plan or shopping list. Shopping for items at reduced price is a worthwhile objective if you have the time, but you also should realize that many people will take your money but few will offer you a good product or service. Be certain that you deal with a reliable firm or individuals you know to be honest. Most bargain hunters are disappointed because they buy poor quality products and because they buy merchandise which they do not need. A low price is no bargain if you have no use for the product. Also, shop to avoid "fraud". Do not go for schemes.

"He who works or sells cheap often does very shoddy work or may not perform and his product often is of poor quality." The merchant and contractor must make a fair profit to survive. The low bidder may run after you make payment, may not pay for materials so that you later have a mechanics lien, etc. Beware. Do not pay before work is done and get lien waivers.

You might use the following before buying.

1. Contact your local Better Business Bureau, lawyer or other specialists as needed.
2. Always obtain estimates in writing and obtain receipts for all payments made.
3. Obtain itemized bills before paying.
4. Deal with reliable contractors.
5. Determine return and refund policy before buying — see it in writing and have a copy.
6. Read fine print in contracts before signing. You may wish to check with the experts.
7. All guarantees should be in writing. All parts of any written contract must be in writing.
8. Check government agencies as to permits granted contractors. Is contractor registered with the necessary government agencies? Does he belong to trade organizations? Is he licensed?
9. Use the three day recision period available in some transactions to check with experts.
10. Know as much as possible about the product being bought. Study consumer products manuals. Go to the library and read about the product, its uses, etc.
11. Know whether the product will meet your needs before buying. Altering a product may affect warranty and physical restraints may limit changes. Will the product fit in your space? Does it have power?
12. Consult with friends who have used the product. Check out references given by the contractor, etc.
13. Will the firm be around to service the product?
14. Drive by the place of business. Does it create confidence? See similar jobs performed by contractor.
15. Be certain that you really want and need the product being sold. Does it offer a long term benefit? Would you be better satisfied with another product?
16. If work is on your property, who carries the insurance for liability, etc.? Insist on lien waivers.
17. If seller retains merchandise, stocks, bonds, etc., is the firm bonded? Is property segregated and in your name? Who is responsible for theft, fire?
18. Is the asking price reasonable? Firm must make reasonable profit if it is to be around in case of warranty problems, etc.?

You also need to be aware that advertising is designed to get you to spend your money rather than save a little of it. Advertising also is needed by a company to get you to spend with them rather than with another merchant. Use advertising carefully to help you find bargains and true value — not to buy things which you do not need. The successful advertiser has learned that:

1. People buy on impulse if you get them into a store. Use shopping lists – buy only what you need.
2. What the ad says is more important than how it is said.
3. Maximum sales per dollar relates with perpetual testing of all variables in sales techniques.
4. The headline attracts readers and customers.
5. Appeals to the readers self-interest are important. Flatter the reader, give news and sell with your ad.
6. Headlines must say something desired by the reader.
7. Specifics are believable and saleable to others.
8. Long copy sells more than short copy.
9. The use of the word "you" is good.
10. Follow the lead of the mail order ad. Look at mail order booklets for leads.

You as a purchaser should be aware of these techniques and resist the impulse to buy when you do not need. Learn to save a little.

Refer to "Consumer Confidential" by Boardroom Books, Box 1026, Milburn, New Jersey 97041 and the Consumer Information Catalogue, Consumer Information Center, U. S. Government, Pueblo, Colorado 81009. Dial 1-800-555-1212 when you need the 800 number of a company.

PERSONAL FINANCE MANAGEMENT

Financial worries usually interfere with our work. Most employers react unfavorably when they receive notices that employees do not pay bills.

Governments can print money – often related with inflation – but individuals and their businesses must live within their respective cash flows or income and their ability to borrow funds. Financial trouble is invited when:

1. Spending more than 10-20% of take home pay on installment debt. This value does not include long term debt such as house payments and rent. Investments also are excluded.
2. Putting off paying of bills until later and later each month and making only minimum payments on outstanding debts.
3. Arguing about money among family members.
4. Using credit for daily living expenses such as buying groceries and paying the rent.
5. Juggling the bills to try avoiding dunning letters from creditors.
6. Buying things that you do not need and which you cannot afford on credit to cheer yourself so that you feel better. Do not buy on impulse or on the spur of the moment. Use a shopping list instead and think out your need or benefits before making major expenditures. Have a plan for buying.

The first thing to do after your realize that you have excessive debt and cannot make payments is to call all your creditors. We each make mistakes and you may have excessive debt because of illness or other events which could not have been anticipated. If past credit and payment record has been good, your creditors will probably be lenient and they will work with you to avoid bankruptcy. Bankruptcy records usually remain on your credit records for a ten year period and should be considered as an action of last resort. You will probably be asked by your creditors to work out a repayment plan and your living style will probably be lowered until the debts are repaid. Most of us do spend money on luxuries which are not essential and discipline is learned which will be useful throughout your remaining days on this earth.

You will probably learn to rearrange your priorities. Saving for the rainy day which enters most lives can be learned. You also learn management of your life and savings. You do need savings capable of meeting necessities during a period of six months as a minimum instead of debts.

There are non-profit counseling centers which can help you organize your spending habits. Books are also available. Look in the telephone book under "consumer" or "credit". You may also write to the National Foundation for Consumer Credit, 8701 Georgia Avenue, Silver Springs, Maryland 90910. Your banker, lawyer and accountant may be willing to help you. If you do not know any of these specialists, contact the welfare groups in your city government for references.

TAXES

The politicians spend other people's money — yours and mine — and they are responsible to voters — you and me. They are controlled by vocal special interest groups who lobby hard and have blocks of voters behind them. Politicians like their power and they will never save taxpayers money unless voters react and make their wishes known. You must out-vote the special interest groups. Such spending increases the national debt.

We each like to receive a free gift. We also do not like to pay taxes and do not like to be regulated. As a result we have districts, cities, counties, states and the federal government. They each pass laws and they each tax and regulate you. Every act seems to require a permit and a tax. Special benefits designed to favor groups complicate law and daily life. If we want less tax, we must demand fewer services.

You should not take a job, make an investment or consider any action without first determining the effects of taxes and regulations. Tax and other restrictions can be understood by reading regulations and contacting those who regulate. You probably will have to fight for what you believe to be correct. Every regulator likes his authority and prestige. He, too, is human.

Your specialists such as lawyers and accountants do not know your business like you do. They never will. Even if they did, they are too busy to sit and sift through regulations while thinking about your interests and looking for money saving ideas just for you. They must make a living and have other clients. You cannot afford to hire a full time specialist. Even if you paid $50,000 yearly, you have no assurance of finding good, honest, reliable advice. You must face your problems and recognize that you alone must know law and tax. In addition to income taxes, you must be aware of sales taxes, property taxes and fees imposed by all governing groups.

State and city income taxes are usually related to the federal income tax as some type of proportion. You can join the wealthy and reduce your taxes by knowing tax law and taking tax avoidance steps known as "Loopholes". Failure to do so will cost you a fortune during your lifetime. These methods include the use of the usual tax avoidance procedures, legal tax shelters, trust, gifts to children and others, etc.

Individuals pay for government either directly, through Social Security, or by higher prices. Corporations will never pay much tax since they must increase prices to pay their taxes if they are to remain profitable. Corporations must remain profitable or they fail. They must pass taxes on to the consumer in the form of higher prices for products made and sold. Tax payments made to the Federal Government are shown below.

FEDERAL GOVERNMENT RECEIPTS

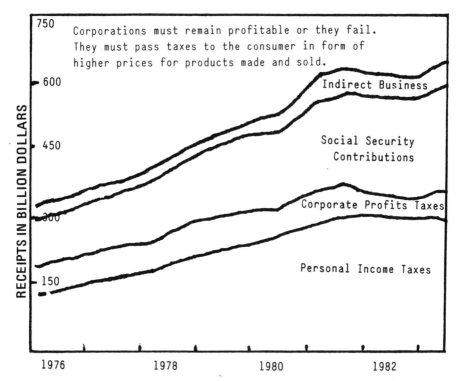

The above was taken from the federal government statistics. Basic economic and financial data are collected and presented in tables and curves by various government agencies and many private organizations. The data are used in stock advisory letters of stock brokers and writers such as Value Line, Standard and Poors, Wall Street Journal, Barrons, Wall Street Digest, Forbes, Fortune, Business Week, U. S. News and World Report and Investors Daily.

Obtain a copy of the federal and state income tax forms. Learn how to complete the basic forms. You are thereafter prepared to analyze and understand the affects of taxes on your lifestyle. Taxes take away a large part of your income and you need to know how to keep taxes at minimum values consistent with the changing laws.

1987 TAX RATES

SINGLE RETURNS		JOINT RETURNS	
Taxable Income	Tax	Taxable Income	Tax
Up to $1,800	$0 + 11%	Up to $3,000	$0 + 11%
$1,801 to $16,800	$198 + 15%	$3,001 to $28,000	$330 + 15%
$16,801 to $27,000	$2,448 + 28%	$28,001 to $45,000	$4,080 + 28%
$27,001 to $54,000	$5,304 + 35%	$45,001 to $90,000	$8,840 + 35%
$54,001 and over	$14,754 + 38.5%	$90,001 and over	$24,590 + 38.5%

1988 TAX RATES

SINGLE RETURNS		JOINT RETURNS	
Taxable Income	Tax	Taxable Income	Tax
Up to $17,850	$0 + 15%	Up to $29,750	$0 + 15%
$17,851 to $43,150	$2,678 + 28%	$29,751 to $71,900	$4,463 + 28%
$43,151 to $100,480*	$9,759 + 33%	$71,901 to $171,090*	$16,265 + 33%
$100,481 and over	$28,678 + 28%	$171,091 and over	$48,998 + 28%

*The top of the 33% bracket is extendd by $10,920 for each dependent claimed on the return.

Study tax laws for details. Tax law for the average individual can be understood by study of PUBLICATION 17 which is free from the Internal Revenue Service. Consultation with a tax specialist also is recommended.

Taxes and inflation are the tools used by governments to keep you poor. You can change government only if you convince sufficient voters to elect officials who will keep both at minimum values.

You should subscribe to one or more tax services so that you are made aware of changes in tax laws made by Congress and in application by the Internal Revenue Service. Such services might be selected from:

1. Tax Hotline, Box 1029, Milburn, New Jersey 07041
2. Kiplinger Tax Letter, 1729 H Street N.W., Washington, D.C. 20006
3. Tax Avoidance Digest, Box 6638, Silver Spring, Maryland 20906

The tax laws are frequently changed.

All of your decisions should be made after you calculate values after adjustment for both taxes and inflation. You do not use your average tax rate but instead you should use the maximum tax rate applicable. Such calculations become feasible after reading IRS Publication 17. Use available tax "loopholes". Tax law is written to benefit some investments and you should pay only the tax due as a result of tax law.

Gift and inheritance tax law at times also affects your decisions. You can give to others tax free under the "unified credit" a lifetime amount of $600,000 by 1987. For amounts in excess of these values, tax rates are 32% to 65% varying with the amount. These values, too, are scheduled to decline by

1987 but the maximum rate will then be 50%. You and your spouse can each make yearly gifts of $10,000 to each of as many people as your desire. Gifts to charity are also tax free within limits prescribed by law. Study tax laws.

Only one-half of the value of joint tenancy property will be included in the estate of the first spouse to die, regardless of who paid for the property. This does not imply that joint tenancy is the best way to hold property. Contact your tax specialist about the use of trusts. Before such contact, read IRS Publication 463 — Federal Estate and Gift Taxes. States may also have tax laws affecting gifts and inheritances. Tax law depends partly on state laws and regulations.

How much federal income taxes do you pay? The average American works four months just to pay federal, state and local taxes. The sequence follows:

Year	Days Worked to pay taxes	Tax Freedom Day
1929	39	February 9
1939	64	March 6
1949	83	March 24
1959	103	April 14
1969	120	May 1
1979	122	May 3
1983	120	May 1

If you are in high tax brackets, the income you earn during the latter part of the year may be taxed at a 33%+ rate for federal government plus state and local income taxes. The incentive to take risks is thereby greatly reduced and the country suffers from inadequate leadership and other qualities.

You also pay social security and other taxes.

Notice of a tax audit should not cause despair. The tax man may accept your explanations, you may be able to handle by sending proof and you have various appeals processes if you believe you are correct.

You may be able to handle yourself if the questions in the audit notice can be handled by proof of evidence such as a copy of a check. If technical evidence and argument involves theory and law interpretation, you should seek and have professionals do the presentation of your case.

You may be able to furnish proof yourself when faced with a "Correspondence Audit" or a simple "Office Audit" involving a few items for which you have written proof such as cancelled checks, statements from loan companies, etc. If a "Field Audit" is your problem, hire a professional.

Always give copies and not originals of your documents. Keep originals for your files.

Keep appointments and be on time.

Take only the items needed to answer the questions in the tax audit notice to meetings. Do not take your entire tax file.

Be prepared and well organized. Have copies of all documents so that the auditor can have them if he so requests.

Do not display hostility or animosity. The auditor is only doing his job and you should cooperate.

Be friendly, personable and cooperative. You should act as a professional at all times.

Never volunteer information. Answer questions and furnish proof only when asked and be brief but courteous.

Never lie to an agent. You need his confidence.

Be reasonable and try to compromise if possible. If you are correct, you can say so and appeal, etc. You can appeal to the IRS Appeals Division. Beyond that you can appeal to the Tax Court or pay the tax and appeal to the District Court or to Claims Court.

You need to be friendly but it does not hurt to let the agent know that you know appeals procedure. He, too, does not like appeals and may compromise.

If you have valid, unclaimed deductions, etc., present your evidence with reasons for failing to do so initially.

When an agent is unreasonable or wrong, ask to speak to his supervisor. You possibly could win the argument.

Know the tax law being discussed. Have copies of the regulation on which you relied when you go to audit.

When the auditor is too unreasonable, ask to leave and advise the auditor that your tax professional will contact him shortly.

Do not yield to pressure to close while in the office. Do not sign Form 870 unless you are willing to agree with the auditor. Have the auditor and his supervisor sign with you. You lose your rights if you sign and so should the Internal Revenue Service.

You can ask to be released from audit if you have been audited on the same subject and won during the past two years.

Never try to bribe an auditor. He cannot go to lunch with you, etc.

Summarizing, you save taxes when you do chores. You pay income taxes when others are hired to do them.

NOTE: Always respond to tax notices within ten (10) days.

RETIREMENT

Retirement is not easy at any age regardless of financial status. Financial independence removes one problem but the emotional strains remain.

During our youth, our salary and job position may seem secure but age will eventually force retirement. The age of forced retirement may not relate with our physical needs. We may not be ready for the necessary emotional adjustment. What do you plan to do after you retire to retain an interest in life and thereby avoid death a few years later? Your wife may love you but she does not need interference with her lifestyle. Your body may not allow you to play golf.

Most workers upon retirement realize that work can be enjoyable — work with our hands and mind is satisfying — and our believed desire to watch more television, go fishing or play golf change to boredom after a few months. Finding other well-paying work is not easy. Employment in a new field of work often requires years of study and thereafter you compete with people who have years of experience and seniority. Social work, which usually offers no pay, and supervision of your own investments, which can be rewarding financially, offers one solution which can make life interesting during retirement.

Changes in tax laws will require more work by you since government-offered pensions are becoming less important and your personal savings — IRA's — are becoming more useful in your plans. Do not depend upon Social Security and company pensions. The first depends upon Congress and companies do go broke and are sold. You should investigate advantages of an IRA and Keogh Plan. Remember that inflation and tax erodes all savings. Learn to manage your assets. Investigate single premium variable life insurance.

Inflation can be a disaster for the retired who depend upon Social Security and company pensions and handouts.

Real property such as homes, land and personal property such as financial documents, jewels, furniture are all transferred to others using legal documents. These assets also require management to protect from ever-changing tax laws and inflation which can decrease or increase value by more than one-fold during a very short time period. Jointly held property, including property owned jointly with family members, cannot be sold or managed properly because unanimous decisions cannot be reached and legal documents cannot be signed. Legal devices such as corporations, legal partnerships, associations, trusts and power of attorney are used to convey to one person the fiduciary authority to make necessary decisions and sign legal documents for the group. A group is useful to obtain advice but a committee is a disaster when unanimous agreement is necessary. Learn to protect your financial "nest egg" by being smart and using legal devices to reduce disagreements or disaster when agreement cannot be obtained between all parties. Also, obtain legal advice before acting and know the advantages and disadvantages of the legal tools. Set up legal devices early when everyone is agreeable and see your lawyer before acting.

Do you have hobbies and interests which will keep you alive and interested in life after retirement? Fishing and television will not suffice for active people.

Plan for your retirement long before you retire. Develop a hobby, join a service organization.

Where do you plan to live? Who will be your friends? Have a plan before retirement and be certain that your plan will make you happy. Think and explore during your vacations.

Plan for possible early retirement. You may lose your employment by whim of your employer, failure of health and accidents. Your job is never secure.

Is your wife trained to take care of assets if you should not be able to do so? Does your plan support her properly? She can be expected to live eight or more years longer than you statistically.

You do not have to become president of a nation or a company. You do need the ambition to take care of yourself emotionally and financially. You also need to be considerate of other people and the natural environment.

You must use discretion and care when handling your financial affairs.

Others willingly take your money and you must always investigate before acting. You must also be fair. Some religions suggest that the meek inherit the earth and that you should turn the other cheek when hit by others. In the living world, few will react in this manner and few will give you the chance to kick them in the rear a second time. Be fair and considerate initially.

There are several reasons for not discussing your personal life, including finances, with others, including close friends. Discuss with a professional only that part needed for him to perform his functions. In the 1980s, there are too many people who wish to share your money using techniques which might include kidnapping.

You will probably be working with insurance agents, bankers and financial consultants. You should ask them:

1. What is their education and experience?
2. What are their professional credentials?
3. Are they licensed? Do they sell insurance or securities?
4. Check on results with references provided by these advisors.
5. Have them show you sample plans and the performance of plans.
6. Do they use other financial assets such as bankers, CPA's, and attorneys?
7. Do they make the plan or do they use clerks or substitutes?
8. How do they arrive at their recommendations?
9. What are the risks associated with the recommended plan?

The retirement plan should be based on hard numbers and facts, and allow for taxes, inflation and recessions. It should provide for quick cash, some safe investment and some investment in growth so that pleasures, safety, growth-profits are provided throughout remaining life. Have some fun, enjoy life and diversify so that you handle risks and have needed money.

WEALTH ACCUMULATION

The natural laws which govern the physical universe also apply to business.

Everything in this world is part of a system. No matter is either created or destroyed. We can rearrange and use but nothing can be without its costs. Nothing is free. Everything in our economic life has a source, a destination and a cost that must be paid.

Government is never the source of goods. Everything produced is produced by people and everything that government gives to people must first be taken from people.

Money that government spends is money taken from people by taxes or borrowed from people. All other sums spent by government creates inflation which reduces the value of assets owned by people. The money created out of thin air by government is paid by the people as a result of a reduced value of money, savings, insurance, etc. owned by people. Taxes and inflation are forms of robbery legalized by government. Government is required to perform a limited group of services.

Excessive taxes result in poor incentives and lower output by both manager and worker. Loss of productivity occurs. Tax avoidance rather than good investment decisions occur and the underground economy which hides taxes grows rapidly.

Inflation transfers wealth from lender to borrower. All monetary dominated investments such as savings and bank accounts and insurance rapidly decline in value.

All decisions are based on after-tax and inflation values. Returns on financial and human investments such as interest, dividends, salaries, and wages are first reduced by the taxes paid to all governments. The maximum tax rate paid on the highest taxed income and last increment of taxable income are used. The return after taxes is further reduced by deducting for inflation.

In our modern exchange economy, all payroll and employment come from customers. The only job security is customer security. If there are no customers, there can be no payroll or jobs. The competition is worldwide and cooperation between labor, industry and government is essential.

Customer security can be achieved by the worker only when he cooperates with management in doing the things that win and hold customers. Job security is a partnership problem that can be solved only in a spirit of understanding and cooperation so that the quality and price are competitive.

Because wages are the principle cost of everything, widespread wage increases without corresponding increases in production simply increase the cost of everybody's living. Management salary can be more damaging than wages when salaries are not controlled and excessive management is allowed.

The greatest good for the greatest number of people in a material sense means the greatest productivity per worker. Small management expense, no waste and spoilage, etc. are part of costs.

All productivity is based on three factors:
1. Natural resources whose form, place and condition are changed by the expenditure.
2. Human energy — both muscular and mental — expended on the product.
3. Tools used to increase the effectiveness of the overall effort.

Tools are the only one of these three items that man can change and increase without limit. Tools come into being in a free society only when there is a reward for the temporary self-denial that people must practice in order to channel part of their earnings away from purchases that produce immediate comfort and pleasure into tools needed for production. We simply must save if we are to make the tools necessary to produce more effectively. A nation which fails to save to create the tools required to remain competitive dies a slow death materially. No nation can exist when everyone has expectations in excess of the nation's ability to produce.

The efficiency of the human energy applied in connection with the use of tools has always been highest in a competitive society in which economic decisions are made by millions of progress-seeking individuals rather than by government. Government is always inflexible and makes bad decisions.

The economy and politics cannot be separated. Politicians like their job and the gifts and "perks" derived therefrom. They also like the power related to telling others what to do. Politicians do not vote against increases in existing benefits and vote in favor of new spending programs demanded by all special interest groups. Tax increases, which handicap the economy, also are voted. Thus, deficits and the "printing of money" constantly increase. Inflation then grows. Can the world live with growing inflation or will it collapse into a depression? That is a good question.

Econometric models and economists using computers have difficulty forecasting the performance of the economy. Their failure suggests that the individual might continue to meet the competition.

CONCLUSIONS AND SUMMARY

You alone must master the art of living and running your business. Learn to manage your life, time, and your investments. You should not delegate the most important aspect of your life. Use specialists but manage by yourself.

You should raise your sights. Realize that you, too, can be successful — possibly rich. At the same time, you can be reasonable and decent to your fellow man and to your surroundings.

Learn to make money in both good and bad times. Study, read, think, decide and act.

Use leverage — use other people's money. The uninformed and timid lend you money at interest rates which enable you to invest it in a way which allows you to make a profit.

Learn the magic of compound interest and growth — study the interest rate and discount tables.

Learn to reduce your taxes. Use the benefits of tax laws and pay no more tax than required. Use leverage, tax shelters, etc.

Use techniques of diversification to reduce your risks. Always be informed and study the rules of risks.

Have a sound plan for your life, your business, your time and your investments. Stick with your plans.

Pay yourself each week. Learn to save a little.

Make investments one of your hobbies. Have fun while watching your business and investments grow.

Have the courage to act devisively when opportunity beckons. Think, decide and act but do CHANGE WHEN DATA INDICATE THAT A MISTAKE HAS BEEN MADE.

Your job places food on the table and shelter overhead but investments and business give you luxury.

Learn to be smart — but do not be a "smart-ass".

Be willing to take risks and do not be afraid of an occasional failure. Learn the satisfaction of producing something of quality at minimum cost. Life includes failure and success. Seek advice as needed, think, evaluate and act. Hope that your big decisions are correct and always consider the rules of risk using data which is reliable and adjusted for both tax and inflation.

Write for:

"Money Matters" by AARP, Washington, D.C. 20049
"Age Pages", Information Center, Pueblo, Colorado 81009.

Management Of Investments

All individuals need to know the basic rules of investment so that they can participate within the business and political world.

Sound management of your savings is probably your best opportunity for financial independence.

HOW YOUR SAVINGS GROW

You may have saved or inherited $10,000 which you invest so that the return is 15% annually. This return is also invested at the same rate. If you pay no taxes — IRA after 1987 — and there is no inflation, your investment will grow as follows:

Years invested	Your assumed age	Value in Dollars
0	30	$ 10,000
10	40	40,000
20	50	164,000
30	60	663,000
35	65	1,332,000

Congratulations, you retire as a millionaire.

Alternately, you are able to save and invest $1,000 each year after you reach age 30 years. You are able to manage your investments so that they perform as defined in the prior example. Your investment grows as follows:

Year after start of investment	Your assumed age	Value in Dollars
0	30	$ 1,000
10	40	23,000
20	50	118,000
30	60	500,000
35	65	1,013,000

Again, you retire with a million dollar nest egg. This is about the same as $100,000 in 1900. The difference is inflation.

The above two examples show the growth of investments when growth is at 15% compounded annually. In 1984, you bought bonds which returned 15% but in more normal times, you would probably have to use some money borrowed from others at low interest to earn this return. Return on borrowed money during many past years has been between 1-2% after taxes and inflation. Taxes often can be avoided by use of an IRA or Keogh Plan. Careful supervision is required to overcome effects of inflation. You probably will have to change the type of investments as dictated by the economic cycles. You need to understand the importance of terms such as interest rates, leverage or use of other people's money and you need to learn the techniques of management of your assets. Learn to "Buy low and sell high". You also need to learn the negative effects of risks, taxes and inflation. Lastly, you need to control your time and learn to act after making a decision. Remember that the 1986 dollar has the same purchasing power as nine cents in the 1900 dollar. Never put your money into a bank and hope to retain purchasing power. Inflation will always be with us and it will ruin your savings if you do not manage properly. Be smart rather than foolish — you can make your savings grow if you try. Spend the time to learn the necessary techniques.

You probably should borrow to increase the return or income earned on your savings. The interest paid for the money you borrow must always be less than the return you earn. This technique increases risks and may not be useable when interest rates are high. In 1987, interest on home loans is tax deductible.

Understanding investments also should make you a better employee and may result in job advancements.

You may not wish to take the risks involved with investments returning 15%. You can readily calculate the return on your investments using other rates of return by using interested tables presented later in this section.

Always remember that savings will double in value, before taxes and inflation adjustment, as follows:

Interest rate	Years to double in value
6%	12
9%	8
12%	6
15%	5

The rate of return often expressed as an interest rate usually increases as the risk increases. Of course, your purchasing power is reduced by inflation and taxes may reduce your returns.

It pays to take a moderate risk to increase earnings if you know what you are doing. Know the rules for investment in the mediums in which you invest.

A DEAL THAT LOOKS TOO GOOD USUALLY IS A FRAUD
EVEN YOUR FRIENDS WILLINGLY TAKE YOUR MONEY.

The interest rate graphs on semi-log paper may be used to quickly determine the growth of your investments, business or any other asset. Simply plot the basic data on the graph. Determine the average growth of your asset by drawing an average line through the basic data points. Thereafter, by aid of triangles, find the interest rate on the base graph which has the same slope as the average line drawn through your basic data. This interest rate is the growth rate of your asset. This is a useful tool for evaluation of stock and mutual fund information and business detail.

Some bad investments will be made. Do try to prevent loss of principle by control of risks. Inflation and taxes do cause a loss of principle unless you have offsetting growth from interest and appreciation of capital.

The life of a company often is like that of a human individual. They are born, develop slowly as management and assets are accumulated, grow rapidly, reach maturity and eventually reach old age, decline and possibly die. The time in each stage varies greatly among companies.

NEED FOR SAVINGS

Do you feel uncomfortable each time you see an old person cleaning your hotel room? Do you say a prayer of thanks and resolve that you will save so that you and those you love do not encounter a similar fate? The reasons for you to save are many. Barring war and other disaster, the individual, by being flexible and watching tax and inflation with intelligence, should experience the joy of watching savings grow. You can, with a little effort, learn to manage your assets and you will find it to be fun. Tax-free saving methods, recently made available by the government, and trusts should make it possible to save for retirement and children's education with moderate risk and effort. Steady growth of savings at moderate rate appears attainable by the average saver. The cards are stacked against the gambler and the speculator since they are competing against the professional investor and his computers. It is hard to make money in short term trading but it is easier to trade using business cycles.

The amount of money to be saved, invested and supervised is a personal decision. However, this should not be an excuse for no savings. You simply must save today if you want freedom and security during your later years. You are a better individual if you learn to manage assets and protect them from government confiscation, high taxes, inflation and poor judgment. It can be fun after you learn the techniques. You must be flexible and change investments as indicated by circumstances.

Social security and company plans may provide minimum existence in your later days. If you want today's lifestyle, you must act and save part of your income when you are young. You must learn to manage assets if you want such comforts when you retire, when you lose your job or are ill. Managing your savings does take a little time and you must learn and study but it can be fun. You become a balanced individual and you will find that the feeling of security is very pleasant when you are old.

You must acquire knowledge of industry, business, statistics, economic trends including inflation, money management and taxes, etc. This knowledge should make you a more efficient worker and may even increase your earning power at the workplace. You are then prepared to vote with intelligence and analyze demands of special interest groups.

You should first determine what you want out of life and how your investment goals fit into such plans. You should learn to obtain advice and remember that your broker is interested in commissions and his pay. Books are available covering many investment mediums and you need to read many of them to avoid bias and poor opinion. You should seek advice, evaluate, decide and then act. You must make the final decision. You, alone, are responsible for your investments. Many people give advice but determining what is true and what is false is more difficult. You can manage.

Individuals who are forced to move often are limited as to type of investments. Real estate is difficult to supervise when you are unable to inspect it. Stocks and bonds can be taken with you when you move.

Investments usually should be bought when prices are relatively low and sold when speculation increases price to unrealistic levels. You also should remember that you are interested in total return after taxes and inflation — look for current income and asset growth combined as your criteria. You can always sell liquid assets when you need cash so high current income should be given low priority.

Growing nations on average save 6% to 20% of gross income and the rate of industrial growth often relates directly with savings. Jobs are created by the savings. Income must be invested in plant, research, new tools and other items if jobs are to be created. Our living standards cannot grow unless we each save and the money is invested in productive ventures. In the United States, we have been investing in the environment and not plants. As a result, we have lost productivity. We need to save, invest in productivity and learn to compete in the world economy. We also have become inefficient and lazy.

Gold, during many centuries, has been a store of value. Today, an ounce of gold will buy about the same amount of merchandise as it did a century ago. Price of gold does vary as most commodities but it is not a true investment for growth.

Summarizing, no country can prosper without savings and investments in greater plant and productivity. Also, individuals need to save for old age and many other purposes. Inflation and other forces tend to increase, in current dollars, the value of assets and you can save and manage your savings if you try. You will find the task to be fun after you learn the necessary techniques. Always think in terms after adjusting for inflation and tax.

SAVINGS IN THE UNITED STATES

Savings in the United States since 1960 have averaged between 14% to 16% of gross national product, or GNP. About two thirds of these savings are made by corporations and the remainder are made by individuals. Since 1983, about half of the individual savings have come from foreign countries since their citizens prefer the stability of our government.

All savings will be eroded by both taxes and inflation if history repeats. You can avoid this problem by sound investment and proper management of savings. We also can reduce both taxes and inflation if people awaken and teach the politicians the need for savings by government. There are always many needs for services and we each pay for service if we do not serve ourselves.

Savings made are detailed on the graph on page 177.

Many people do not save. The very poor do not have income sufficient to save. Most individuals do have savings but most of us do not understand what will happen to us as we become ill or old. Individuals who borrow for short term enjoyment are asking for unnecessary problems. Consumer debt is very damaging but mortgage debt often enables us to buy homes which is a form of saving. Debt of individuals is shown on the graph on page 178 entitled "Household Debt".

A graph showing the history of debt in the United States follows on page 179.

SAVINGS IN THE UNITED STATES

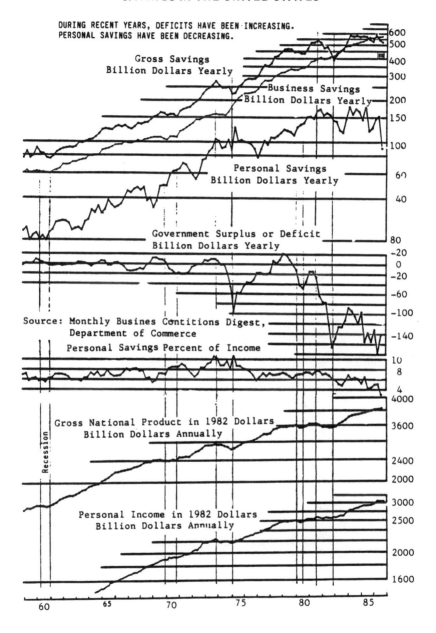

DURING RECENT YEARS, DEFICITS HAVE BEEN INCREASING.
PERSONAL SAVINGS HAVE BEEN DECREASING.

Gross Savings
Billion Dollars Yearly

Business Savings
Billion Dollars Yearly

Personal Savings
Billion Dollars Yearly

Government Surplus or Deficit
Billion Dollars Yearly

Source: Monthly Busines Contitions Digest,
Department of Commerce

Personal Savings Percent of Income

Gross National Product in 1982 Dollars
Billion Dollars Annually

Personal Income in 1982 Dollars
Billion Dollars Annually

Recession

HOUSEHOLD DEBT
(in 1984 dollars)

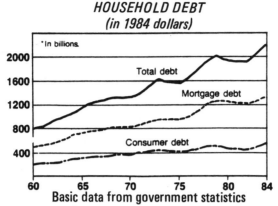

Basic data from government statistics

Population in "undeveloped countries" is growing very rapidly as shown below and this growth affects the economy of nations throughout the world.

POPULATION OF THE WORLD

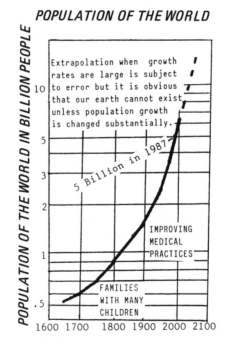

This rapid growth affects the worldwide natural environment. Hungry people tend to migrate illegally and influence all nations on earth. Some analysts see the mixture of people in the U.S. to be mostly Spanish and Asian after several generations. Birth in the U.S. is 1.8 children per family which is not sufficient to maintain present population without immigration. Illegal immigration is required to supply low paid workers and the construction industry will die when population does not require new building.

SPENDING AND DEBT IN THE UNITED STATES

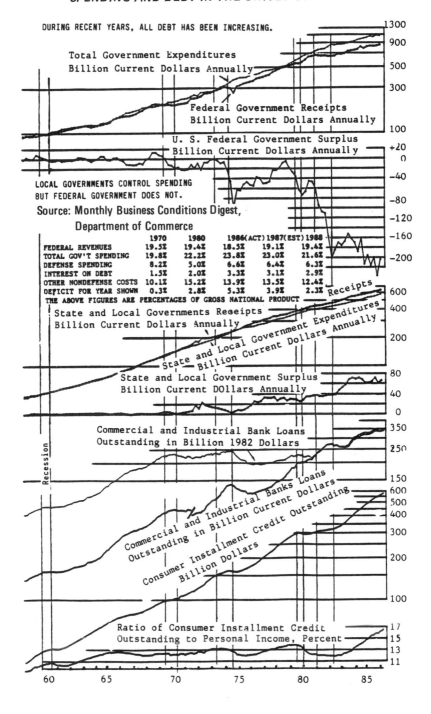

DURING RECENT YEARS, ALL DEBT HAS BEEN INCREASING.

Total Government Expenditures
Billion Current Dollars Annually

Federal Government Receipts
Billion Current Dollars Annually

U. S. Federal Government Surplus
Billion Current Dollars Annually

LOCAL GOVERNMENTS CONTROL SPENDING
BUT FEDERAL GOVERNMENT DOES NOT.

Source: Monthly Business Conditions Digest,
Department of Commerce

	1970	1980	1986(ACT)	1987(EST)	1988
FEDERAL REVENUES	19.5%	19.4%	18.5%	19.1%	19.4%
TOTAL GOV'T SPENDING	19.8%	22.2%	23.8%	23.0%	21.6%
DEFENSE SPENDING	8.2%	5.0%	6.6%	6.4%	6.3%
INTEREST ON DEBT	1.5%	2.0%	3.3%	3.1%	2.9%
OTHER NONDEFENSE COSTS	10.1%	15.2%	13.9%	13.5%	12.4%
DEFICIT FOR YEAR SHOWN	0.3%	2.8%	5.3%	3.9%	2.3%

THE ABOVE FIGURES ARE PERCENTAGES OF GROSS NATIONAL PRODUCT

State and Local Governments Receipts
Billion Current Dollars Annually

State and Local Government Expenditures
Billion Current Dollars Annually

State and Local Government Surplus
Billion Current DOllars Annually

Commercial and Industrial Bank Loans
Outstanding in Billion 1982 Dollars

Recession

Commercial and Industrial Banks Loans
Outstanding in Billion Current Dollars

Consumer Installment Credit Outstanding
Billion Dollars

Ratio of Consumer Installment Credit
Outstanding to Personal Income, Percent

WHO SHOULD SAVE AND MAKE INVESTMENTS

Each individual who expects a lifetime of comforts above average must make an above average contribution to society and industry by hard work — consistent and intelligent work. He also must learn to save, invest and manage part of his rewards. The following sound advice is often quoted:

"If you have the things you need to live in reasonable comfort,
If you have adequate insurance to cover risks,
If you have cash in the bank to cover short-term emergencies,
Then you should make investments — have savings."

It is easy to become comfort prone — to never learn to save or invest. You waste your time and life. You do not plan your life, your time or your investments. Also, you can spend so much on insurance that there is no money for investments. The competition for your income is severe. You must budget your money and time so that you save a little and learn how to manage assets.

Insurance is required to protect from unexpected risks which normally do not occur to an individual but are catastrophic when they hit, such as a death of a parent with small children. Permanent disability is a greater disaster particularly when associated with a long illness. Illness and accidents do occur and doctor bills can be very large. Elimination of risks of property resulting from fire, weather, lawsuits, etc. is a good use of insurance. You can become "insurance poor" when you over-insure because insurance only protects from risks and is not an investment. Consider the use of term rather than 20 year life insurance when making purchases. The insurance salesman works for commissions and he, too, can be biased.

Some ready cash should always be available in interest bearing accounts — often six months living costs is a recommended amount for such emergencies. Such types of investments often have a lower rate of return than that available from "true investments with higher risk". Interest rate tables show that earnings from investment increases rapidly as the rate of return increases. Money earning a low rate of return should be kept at minimum values consistent with your financial needs and your emotional capacity to live with risks. Greater growth rates usually relate with higher risks and you must learn to live with some risks when you supervise your investments. You might wish to set up an imaginary or paper group of investments today. Watch it make and lose money. This is a way for you to learn to manage assets and accept risk while you never take any risk. After you have learned techniques and have a feel for risks, you may start changing your imaginary paper assets to stocks, bonds and other true investments.

When interest rates are high — often when inflation is also high — interest bearing investments bought with high interest rates should offer high return and safety, although the return after inflation may not be too good. Municipal bonds may be attractive to people in high tax brackets when they are tax free. You should learn to think in after-tax and inflation terms. Learn to adjust for tax and inflation. Also, remember that you must investigate carefully before making investments since investments which have a return greater than that expected from investments having comparable risks are often frauds. Many people do not know the art of finance and even your minister or closest friend can mislead you. ALWAYS INVESTIGATE CAREFULLY BEFORE INVESTING OR GIVING.

You should recall that investments differ in rate of return and risks. Some stocks, bonds and business ventures will outperform others. Your job is to select properly. Some investments have tax benefits which are important when you are paying high taxes. When inflation is high, property such as your home may be a good investment. It should be obvious that consumer purchases such as vacations, cars, recreation, medical/dental costs are not investments which earn you money but may be necessary for you to earn a living and enjoy life. Keep these at minimum levels so that you do make true investments. Gifts to family members and charity are not investments but they may be needed in estate planning and in family relations. Learn to think and manage.

CHARACTERISTICS OF INVESTMENT MEDIUMS

Many variables are encountered when you try to determine the relative rate of growth of various investments. The following values are one estimate for an investment made in 1948 of $13,820 in various investment mediums which has been allowed to grow without change during the following 36 years.

Inflation value during 38 years	$ 57,000
Investment in silver	182,000
Investment in gold	220,000
Investment in average real estate	210,000
Investment in NYSE Stocks	145,000
Savings and Loans, etc.	106,000
Diamonds	99,000
Bareford Rare Coin Collection	5,454,000

Since 1984, stocks have performed well while real estate has found bad times. However, investments have a habit of again meeting their average growth values during another time period.

Unsupervised investments usually do not perform well and often do not approach the effects of inflation and taxes. To find real growth of your savings, you must learn to "buy near temporary lows" and sell when price reaches temporary "highs". You can learn these techniques if you study the characteristic patterns of your investments.

Our home may be our best investment. It provides shelter and tax advantages. IRA's also are useful since taxes are deferred. The same applies to company savings plans and Keoghs.

Low taxes and high return rate are both desired.

Tend to concentrate your investments into "what you know best". Diversification is a form of insurance but it tends to reduce return when the investor really knows what he is doing.

Be on the offensive rather than on the defensive, particularly during youth when you often can afford more risk. Concern with security is required with a part of your investment. Try to be informed and know what you are doing so that risks are reduced and your investment return is high without undue risk.

Your investments must grow at a substantial rate after taxes if you are to offset the effects of inflation. Taxes and inflation can consume all of your return even when return is high. On average, interest received is often 1%-2% after taxes and inflation unless you "buy low" and "sell high".

Promise of very high — higher than normal for the type of risk — return is usually a fraud. Promoters may use churches, charities, real estate syndicates to gain public acceptance. Always investigate before investing. To obtain an overall high rate of return, you may consider borrowing money to use for investment. If your "safe" return is above the cost of borrowing, you can make a profit on other people's money. You use leverage — the same as large corporations. You need to know what you are doing and carefully evaluate before you borrow. You borrow money from those who are afraid, timid and uninformed — who are afraid to invest — and you make a return greater than the cost of borrowing.

Investments have different characteristics and you should recognize these differences. Some follow:

	LIQUID	STABLE	LEVERAGE POSSIBILITY	INFLATION HEDGE	DEFLATION HEDGE	PORTABLE	CASH FLOW
HARD ASSETS:							
Gold	*		*	*	*	*	
Silver	*		*	*	*	*	
Coins	*	*	*	*	*	*	
Art		*		*		*	
Antiques		*		*		*	
Stamps		*		*		*	
LIQUID MONEY:							
Savings	*	*			*	*	*
T-Bills	*	*			*	*	*
Money Market Funds	*	*			*	*	*
PASSIVE & GROWTH CAPITAL:							
Stocks	*		*			*	*
Mutual Funds	*	*	*			*	*
Commodities	*		*	*			
Bonds	*		*		*	*	*
Discounted Mortgages	*	*	*		*	*	*
ACTIVE CAPITAL:							
Business			*				*
Real Estate		*	*	*			*

NOTE: Municipal bonds, business and real estate offer tax shelter advantages. Business and real estate have management needs greater than other investments.

Leverage involves interest which may be tax deductible.

In 1983, the assets of families and individuals are believed to be distributed as shown below:

TANGIBLE ASSETS IN BILLION DOLLARS

Residential structure	2,227
Land	1,226
Autos, consumer durables	1,151
Remainder	208
TOTAL	4,812

FINANCIAL ASSETS IN BILLION DOLLARS

Deposits and currency	339
Time, savings deposits	1,674
Money Market funds	163
Savings bonds	72
U. S. Treasury and agencies	354
State and local bonds	160
Corporations, Foreign	59
Mortgages	184
Corporate stock	1,519
Life insurance, Pension	1,368
Other financial assets	2,386
TOTAL	8,277
GRAND TOTAL	13,069

ACCUMULATION OF WEALTH

Learn to take care of what you have. The individual who does not learn to take care of his toys such as a car, a home or his tools at an early age is handicapped throughout life. Insurance is no substitute but it can be used to reduce risks and somewhat reduce effects when you are reckless or careless. You should be aware of accident-prone situations and reduce accidents.

Don't count your dollars before effects of taxes and inflation have been deducted. Always think in terms of real money — after deducting all taxes and inflation. Never make decisions based on fake money such as total salary, dividends, interest or profits from business. Tax laws are complicated but reasonably accurate effects for city, county, state and federal taxes are usually obtained rather easily. Taxes are usually applicable to inflated income and the effect of inflation is a simple deduction from after-tax income.

The wealth-seeker sacrifices instant gratification and does not seek "the appearances of wealth". He does not borrow to buy a car, boat and he chooses to make an investment rather than to buy today's pleasures. He always remembers that gifts and consumer-type purchase are never true investments. The man of wealth has learned to count his nickels. He saves a little for tomorrow. He has learned to manage his affairs and finds investments which retain value after he has paid taxes and deducted for inflation. He knows tax laws in sufficient detail and pays no more tax than required by law. He uses tax shelters which are legal. He usually is buying his home since it offers a roof overhead and often has tax advantages plus a possibility of appreciation in value.

Many investors in real estate have become millionaires and long-term inflation is favorable to real estate. The investor must manage, maintain and know the rules. Study by reading the manuals of the State Real Estate Commission and go to the library and read books related to purchasing, financing and management before buying any real estate. Sale of property may be difficult.

You invest wisely, you become rich while the timid remain poor. This is their reward for failing to study, to gain knowledge and because of their fears of risk. Study a good text on risk analysis.

There is no ideal investment and all investments as well as life are filled with risk. Different types of investments advance and decline in various cycles — some cycles seem to vary with business but the time lags differ between investments as will be discussed later. An astute investor knows the time on the clock for each investment category in which he maintains an investment interest.

Do not allow anyone to take control of your investments. Carefully watch your "nest egg", nurture it, control and manage it wisely using your knowledge and ability acquired during a lifetime of observations. Manage soundly and your investment will grow so that you become financially independent at an early age.

Study the cycles of your investments and of business activity. In the past, as an example, three changes in the same direction of the discount rate used by the Federal Reserve Bank have resulted in a change in the direction of the nation's economy. Also, in a "bull market" period, the stock market often advances in three upward steps with declines in between. Each industry and investment type has its own history of cycles. Be aware of them before investing. In other words, know the rules of the game in which you play at all times — read as much as possible by reading many books on the subject.

SUGGESTED COMPOSITION OF INVESTMENTS

We each have different financial objectives and our investment should so reflect. In general, four types of investments are recognized:

SPECULATIVE INVESTMENTS Speculative investments include volatile stocks, low valued bonds, call options and similar investments. Try for 20%+ return.

AGGRESSIVE INVESTMENTS Higher risk stocks, somewhat risky bonds, real estate, etc. Try for 15% return.

CORE INVESTMENTS High grade stocks and bonds, mutual funds, safe investments. Try for 10% return.

FOUNDATION INVESTMENTS Equity in home, insurance, a car, social security, IRA, HR 10 — Keogh Pensions, company pension funds, etc.

Your investment portfolio should vary with economic conditions. Diversify as needed.

You should select and manage your investments yourself after you have obtained the knowledge to be successful. When money available is small and you do not have the necessary expertise, you might consider mutual funds as managers. You need three types of growth mutual funds, one bond fund and a money market fund. When times are good, you might have:

1. Thirty percent in aggressive stock fund
2. Twenty percent in conservative growth funds
3. Twenty-five percent in equity-income funds
4. Five percent in money market funds and twenty percent in fixed income funds.

The various types of investments often have lives and rates of return as shown below:

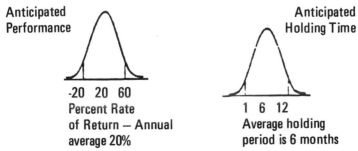

CORE INVESTMENTS

Anticipated Performance

-10 10 30
Percent Rate of Return — Annual Average 10%

Anticipated Holding Period

Hold for long term
Average return 10%

AGGRESSIVE LAYER OF YOUR CAPITAL STRUCTURE

Anticipated Performance

-10 15 45
Percent Rate of Return — Annual Average 15%

Anticipated Holding Period

6 12 24
Average holding period is 12 months

SPECULATIVE LAYER OF CAPITAL ASSETS

Anticipated Performance

-20 20 60
Percent Rate of Return — Annual average 20%

Anticipated Holding Time

1 6 12
Average holding period is 6 months

Watch your investments and change when necessary. You should never marry an investment or become involved emotionally. Some investments are safe long term but most should be reviewed on a routine basis. Use "stop orders" when dealing in financial type investments to reduce risks resulting from a major price decline.

In addition to tailoring investments to objectives, you should make investments in areas where you feel comfortable with related risks. Your sleep should not be disturbed. Risk might be reflected in investments by the percentage relations between various types of investments. One possible relation is presented below:

	PROTECTED GROWTH RISK		*SPECULATIVE RISK*	
Normal	30%	Speculative	40%
economic	40%	Aggressive	40%
certainty	30%	Core	20%
Increased	20%	Speculative	30%
economic	30%	Aggressive	40%
uncertainty	50%	Core	30%

(Expectations About The Future)

You might sell stocks and switch money into interest bearing funds when a decline in business activity is anticipated. If you own funds, you might switch from stock funds to money funds. Switch only when economics of nation and companies change or you have good reasons.

The value of any investment is the value of all future returns adjusted for risks, taxes and inflation. An investment is valued in terms of (1) how much will it pay back in the future, (2) how much risk attaches to the expectation, and (3) the cost of waiting — the interest rate. Risk and interest rate both have a component which varies with time. All values must be evaluated before and after taxes and inflation using available techniques. Some of these are discussed in the previous sections under Business.

Careful selection of stocks and bonds and selection plus location with real estate are important.

Lending to friends and relatives invites disaster.

TYPES OF INVESTMENTS

The types of investments are many. Your library and bookstore contain many texts describing details of specific types of investments. You should study and become familiar with all and become an expert in several.

The total gain — current income and the increase in value of the asset, known as appreciation, should be combined — before and after taxes and inflation. You also need to apply the present day value concept to each in your evaluations. Remember that income received is worth more than income received at some future date.

Major investment types may include:

Type of Investment	*Name of Investment*	*Principle Sales Group*
Principle remains constant	Checking Accounts	Banks and Savings and
except for inflation effects	Passbook Savings	Loan Associations.
	NOW Accounts	Also, Credit Unions.
	SUPER NOW Accounts	

	7-31 Day Deposits	
	Money Market Deposit	
	Short Term Certificates	
	Long Term Certificates	
	IRA Certificates	
	Annuities	Insurance salesmen
Daily value of Principle	Money Market	Fund Manager
depends upon daily action	Mutual Funds or	Stock Broker
of marketplace	Trusts	Banks
	Bond Funds	Fund Manager
	Tax Exempt	Stockbroker
	Bond Funds	Banks
	Stock Funds	
	U.S. Savings Bond	U.S. Government
	Treasury Bills	Agencies
	Treasury Bonds	Banks and others
	Corporate Bonds	Banks
	Top Quality	Stockbrokers
	Low Grade	Mortgage Brokers
	Zero Coupon	
	Sinking Fund	
	Common Stocks	Stockbroker
		Discount Broker

Recall that each group of salesmen often work on a commission basis and that their primary objective is making a living. Your interest and their interest often differs. They are taught that a sale which results in your making a saving effort is worthwhile and may not recommend or advise the safest and best investments. It is your duty to yourself that you investigate before selecting your investments. You can find the necessary information, make the necessary judgments, reach decisions and act to buy. This is your obligation to yourself.

Stocks should be evaluated using a combination of dividends and present value of future capital appreciation. Total income to maturity — interest plus present value of price increase — is used for poor bonds, since all bonds are redeemed at face value at their maturity date shown on the face of the bond. The very small investor may prefer mutual funds to obtain advice and diversi- fication.

Changes in tax laws during the early 1980s make it possible for the small investor to save without paying taxes immediately. Your tax consultant and the IRS should be contacted for literature explaining these techniques for delaying taxes. The financial industry is being deregulated. The rules are complicated and you should be aware of the changes and the lower level of supervision of their operations.

General remarks about investments include:

IRA Money. These tax-delaying investments are limited to insurance annuities, mutual funds, deposits in banks, savings and loan organizations, and self-directed brokerage accounts. U. S. gold coins have recently been added.

Annuities are relatively unappealing because the setup charge and service charges are high while the guaranteed interest rate often is on the low side.

Savings deposits also have drawbacks if you withdraw early. They do have government insured safety. You must shop for interest rates and manage your accounts.

Good "no-load" mutual fund "families" are favored by many investment advisors. You may switch between a group of funds at little cost as the economy changes. The objectives of the groups within the family may differ — one may be in bonds, another in stocks, etc. These funds make no charge for entry or withdrawals. Investigate for other charges by fund.

Self-directed IRA's are good if you are willing to work and manage in detail. You must select individual investments and manage. Owning mutual funds only requires change between funds within the family while you must select, sell, evaluate and manage your IRA yourself.

Tax shelter investments do not make sense for IRAs.

You should delay taxes by investing in IRAs and Keogh plans. You should select with care. In 1987, review single premium variable insurance.

The daily value of most assets is determined daily by actions of buyers and sellers in the marketplace. Short term financial instruments have lower risks because they are redeemed quickly. Change occurs rapidly and you must keep informed so that you can react as needed.

Inflation erodes all investments even when no taxes are paid.

Bonds and money type investments. Banking and other financial institutions are changing rapidly due to deregulation. Treasury bills and certificates are issued regularly by the government and its agencies. Many are insured by the full assets of the federal government and others are based on real property such as real estate. These may be bought directly from the government and most are available from bankers and stockbrokers. Mutual funds, which allow switching among their funds, and stockbrokers, bankers, etc. offer money market funds. The "no-load" funds charge no entry or sales fees. Utility stocks and convertible stocks offer characteristics similar to money accounts. Municipal bonds and funds dealing in them offer tax advantages which should be investigated by people in high tax brackets. You may contact your stockbroker, banker, and savings and loan officers for details. Returns and rules often change daily under deregulation.

Stocks and investments based on stocks. Contact your stockbroker and mutual fund manager for details. Many thousands of stocks are traded daily on the stock exchanges and most stocks are easily sold and bought. You may have such investments through your company pension plans. You can also form investment clubs by contacting The National Association of Investment Clubs. You may own stocks directly using a stockbroker or discount stockbroker. Learn to avoid tips. You can find data in offices of stockbrokers. You may buy Value Line and Standard and Poors services for basic data. Other services also offer investment charts and some data and advice. Contact your stockbroker.

A mutual fund might make the stock selections for you. The growth of mutual funds is easy to track and you can know when to change fund type if you track the economic cycles and order fund switches within the "Fund Family".

The speculator may be interested in *puts, calls, options of various stock groups* but this is not for the uninformed or average investor. Study these techniques in great detail before using. You can sell options on stocks which you own and this may be useful since loss occurs only if the stock advances rapidly and some money is made even if the stock is sold as a result of exercise of the option. You also can use this technique to hedge stocks owned.

Commodity trading. This type of investment is not for the small investor. Risks are high and few people make money over the longer term. Most trading in stock futures and indexes is very similar.

Gold, silver and collectibles. Some gold and silver may be desired as an insurance against a collapse of the financial system. Coin is the usual medium. Rare coins, in the past, have a good history of growth. Contact the offices of Deak-Perera for additional information and prices. There are also other companies in this field — some in your city. Do not rely on one source of data. Other collectibles vary in value and appraisals vary widely depending upon the appraiser.

Real estate. During the inflation of the 1970s, home prices increased rapidly, However, older individuals can remember long periods when homes depreciated rather than appreciated. Homes and other buildings do offer tax shelter advantages and a home offers work with many satisfactions to the average family. You should contact the Internal Revenue Service for literature explaining taxes before buying.

Know how to evaluate property before purchasing any real estate. Do not believe all that you read in books in your library — much is written to sell books. The real estate agent usually represents the seller unless you hire your buyer's agent. You might consider real estate trust and partnership if you are looking for tax shelters and are not too interested in income and management costs.

General advice. All investments involve some risk. You should carefully investigate before making any investment. Do not hesitate to contact your real estate agent, your stockbroker, your banker, your lawyer, your accountant and successful investors before buying. Often they will give free advice but you must evaluate all. Start with small amounts of money or with an imaginary paper investment to learn the techniques with minimum risks. Read, study and gain esperience so that you master the techniques of risk, investing and management. All advice must be tempered. It is your money and you must decide. Buy and sell when necessary. ALWAYS THINK ABOUT TAX AND INFLATION EFFECTS. GO TO THE LIBRARY AND ASK FOR BOOKS ON INVESTMENTS BEING CONSIDERED.

PROTECTING INVESTMENTS AND SECURITIES

You should protect your investments from loss due to mismanagement and loss from fire and theft. The successful investor manages by:

    1.   Being patient — determining objectives and sticking with the plan

in good times and bad.

2. Being steady — he is not a chronic switcher. He learns to buy when the price is low and sell when the price is high. He makes sound judgments and sells when needed.

3. Being unconcerned with short-term market changes unless long-term economic changes are indicated. He sells when his original objectives have been met, when his original judgment is indicated to be in error and when basic economic trends affecting his investment has changed.

4. Investing in growing companies in growing locations when the price is correct.

5. Looking for real sleepers. He discovers new trends before others do.

6. Buying only when the price is reasonable. Preferably, when the price is low based on long term values.

7. By reaching only for yields which are fair. He suspects fraud when yields are high for risk indicated. An investment offered at a yield several percent above that of similar investments usually is a fraud or loss.

8. Being wary of promoters who claim low price. Do not be pressured by promoters, by phone calls, etc. Instead, always study, wait and think before acting.

9. Being slow to buy more when prices are falling. Do not average down unless you know the cause of a price decline. Do be the first to buy during turn-around.

10. Searching for value — do not insist on active leaders. Use good judgment before deciding but do decide rather than "put off".

11. By keeping some liquid assets to carry through a bad time and for investment at start of "booms".

12. Facing mistakes firmly — use stop orders freely.

13. Reviewing your investments regularly — sell and buy when the time is indicated to be appropriate.

14. Diversifying but not widely. Make investments of a size which force review and action. Learn to make decisions and act. Know the rules for management of your investments so that decisions are made with confidence.

15. Making investments grow. Study, work, decide and learn to act.

Your securities are valuable pieces of paper. To avoid loss and inconvenience, keep them in a single safe place such as a bank safety deposit box which is fire and theft proof. Securities can be replaced but a surety bond costing about 3% of face value of securities is demanded by the transfer agents. Usually you must deal with the transfer agent for your stocks and bonds — not the company. You should never sign your securities. Use transfer documents such as power of attorney when you mail and do insure for loss in mails. Demand a receipt of documents from the transfer agent. Carefully record your certificates using number, number of shares and other data. Keep proof of cost for tax purposes when selling. Keep two sets of records. One with the certificates and the other at another place.

Keep records necessary for tax needs. Most companies send income tax information with their quarterly income checks during past years.

INTEREST RATE CHARTS

Money, like all commodities, has value. Learn how to calculate interest returns. Know the benefits available from growth at compound rate. Review the criteria used in business. Take the time to plot growth curves.

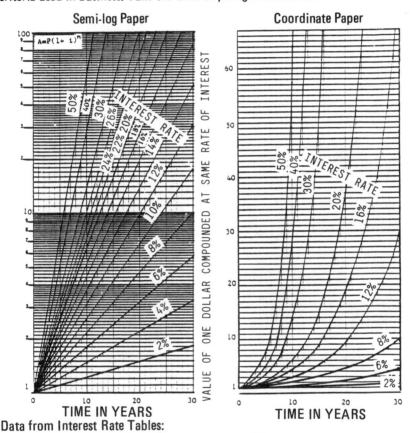

Semi-log Paper   Coordinate Paper

TIME IN YEARS   TIME IN YEARS

Data from Interest Rate Tables:

SIMPLE INTEREST

If P is the principal placed at interest at a rate i (expressed as a decimal) for a period of n years

The amount,
$$A = P(1 + ni)$$

Present value,
$$P = \frac{A}{1 + ni}$$

COMPOUND INTEREST

At interest compounded annually, the amount, —
$$A = P(1 + i)^n$$

At interest compounded q times per year, —
$$A = P(1 + \frac{i}{q})^{nq}$$

At interest compounded annually, the present value, —

$$P = \frac{A}{(1 + i)^n} = A(1 + i)^{-n} = Av^n, v = \frac{1}{1 + i}$$

At interest compounded q times per year, –

$$P = A (1 + \frac{i}{q})^{-nq}$$

Nominal rate convertible p times per year equivalent to effective rate i, –

$$jv = p[(1 + i)^{vs} - 1]$$

Amount for year of p deposits of $1/p$, p times per year, $-i/jv$

DISCOUNT FACTORS

The discount factor is an inverse of interest rate and these values are often easier to use then interest tables. These, too, are straight lines on semi-log paper.

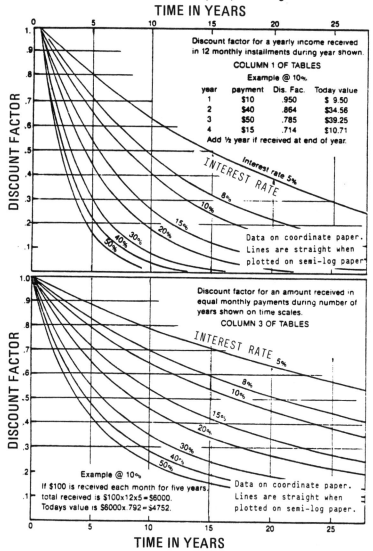

TIME IN YEARS

ANALYSIS OF INVESTMENTS

Many tools are used to evaluate the performance of various investments and they differ by investment medium and preference of the investor. Some of the tools used most often are discussed in the following.

You might consult your broker, real estate agent, banker, lawyer or accountant. Do recognize that their interests are different than yours.

Until very recently you purchased stocks from your stockbroker, bonds from a bank, real estate from real estate brokers, etc. In 1984, many firms have bought all of these investment vehicles and you can walk into offices of Prudential Life Insurance, Merrill Lynch and Company, Citicorp and Sears to buy almost any type of investment medium.

The National Association of Investment Clubs, 1515 E. Eleven Mile Road, Royal Oak, Michigan 48067, has prepared one of the many forms useful in evaluating most investments. Other techniques are available from texts in your library. Naturally, the form for evaluating real estate may be different than that used for stocks or for bonds. You need to use evaluation techniques and you should not trust your agents who are interested in sales commissions. Be careful — be informed and do the work necessary for decisions.

Do you need a quick and easy method for tracking growth of your assets, price of stocks, profits, sales, expenses, income, earnings, inventory, etc.? Try using the graph on page 194. This graph may be used to determine:

Example 1:

The value of an investment earning the indicated rate of return during years indicated when return is reinvested at same rate of return. Example 1 shows that a dollar invested at 10% annual return would be worth $2.60 in 10 years with reinvestment.

Example 2:

The rate of return when value at a specified time is known. Using Example 1, if a dollar invested during 10 years with reinvestment of return at same rate is $2.60, rate of return equivalent to interest rate is 10%. Alternately, plotting the history of the value or change in the value on a graph as shown in Example 2 may be useful. Draw the best average straight line through the plotted points. Take two triangles and compare the slope of this line with the slope of the lines on the base graph. The growth or rate of return of venture represented by points as plotted is 10%+. Many stocks, mutual funds and financial reviews use semi-log plots. Extend lines to 1 or 10 and use 1 or 10 as starting points to read values of growth directly as on Example 4.

Example 3:

The damage to an investment caused by inflation. Read directly from base graph using published values for inflation. If inflation rate is 5%, see Example 3, you have lost purchasing power equal to $0.65 for each dollar invested for 10 years because of a "hidden tax" called inflation. Value of dollar declined $1.00/ $1.65 = $0.60.

Caution for Investors:

This graph does not adjust for effects of taxes paid on reinvested income. If you pay federal or state taxes on income, growth of your investment will be

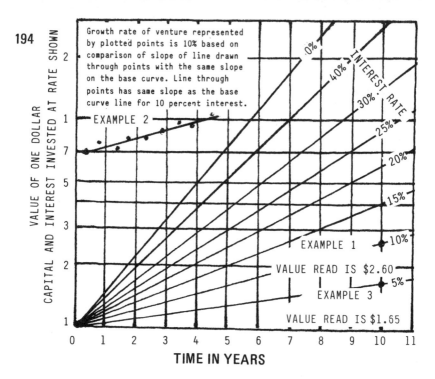

Growth rate of venture represented by plotted points is 10% based on comparison of slope of line drawn through points with the same slope on the base curve. Line through points has same slope as the base curve line for 10 percent interest.

194

VALUE OF ONE DOLLAR CAPITAL AND INTEREST INVESTED AT RATE SHOWN

EXAMPLE 2

INTEREST RATE
.0%
40%
30%
25%
20%
15%
EXAMPLE 1   10%
VALUE READ IS $2.60
5%
EXAMPLE 3
VALUE READ IS $1.65

TIME IN YEARS

NOTE: THE ABOVE GRAPH IS CONSTRUCTED USING INTEREST RATE DATA

EXAMPLE 4
Method is identical with that used to evaluate oil field decline curves

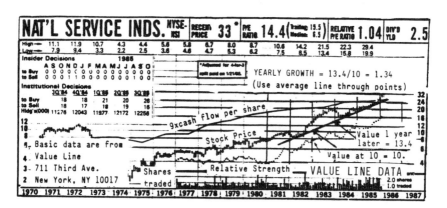

Extrapolation for future

Start	10.0
1 Year Later 10x1.34	13.4
2 Year Later 13.4x1.34	17.9
3 Year Later 17.9x1.34	24.1

Assumes that slope
does not change

much less. Study your tax return and devise legal methods to reduce your taxes. Also, remember that your return is composed of dividend, interest and similar return plus the growth in value of your original principle. You can sell principle if you need added income. Always look for overall or total return after adjusting for both taxes and inflation. Protection of principle is important but protection from taxes and inflation is equally important. Inflation and tax must be minimized. Your job puts food on the table but your investments properly managed make you rich and give you a pleasant retirement. Try.

There are many investments, evaluation methods and investment procedures. You alone must learn how to use them. Some of the methods for determining the value of a business have been given previously. A quick method might involve the simple determination of the price earnings ratio, the company's earnings and revenues during the past 12 months on a per share basis. Also determine the company's sales and book value on a per share basis. These criteria are often given in stock market statistics for the company. A total market value should be less than 75% of sales, less than 12 times earnings and 1½ times book value or less for the conservative investor.

The very conservative investor might buy only during recession periods when ratio of current assets to liabilities is 2 to 1, total debt is not greater than twice net current asset value, total debt is less than tangible book value, earnings double in 10 years, no annual losses have occurred in past 5 to 10 years, earnings are twice interest rate on AAA bonds, dividends exceed 2/3 interest on AAA bonds, etc. Others would add return on equity growth rate of 15-20 percent and a price to earning divided by growth rate of less than one.

Investment in the stock depicted on Chart 1 (below) is more profitable than Chart 2 (on page 196).

CHART 1

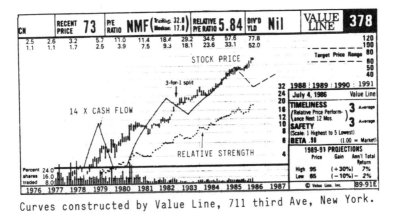

Curves constructed by Value Line, 711 third Ave, New York.

You might write to the National Association of Investment Clubs for the methods and forms used for selecting stocks. The address is 1515 East Eleven Mile Road, Royal Oak, Michigan 48067.

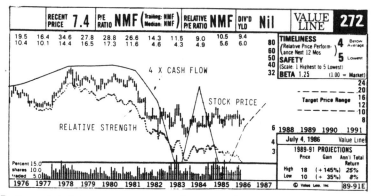

Ratios related to company operations are often used by both company managers and investors. Some of the average values were presented in other sections.

Ratios usually are classified into three major categories which are solvency, efficiency and profitability. These are defined as follows:

1. Solvency ratios.

   Short term creditors are interested in the liquidity of a company. Liquid assets are assets which can rapidly be converted into cash when necessary. The following ratios are used:

   a. Current ratio is the current assets divided by current liabilities. A high value is desired.

   b. Quick ratio is current assets divided by current liabilities after exclusion of inventory. Inventory may be difficult to sell quickly at a fair price. A high value is desired.

   c. Current liabilities divided by net worth ratio. This ratio contrasts the funds short term creditors are risking and the funds permanently invested by owners of the company including common stock, preferred stock and retained earnings. A low to moderate value is desired.

   d. Total liabilities divided by net worth. This ratio shows the amount invested by total creditors compared to investment of owners of the company. Investments by creditors represent interest that must be paid by company before dividends to owners are possible. Interest usually is taxed as an expense for company, while dividends are taxed to both company and individual. Nevertheless, too much debt can be dangerous in bad times.

2. Efficiency ratios.

   Assets which are too high compared to sales are costly and tend to reduce company profits. When they are too low, the company possibly is losing business because it does not have necessary merchandise to show buyers. These ratios are shown below:

   a. The collection period can be determined by dividing accounts receivables by sales times 365 days.

   b. Inventory turnover ratio is obtained by dividing sales by inventory. This enables us to know how rapid merchandise moves to customers.

   c. Sales divided by total assets ratio. Total assets includes plant and equipment. This ratio shows total investment to generate sales.

   d. Sales divided by net working capital.

3. Profitability ratios.

These ratios measure the effectiveness of the total operation and also the firm's ability to withstand adverse conditions. These ratios are discussed as follows:

   a. Return on sales ratio. A good indicator of a company's ability to weather bad times is given when net after-tax profit is divided by sales.

   b. Interest coverage ratio. The company's ability to meet interest obligations is given by dividing profit before tax and interest by interest expense.

   c. Return on assets ratio. A key indicator of profitability is obtained by dividing net profit after-tax by total assets.

   d. Net profit after tax divided by equity is another good profitability indicator. Every company must earn an adequate return on the common stockholder's equity.

The literature contains many other important indexes as discussed under the section related to "Business".

Ratios are very important tools but they must be used with caution. They all use accounting information which often is not consistent between companies and industries. Inventory evaluation is often different between companies. Also, seasonal factors often influence values shown in reports for different industries.

Deviation from industry averages requires careful inspection of basic data. We need to recognize that companies use different interpretation of accounting rules. Study reports such as Value Line for average values by industry.

Many different indexes are used to evaluate a company. Rate of return is a useful index which is influenced by all ratios discussed previously but return on sales ratio and sales to total assets ratios are most important. The value of money often is desired in evaluations.

A large profit margin is needed to achieve a satisfactory return on assets when the company requires large investment in assets. Manufacturing often is in the category of industries such as steel.

Companies with slim profit margins, such as grocery stores, must have low assets compared with sales. They must "turnover" inventory quickly to make a satisfactory return.

Managers use indexes to control operations and attain objectives. Higher margin products are promoted while low volume and low margin products are removed. This explains why the product you use often no longer can be found in stores. The ratios used include (1) product gross margin percentages, (2) sales and administrative costs to sales ratios, (3) inventory turnover, (4) operating profit to sales ratios, and (5) return on assets. Use of these ratios when selecting merchandise to be placed on shelves often increases values on income statements and balance sheets.

Book value is an index often used by investors. In 1927, investors paid 2.6 times book value for stocks. The value increased to 4.18 before the 1929 crash and fell to 0.5 in 1932. In 1981, stocks sold at 1.05 book value. For many years, stock prices corrected when book value reached 1.5 but this value was exceeded in 1986 when stock buyers became optimistic and too much money started chasing too few stocks.

BUSINESS CYCLES

Economists attempt to relate business with both long term and short term cycles. Business does seem to ebb and flow in a fairly regular pattern called cycles. Booms give way to busts and the cycle repeats.

A long term — two generation cycle — seems to be recognized. Business has the following characteristics:

Peak year	Bottom year	Length — years	
		up	down
1815	1835	20	
1866	1883	17	31
1920	1935	15	37
1966	1983	17	31

There also appears to be a 4-5 year cycle which some individuals relate with money manipulations by the Federal Reserve Board and U. S. presidential elections. These changes can be obtained from the following data:

Year	% Change Real GNP	
1958	−0.4	Recession ended, May
1959	6.0	
1960*	2.2	Recession began, May
1961	2.6	Recession ended, March
1962	5.8	
1963	4.0	
1964*	5.3	
1965	6.0	
1966	6.0	
1967	2.7	
1968*	4.6	
1969	2.8	
1970	−2.9	Recession, Jan.–Dec.
1971	6.2	
1972*	5.7	
1973	5.8	Recession began, Dec.
1974	−0.6	
1975	−1.1	Recession ended, April
1976*	5.2	
1977	4.5	

1978	5.0	
1979	2.8	
1980*	−0.4	Recession, Feb.—Aug.
1981	1.9	Recession began, August
1982	−1.7	

*Presidential election year

Study the ELLIOT WAVE THEORY for other waves.

The source of business cycles can be traced to governmentally-established principles such as fractional reserve banking, fiat paper money, and other actions of the Federal Reserve Board. They have exclusive control over the money and credit of this nation. The Fed can and does inflate or deflate, increase or decrease, the supply of money and credit at will. Fractional reserve banking allows banks to loan out money without having the monetary reserves to back the loans. Fiat paper money allows the Fed to increase the supply of money infinitely and without restraint by purchasing debt. The dollar has no real definition in terms of gold. Under such restraints, there is a virtual guarantee of large swings in price, interest rates and economic activity. The less restraint put on the Fed, the larger the swings become. This is why the cycles have gotten much worse since 1973 when the dollar's loose link to gold was severed.

Many forces influence the economy of the world including the United States, which is a world leader. However, the short term cycle is considered to have three phases — growth, inflation and recession — which often are explained somewhat as follows:

The cycle begins at the bottom of the recession illustrated on a later figure. Near the end of the recession, government reacts to the growing discomfort of the people by having the Federal Reserve Board lower interest rates. The FED aggressively buys Treasury securities from commercial banks which bids up prices. The FED credits the bank's reserve account when such securities are bought. This creates credit out of thin air since the banks can increase this reserve and lend the money to others. The bankers do not leave the credit at the Fed where it earns a low rate of interest. Instead, the commercial banks lend out as much money as they prudently are able to lend while satisfying the reserve requirements of banking laws. Since various federal insurance methods tend to protect banks, the amounts made available often are the maximum permitted by the federal regulators who enforce banking laws. The overall operation expands credit and money supply and the economy picks up as bank customers spend the loan money. Prices stop falling and head higher as the fake money is placed in circulation. Each dollar spent for wages increases two to four times as it works through the business system. We now have an economy with good growth characteristics.

Eventually, the economy speeds up to a point where business and individuals begin to make unwise expenditures. Factories run above 85% capacity and labor makes unrealistic demands. Management pays itself unreasonable salaries and the economy reaches unsustainable levels. Real interest rates — rates after inflation — still seem low and plants are constructed to "keep up with the demand". Individuals buy too much on credit. The business is good and demand for loans enables lenders to increase interest rates. Prices paid for all goods moves up as too many dollars chase too few goods. Labor and cost of goods also contribute to inflation. The price of everything is increasing rapidly — inflation is in full control. Management fails to control so that "too much money is available to buy too few goods", salary and wages are far greater than productivity, and costs in general are rising too rapidly. Business and consumer both buy to protect against future price increases. Inflation is feared and the government again reacts because the average person is being hurt by inflation in excess of wage increases.

The government moves by having the Fed get stingy about supplying funds needed for continued growth. Study of money supply shows that the Fed adds 5%-10% annually to the money supply to allow growth in a normal economy. The Fed may also use other tools such as a change in the discount rate charged banks. Consumers reach their borrowing limits as credit tightens and purchases drop. Industry profits decline but time lag causes expenditures for new plant to continue so that construction is completed. Business slows and the recession begins. Everyone begins to pay off debts rather than borrowing and the recession deepens. Business lays off workers, dividends and interest rates provide less money for investors, inventory is slashed, raw product prices decline. The slowdown continues until government decides that people want a change and the process is repeated.

Government is controlled by people who like their jobs. The politician wishes to get reelected and he reacts to public pressure rather than doing what is best for the country. Individuals are responsible since we look at the short term rather than our long term needs. We want our pleasures today and are willing to allow our children to pay for our pleasures. With the increasing deficit and its interest burdens, the only way to pay and continue our luxury is inflation. This robs the investor when uninformed, timid and managing poorly, but he is a minority who does not complain sufficiently. The average worker does not realize that his pension fund is the principle contributor and that the worker is paying for his excess with his savings because managers of pension funds, by law, are required to be conservative. Each of us needs to become informed, demand better management of our pension funds, manage our own IRA, etc.

We should each constantly remember that the 1900 dollar is worth nine cents today, that the 1939 dollar is worth less than fifteen cents, that the 1972 dollar is worth about forty-five cents and the year 2000 dollar is expected to be worth 2.5 to 10.0 times less than today's dollar. We must take care of ourself during our old age since the government will not be able to do so. We should demand a more responsible government which is possible only if we demand less today. Learn to manage your own assets and demand that government become responsible and live within its means. Excessive taxes are not the answer since people must have rewards from their labor and taxes will be paid willingly only when they are reasonable and fair.

The Federal Reserve Board, an independent agency appointed by the president, manages the banking system in the United States and should be relatively independent of politics. Nevertheless, business, as indicated by the

Dow Jones Industrial Index, which is an approximation for all U. S. business, often has high values at election time and politicians are pleased.

BUSINESS TRENDS

Economists in the early 1900s tried to find indexes which would forecast major turns in business. Continued study accepted the following indicators as significant.

THE 12 LEADING INDICATORS

1.	Average Hours Worked	1920	U. S. Dept. of Labor
2.	Unemployment Claims	1945	U. S. Dept. of Labor
3.	Net Business Formations	1945	Dun & Bradstreet
4.	Durable Goods New Orders	1920	U. S. Dept. of Commerce
5.	P. & E. Contracts, Orders	1948	U. S. Dept. of Commerce
6.	Housing Permits	1918	U. S. Dept. of Commerce
7.	Mfg. & Trade Inv. Chge.	1939	U. S. Dept. of Commerce
8.	Ind. Materials Prices	1919	U. S. Dept. of Labor
9.	Common Stock Prices	1871	Standard & Poors
10.	Corporate Profits Net	1921	U. S. Dept. of Commerce
11.	Price/Unit Labor Cost	1919	U. S. Dept. of Commerce
12.	Consumer Debt Change	1929	Federal Reserve Board

8 COINCIDENTAL INDICATORS

13.	Nonagricultural Employment	1929	U. S. Dept. of Labor
14.	Unemployment Rate	1929	U. S. Dept. of Labor
15.	GNP (Current Dollars)	1921	U. S. Dept. of Commerce
16.	GNP (1958 Dollars)	1921	U. S. Dept. of Commerce
17.	Industrial Production	1919	Federal Reserve Board
18.	Personal Income	1921	U. S. Dept. of Commerce
19.	Mfg. & Trade Sales	1948	U. S. Dept. of Commerce
20.	Retail Sales	1919	U. S. Dept. of Commerce

THE 6 LAGGING INDICATORS

21.	Unemployment Rate, 15 Weeks	1949	U. S. Dept. of Labor
22.	Plant & Equipment Expenditures	1915	U. S. Dept. of Commerce
23.	Mfg. & Trade Invent.	1939	U. S. Dept. of Commerce
24.	Unit Labor Cost	1919	U. S. Dept. of Commerce & FRB
25.	Comm. & Industrial Loans	1937	Federal Reserve Board
26.	Bank Loans Rate	1919	Federal Reserve Board

The indexes and their definitions have changed with time.

Business in the United States has grown since the early 1930s.

There have been many recessions but no major depression or upheavals. Wars have occurred without severe upsets since the 1936 depression.

Recessions are often preceded by tight money, increasing discount rates, surging inflation, plants at full capacity, small unemployment and high inventories. A major downward change in GNP, a upward change in Federal Funds Rates, excessive speculation in low priced stocks, and a large number of favorable recommendations are other signals.

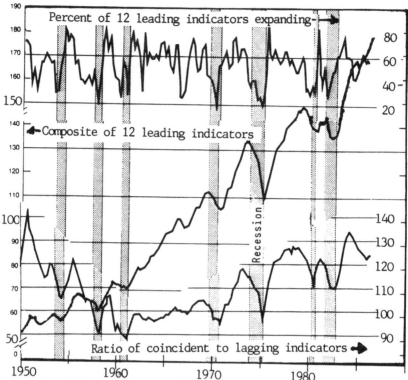

Taken from Federal Government Statistics. Basic economic and financial data are collected and presented in tables and curves by various government agencies and many private organizations. The data are used in stock advisory letters by stockbrokers and writers such as Value Line, Standard and Poors, Wall Street Journal, Barrons, Wall Street Digest, Forbes, Fortune, Business Week and U. S. News and World Report.

TAXES, INFLATION AND INTEREST RATE RELATIONS

Taxes and government borrowing both take money away from the economy. Both have a negative impact on jobs and business. Borrowing also increases the interest paid to lenders. High interest rates in one part of the world compared to that of other countries affects international trade. The entire process is very complicated and is probably not understood by anyone. Relations between tax, inflation and interest may be as shown below and on page 203. Other data indicates that average tax approaches 25% as an average in 1985.

Unadjusted return if investor is to obtain
2% return after inflation and taxes.
Values taken from figure below

Inflation, %	2			5			10		
Tax rate, %	0	25	50	0	25	50	0	25	50
Return, %*	4	5	8	7	10	14	12	16	24

*Return to investor before tax and inflation.

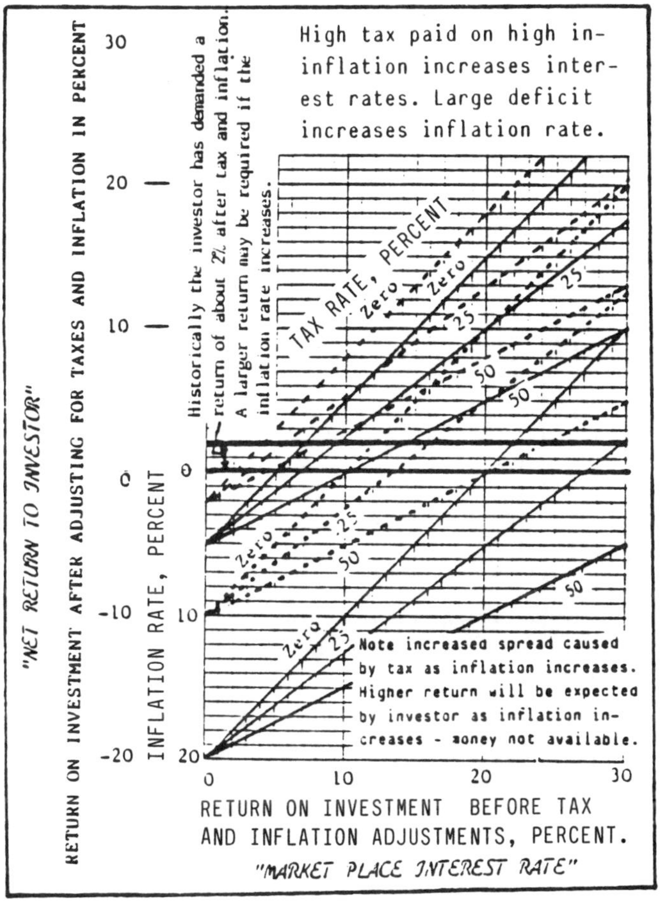
High tax paid on high inflation increases interest rates. Large deficit increases inflation rate.
Historically the investor has demanded a return of about 2% after tax and inflation.
A larger return may be required if the inflation rate increases.
TAX RATE, PERCENT
Zero
25
50
Note increased spread caused by tax as inflation increases. Higher return will be expected by investor as inflation increases - money not available.
"NET RETURN TO INVESTOR"
RETURN ON INVESTMENT AFTER ADJUSTING FOR TAXES AND INFLATION IN PERCENT
INFLATION RATE, PERCENT
RETURN ON INVESTMENT BEFORE TAX AND INFLATION ADJUSTMENTS, PERCENT.
"MARKET PLACE INTEREST RATE"

Values for 25% tax rate may be most reliable.

High taxes and inflation are very important factors in all business and investment decisions. Congress is constantly changing tax laws and inflation seems to be cyclical as the Federal Reserve Board adjusts money supply.

HOW MUCH INFLATION DO YOU WANT? HOW HIGH DO YOU WANT YOUR TAXES? Both are determined by elected politicians. Government controls your life. Vote!

GOVERNMENT INTERFERENCE

Local, state and federal governments enforce many rules, regulations and laws which affect your investments. The number is so great that many people do not know of the laws. Major influences caused by the federal government might include:

FINANCIAL DEFICITS AND TAXES

There is a large underground economy or business effort in most countries with high taxes. This economy does not pay taxes and the income tax loss to the U. S. Federal Government is estimated to be between one and 400 billion dollars depending upon source of the estimate. Additional lost tax includes social security, state taxes and possibly property taxes owed counties and cities.

High taxes distort business decisions. People also spend time trying to avoid high and unnecessary taxes as permitted by a very complicated tax law. People do not pay when tax is unfair.

THE TOP INCOME TAX RATE FOR INDIVIDUALS

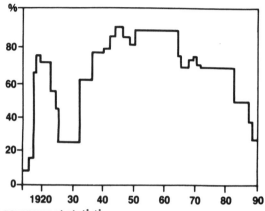

Basic data from government statistics.

FEDERAL REVENUES, OUTLAYS AND DEFICITS
Congress is trying to control deficits during 1986.
Many analysts do not believe they will be successful

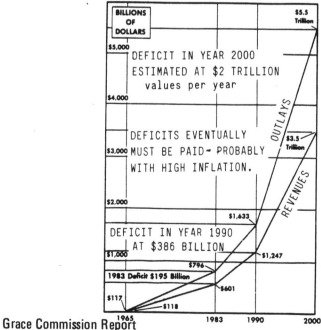

Grace Commission Report

Prior to 1970, the Federal Government tried to control the national debt by allowing debt to increase during poor economic times and war. During better or normal times, the debt was actually decreased so that overall growth in national debt was small. Since about 1970, the debt has always grown and interest on the national debt now approaches 3.0% of gross national product. This approaches the savings of all individuals in the U. S. in 1987.

GROSS NATIONAL DEBT ADDITIONS – B $

Year	Billion Dollars	Year	Billion Dollars
1977	53.6	1981	78.9
1978	59.0	1982	127.9
1979	40.6	1983	207.8
1980	73.8	1984	185.9

The preservation of our nation is the real reason for taxes and government. An adequate defense to protect us from other nations who want our wealth is of first importance. During recent years, our government has also accepted responsibility for curing many social ills because of moral considerations in a wealthy nation and a desire to control the internal, highly organized, special interest groups.

Expenditures now greatly exceed revenues from all types of taxes and the difference creates the growing national government debt. The forecast values assume that people will continue to "live high" today and transfer the debts to their children. We do not want to pay the taxes needed for social programs but we do not force government to change its free-spending habits. If forecasts prove correct, taxes by the year 2000 will approach $48,000 per family. All values also assume some further inflation.

During past years our debt has in part been financed by foreign investors who like our stable government. We probably should expect financial trouble if they change their concepts and decide to invest their money elsewhere.

The National Debt can be paid in three ways:
1. Getting money from individuals and companies through taxes which reduces the economy when taxes are high.
2. Repudiation of the debt which probably is accompanied by a major depression.
3. Inflation which is a hidden tax on everyone as illustrated by events in Germany after World War I, and in the Roman Empire in 0-400 A.D. Money usually is recalled and the face value of the unit may be identical but its purchasing power in goods and products may be less by factors of 100 to as much as 1000.

INFLATION PROBABLY IS THE LEAST DIFFICULT ALTERNATIVE FOR POLITICIANS TO ACCEPT.

A chart showing the inflation index and gross federal debt follows on page 206.

INFLATION INDEX AND GROSS FEDERAL DEBT

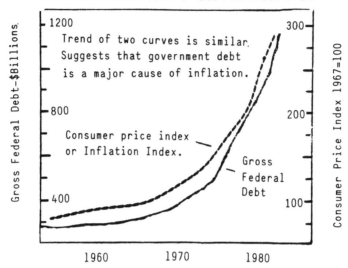

Basic data from government statistics

The financial record of the U. S. Government may be expressed as a percent of the Gross National Product.

	1970	1980	1986	Est. 1987	Est. 1988
Federal Revenues	19.5	19.4	18.5	19.1	19.4
Total Government Spending	19.8	22.2	23.8	23.0	21.6
Defense Spending	8.2	5.0	6.6	6.4	6.3
Interest on debt	1.5	2.0	3.3	3.1	2.9
Other Non-Defense Costs	10.1	15.2	13.9	13.5	12.4
Deficit for Year	0.3	2.8	5.3	3.9	2.3

The national debt and deficit causes government to borrow money in competition with business and the private sector and often increases interest rates above desired levels. Congress wishes to be elected again and they continue to create excessive spending which eventually may result in "run-away" inflation and ultimate destruction of our economic system. Have we created a spending engine which cannot be stopped even if we have the will to do so?

Please note that all of these curves have the same general shape as the compound "interest rate curves". They approach straight lines when plotted on semi-log paper. Government spending is increasing at an ever-growing rate which cannot be supported when values are very large. The above unpleasant solutions with hardship for everyone is the only result.

Can government spending be controlled?

Problems Related to Large Size of Government

The problems of large size and the actions and reactions to reducing benefits, once started, must be analyzed. People hate to give up what they have and are receiving. Also, a large engine once operating at full speed stops slowly. Correction by large inflation may be the political solution to large government.

Natural laws and industrial procedures, including large government, usually can be presented as straight lines on one of four types of graph paper. These are coordinate, semi-log, log-log and probability. An example of the coordinate paper usage is shown as a graph.

SIMPLE GROWTH METHOD
Straight Line on Coordinate Paper

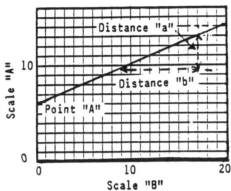

EQUATIONS:

Slope of line is: "c" is $\dfrac{\text{Distance "a"}}{\text{Distance "b"}}$

All points on line are:

Point is "A" + "B" x "c"

Example:

If "A" is 6 and Distance "a" is 3.5; Distance "b" is 8.5; Slope is 3.5/8.5 or .41. The value of "A" when "B" is 10 is 6 plus 10 x 0.41 or 10.1.

Simple growth relates with a fixed base growing at a constant rate. Unfortunately, governments grow with both an expanding base and an expanding rate of growth. These plot as straight lines on semi-log paper rather than on coordinate paper. Some trend to log-log which suggests instability.

Analysis of Compound Growth graph is on page 208.

Curves showing growth of population, U. S. National Product, U. S. Government Expenditures and many other time dependent indexes all have the same general shape. They all conform with the interest rate curves of compound growth. All plot as straight lines on semi-log paper. Most involve very large numbers growing at "high" compound rates. A few examples are shown on the graph on page 208.

The U. S. National Product has been growing at about 8 percent before adjustment for inflation. After inflation adjustment, the rate of growth has been 3.1 percent during the past 90 years. During recent years, U. S. Government Expenditures have been growing almost 10 percent yearly, which is greater than the National Product. The difference, if continued into the future, will result in the U. S. and local governments consuming all U. S. wealth. In time there will be no income available to the average worker who produces our goods and services. Will citizens of the United States allow those who work for the govern-

ANALYSIS OF COMPOUND GROWTH
HUNDREDS CAN BE DOUBLED WITHOUT CONSEQUENCES
DOUBLING BILLIONS OFTEN CAUSES MAJOR CHANGE
DOUBLING TRILLIONS CHANGES HISTORY OF MANKIND
Curves from Commerce Department

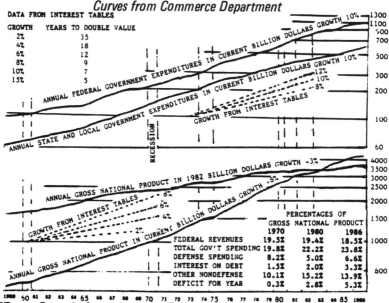

DATA FROM INTEREST TABLES

GROWTH	YEARS TO DOUBLE VALUE
2%	35
4%	18
6%	12
8%	9
10%	7
15%	5

ANNUAL FEDERAL GOVERNMENT EXPENDITURES IN CURRENT BILLION DOLLARS GROWTH 10%

ANNUAL STATE AND LOCAL GOVERNMENT EXPENDITURES IN CURRENT BILLION DOLLARS GROWTH 10%

GROWTH FROM INTEREST TABLES

RECESSION

ANNUAL GROSS NATIONAL PRODUCT IN 1982 BILLION DOLLARS GROWTH -3%

GROWTH FROM INTEREST TABLES

ANNUAL GROSS NATIONAL PRODUCT IN CURRENT BILLION DOLLARS GROWTH

PERCENTAGES OF GROSS NATIONAL PRODUCT	1970	1980	1986
FEDERAL REVENUES	19.5%	19.4%	18.5%
TOTAL GOV'T SPENDING	19.8%	22.2%	23.8%
DEFENSE SPENDING	8.2%	5.0%	6.6%
INTEREST ON DEBT	1.5%	2.0%	3.3%
OTHER NONDEFENSE	10.1%	15.2%	13.9%
DEFICIT FOR YEAR	0.3%	2.8%	5.3%

NOTE: Growth from Interest Tables can be used to quickly determine growth of basic data. Place triangle along the average curve of interest, with two triangles slip the triangle to the Growth From Interest Tables until a curve match is obtained. The match is the growth for original data curve.

ment to be the only people who eat well? This condition exists in many countries today. The military and people with influence all "work" for government. Everyone else receives a very low subsistence wage and lives in poverty. The growth trend of U. S. Government Expenditures, when expressed as a percent of the Gross National Product, must be reversed so that it is negative if the United States is to survive.

Problems Related to Large Size of Population

A rapid increase in the number of people is one cause of all growth problems. The world has easily accommodated growth during thousands of years but it is stressed in most parts of the world today at five billion people. Growth from five to ten billion, which is expected from extrapolation of current trend to occur within 25 to 35 years, will severely distort living conditions and cause very rapid deterioration of the environment of planet earth. Man is harming plants and animals today and the damage will accelerate rapidly unless population is controlled by law, war, accident or disease. Pollution of air and oceans is not limited to national boundaries and poor countries who cannot feed their people have no money for pollution control.

Control of the number of people is complicated and difficult. Couples want children, doctors want income and recognition and we all live longer with improved medical practices. The following graphs assume a lifespan of 75 years and births at an average age of 25 years. If a single family were the only people present, we would double our offspring every 25 years for 75 years if we only reproduced ourselves with two living children per family. The world has existed for many years so that deaths do occur during this time and population actually grows more slowly as illustrated by curves presented for time after 75 years on the first graph. However, deaths always lag births in societies who control disease and wars. Curves depend upon lifespan and birth rates.

EFFECTS OF NUMBER OF CHILDREN

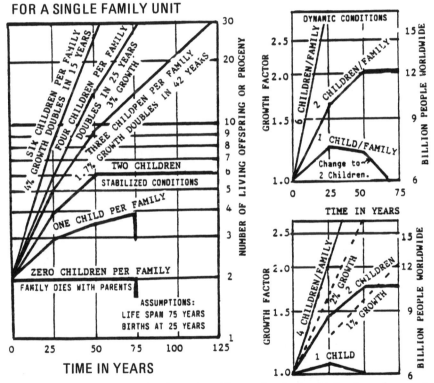

The other two graphs show the effects of reducing births from four and six living children to two and one children per family. Data are approximation for dynamic conditions of growth. The curves show that population can be stabilized in a constant value with two live births per family but the required time is long. If started throughout the world today, worldwide people would probably double today's numbers. Can the world support twice today's population?

Population growth in the developed western world may be approximately one percent yearly, which implies that population doubles every 70 years. Will life be worthwhile and pleasant at that population density? In many undeveloped countries, population is doubling every 15 years and their density is already very large. Trees are disappearing and used for cooking, poverty is severe, and foreign aid given by the western world must be used to feed the newborn today. Their living conditions can only deteriorate with time since resources are simply not available and no money is available to build plants and facilities. Our aid only adds to their long term problems unless we also insist that the population be stabilized at constant values immediately. Our aid is simply wasted and in time they will consume all the wealth of the world if we are so foolish as to continue our aid indefinitely. Should western nations continue their aid when it encourages more people to be born into lifelong poverty and our aid only benefits the rulers of the countries? We may benefit from short-term political stability but that, too, will eventually disappear. Nature reduces lifespan when population is too large for the local environment.

Today China recognizes the problem and their policy of one child per family is criticized by people who do not think before talking. Some Tibetan's have solved the problem during many years. Men inherit the family land collectively and all sons marry the same woman. Most women remain unmarried and childless but population remains constant as required in the harsh mountain climate. China temporarily feeds its people. Today many similar countries have high birth rates, severe poverty and are drifting toward chaos and internal wars.

The concepts of citizens, political leaders and religious leaders must change to meet the needs of the 1987 world environment. Population must stabilize at a constant value which creates an acceptable equilibrium with earth's ability to support people, animals and plants.

We can expect advances in agriculture from genetic advances. We may find an abundant and inexpensive source of energy and "poor" minerals will be used. Social problems, space problems, smog, waste disposal, traffic problems and pollution problems will present real challenges and probably in time will not be manageable. Population growth can always be increased but delay in reducing growth will double the population of the world each 25 to 50 years. It is obvious that many countries today have reached their present limits and must be forced to accept fewer children so that the world remains alive, healthy and livable. Poor people migrate and transfer problems to rich nations.

All nations must work together to protect the world from destruction by retaining a living environment. If we fail, man, plants and animals will no longer live on earth. Foreign aid and the flow of goods and money must be distributed fairly but everyone must recognize the need to use resources to control people and thereby protect the environment of the earth. Our population will be controlled by nature if man does not have the will and courage to control his destiny. Nature, even today, uses many tools, including famine, to reduce and control man and the environment.

Can government solve our problems? All large corporations have problems implementing ideas and decisions of top management at the operating levels. Ideas get distorted as they are interpreted at various levels of management. People are reluctant to accept change. The problems are compounded in government where workers are more protected by politicians and reporters who seek personal glory and advancement rather than the welfare of our country. Lawsuits, hearings and objections by people of influence all interfere. Also, the large, rather independent bureaucracy refuses to obey orders of elected officials.

Democratic governments always seem to "muddle through" and our problems will be solved. Finding correct solutions to problems makes our life interesting. The need for correct solutions is more critical at times of major political and economic change. Today, heads of at least five governments have the raw power to destroy all plant and animal life on earth with a single order or mistake. They also control the political power to cause recessions and depressions. We must strive for internal and external peace so that our freedoms, independence and living standards are retained and hopefully improved. Government, too, must be controlled and we must each learn to elect responsible leaders and keep them informed of our wishes and then accept needed compromise with tact and good grace. We need to prevent problems rather than use "bandaids".

The young student often is an idealist and he or she has not experienced the practical world where compromise is basic to solutions of problems. Some idealists never grow up.

It is obvious that we who live in the United States need to review our individual and collective priorities and make the adjustments needed to compete in a worldwide society. Examples of some possible adjustments include:

1. Today, information, finances, jobs and distribution of products occurs worldwide and is managed as a single unit by international companies. Governments are relatively impotent and usually react slowly in each country's self interest. Should nations and their governments cooperate and unite economically-politically to control larger industrial units? Such cooperation requires that governments and individuals create national policies which permit political leaders to act for the national interests while also cooperating with other nations.

2. Individuals need to recognize that they live in a single nation and must be part of that nation. We cannot each obtain all of our ideals but must compromise with neighbors to determine a plan acceptable to the entire nation. Do we need a single language, common customs and common goals to survive as free individuals and nation? Special interest groups seem to be tearing our nation apart as they strive for their views regardless of the consequences for others.

3. Individuals need to evaluate their true needs — possibly determine their minimum needs — and make the compromises and adjustments. We also must share part of our wealth with poor nations by paying a fair price for the imports of oil, minerals and other products needed to keep our nation operating. Can we adjust to a one world economy without lowering our standard of living? Should we be building houses near work instead of roads? Oil is a non-replaceable resource. Which alternative — alcohol, oil shale, coal, electricity

— will we use?

4. People are rapidly damaging the earth's fresh water, oceans and air. One hundred percent cleanup, too, is an ideal which is very expensive and unattainable. How can the poor nations find the money for cleanup when their people are actually hungry? International cooperation is again required. Cooperation can reduce the need for defense and make money available for other needs.

5. As part of this review, we also need to determine how we will share with the poor in the United States. Are we each too greedy and do we want too much? Do we actually need two cars and many television sets? Do we eat too much and suffer poor health and overweight? Is the pay of lower level workers fair when compared with the salary of our political and economic leaders? Is our definition of "poverty" correct or do we encourage our poor to be non-productive because of excessive aid? How can we make work attractive to everyone? How can we provide and get people to work — particularly at low pay — performing jobs needed by society?

6. Are we willing to spend the time and effort required to understand the problems of our society? We need to vote after making intelligent decisions in a complicated and technical world. Our freedoms and choices are being reduced as government satisfies special interest group demands. Additional freedoms will be lost if we continue to depend upon government for solutions to our problems instead of taking charge of individual and local group efforts. It should be obvious that no government can meet all of our individual desires since national wealth and income simply are not sufficient to satisfy the demands of everyone. Ideals are dreams and we must accept the workable and the attainable in a practical world.

7. Do we have the proper separation of power between the President, Congress, the "press" and big business. The President is elected to manage the country and no one else should be powerful enough or be permitted to usurp his powers. The President must manage and the remainder of us should give him the right to handle his responsibilities without criticism of every detail of action. We each make mistakes and the "press" should recognize that they, too, have self interests and judgment "after the fact" is always easy. They should not act as President.

MONEY SUPPLY

Since Congress and the people who elect our officials do not have the will to control spending, the Federal Reserve Board tries to control inflation and recession by adjusting the money supply, the discount rate and the federal funds rate. These methods have, during recent years, reduced the rate of inflation but interest rates remain at high values relative to long term averages. In a one world economy, control by foreign financial institutions, including bankers and governments is a definite possibility.

Graphs showing the growth in money supply follow:

HISTORY OF MONEY SUPPLY AND INTEREST RATES

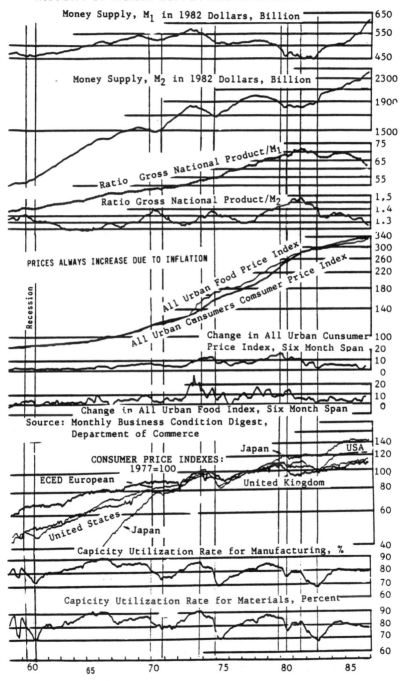

Money and how it is spent is the fuel that drives the economy.

The national economy is also influenced by the way we use our money. The velocity of the money supply or the turnover of money, too, is a variable. The general relation is:

Rate in growth of money supply plus velocity plus a factor
equals the rate of growth in GNP.

GNP is the gross national product. The turnover has been variable but consistently has averaged about 2% since 1953. The value for the factor has averaged about 2% in the 1960s and is closer to zero during the 1980s. Money supply has been growing. Real GNP growth rate hovers around 3%. Growth before adjustment for inflation has been larger as shown by the graph on later pages. Inflation helps pay the ever-increasing government spending.

FOREIGN TRADE

We live in a one world environment and goods move freely throughout the world unless the movement is restricted by governments who may use local customs, trade barriers and other devices. The value of the dollar varies widely and this influences trade among nations.

U. S. DOLLAR TRADE-WEIGHTED EXCHANGE RATE

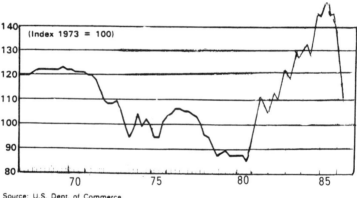

Source: U.S. Dept. of Commerce

Federal Reserve Board records a substantial decline in exchange rate during 1985 to 1986. This is true for major trading nations. However, trade with other nations has been increasing very rapidly and the Federal Reserve Board in Dallas suggests that the average decline, when all exchange rates are averaged on the basis of overall trade, has been very small.

Worldwide money flows overnight to the country and assets which offer the highest rate of return after correction for inflation and taxes if business and political conditions are identical. Movement of money is fast and flexible.

The effective exchange rate varies by country. Most currencies are valued by the market and reflect many different conditions in the respective countries. A few countries seem to control the value of their currencies so that they move with the U. S. dollar.

Based on history, a 10% decline in the value of the U. S. dollar adds 2½% to the U. S. Gross National Product, or GNP. A 10% in value of the dollar adds one-half point to inflation one year later. A billion dollar trade gain also adds 25,000 U. S. jobs.

U. S. FOREIGN TRADE BALANCE

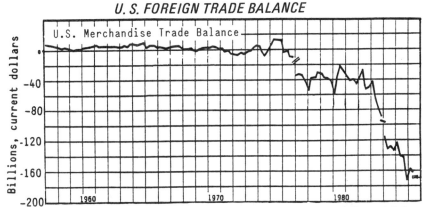

Taken from Federal Government Statistics. Basic economic and financial data are collected and presented in tables and curves by various government agencies and many private organizations. The data are used in stock advisory letters of stockbrokers and writers such Value Line, Standard and Poors, Wall Street Journal, Barrons, Wall Street Digest, Forbes, Fortune, Business Week and U. S. News and World Report.

The United States merchandise trade balance in 1986 was at an all time low with a negative value of 169.8 billion dollars. This is part of the debt which we owe to other nations. Values shown are yearly additions.

A graph showing the history of foreign trade follows on page 216.

Our interest rates, prices and wages are high relative to other parts of the world and our plant is older. As a result, the United States is not able to compete in the world marketplace and our industry is shutting down as product imports increase. Other nations are doing our work and we have a permanent loss of jobs and exports with increasing imports and a large trade deficit. We eventually will have to settle accounts with other nations and we will pay dearly for our folly which we create by high excessive living standards.

A strong dollar, which results from our high relative interest rates paid on borrowed money, and our stable government causes money to flow into the United States from abroad. This helps pay our debts today but foreign money someday will flow elsewhere. We then pay the price.

We import too much. How do we again control our economic life? How do we again compete in the world markets? Good products at a price which meets the worldwide competition is the probable answer. Improved plant, improved efficiency and possibly lower pay are required.

HISTORY OF FOREIGN TRADE

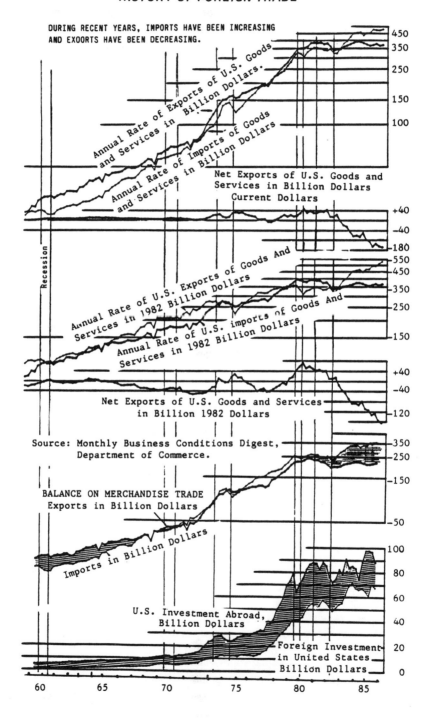

DURING RECENT YEARS, IMPORTS HAVE BEEN INCREASING
AND EXOORTS HAVE BEEN DECREASING.

Annual Rate of Exports of U.S. Goods
and Services in Billion Dollars.

Annual Rate of Imports of Goods
and Services in Billion Dollars

Net Exports of U.S. Goods and
Services in Billion Dollars
Current Dollars

Recession

Annual Rate of U.S. Exports of Goods And
Services in 1982 Billion Dollars

Annual Rate of U.S. Imports of Goods And
Services in 1982 Billion Dollars

Net Exports of U.S. Goods and Services
in Billion 1982 Dollars

Source: Monthly Business Conditions Digest,
Department of Commerce.

BALANCE ON MERCHANDISE TRADE
Exports in Billion Dollars

Imports in Billion Dollars

U.S. Investment Abroad,
Billion Dollars

Foreign Investment
in United States
Billion Dollars

INFLATION AND CONSUMER PRICE TRENDS

Most of the increases in prices, increase in wealth, increase in assets and pay are the result of inflation and are not true increases in purchasing power. Inflation increases all values and is an easy way to transfer wealth from the lender to the borrower. Government uses this technique to create a false illusion and make people feel good. True values vary with time and place and one should buy when price is low and sell when price of a single asset is relatively high so that money is made and wealth is increased. Gold and many other assets will purchase the same amount of goods as they purchased in about 1900.

The inflation index correlates with the national debt after adjusting for a time lag of several years as shown on a previously presented graph.

INFLATION – 1914 TO 1983

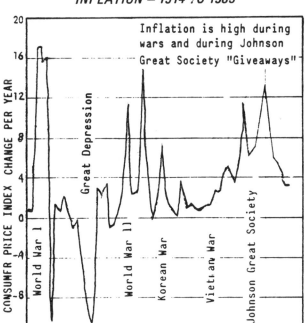

The Federal Reserve Board in the past has controlled the money supply as part of its effort to control inflation. Definitions have changed so that M_2 is probably a useable record of this effort.

Graphs showing the growth of money supply and the U. S. economy, the Gross National Product — Constant, 1972, Dollars, and Industrial Production, 1900 to 1980 follow on page 218.

The United States seems to prosper when the Gross National Product grows at a compounded rate of 3.1%.

The total Fed credit or the total reserve (Federal Bank Credit) is reported weekly in publications of the Federal Reserve Board. Basic information is also published weekly in Barrons' and the Wall Street Journal (Friday issue). You

GROWTH OF MONEY SUPPLY AND THE U. S. ECONOMY

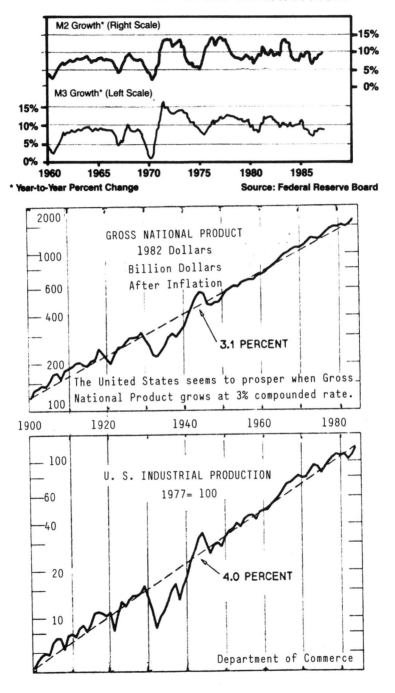

M2 Growth* (Right Scale)

15%
10%
5%
0%

M3 Growth* (Left Scale)

15%
10%
5%
0%

1960   1965   1970   1975   1980   1985

* Year-to-Year Percent Change   Source: Federal Reserve Board

2000
1000
600
400

200

100

GROSS NATIONAL PRODUCT
1982 Dollars
Billion Dollars
After Inflation

3.1 PERCENT

The United States seems to prosper when Gross National Product grows at 3% compounded rate.

1900   1920   1940   1960   1980

100
60
40

20

10

U. S. INDUSTRIAL PRODUCTION
1977= 100

4.0 PERCENT

Department of Commerce

might wish to continue the following table at least on a monthly basis. These data may be used to forecast changes in inflation.

Date	TOTAL FED CREDIT Billion Dollars (end of month)	Change in Dollars (Annualized basis)
December 1978	124.0	——
December 1979	140.7	13.5
December 1980	143.3	1.8
December 1981	151.9	6.0
December 1982	161.5	6.3
December 1983	173.0	7.1
December 1984	184.0	5.2
December 1985	204.5	11.1
December 1986	232.9	13.0

Some money growth is required to support a growing economy. When the increase in money supply is too small, the economy declines. When it is excessive, inflation often is the result. This index is one of the best tools to reflect possible inflation. Money supply in excess of GNP may increase stock prices.

A rapid increase in the Total Fed Credit often produces a spurt in business and product shortages which increase inflation. Gold prices often move in parallel with this index but there may be substantial time lags. Also, the Fed Credit may be changed before the effects are reflected in gold prices since the Federal Reserve Board tries to control the economy and business by use of changes in credit. Stock prices tend to increase during early stages of inflation when inflation is relatively low, say around 5% but high inflation is detrimental to stock prices. A decline in inflation is often associated with a decline in interest rates so that bond prices increase. Alternately, bond prices decline when inflation and interest rates are increasing.

In a one world economy, a change in business conditions in one country is reflected in the economy throughout the world, with major industrialized countries having the most importance. The changes do not always occur at the same time and the astute investor can make money by taking advantage of these differences. Watch changes in inflation indexes such as the changes in the consumer price index which is published for many countries on a monthly basis by the Department of Commerce.

Over long term history, inflation occurs when too much money chases too few products. Cost-pull inflation occurs when increasing cost of goods and labor push up prices which usually is associated with organized groups making unfair demands on society.

Three indexes are used to track inflation behavior:

1. Consumer Price Index or CPI
2. Gross National Product Deflator or GNP Deflator
3. Personal Consumption Expenditure Deflator or PCE.

Curves for inflation have been presented previously and the cumulative effect is shown on the graph on page 220.

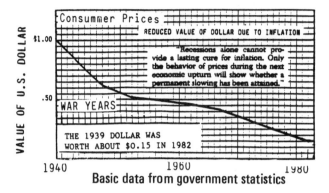

Basic data from government statistics

PURCHASING POWER

Year	Equal Value
1984	$1.00
1972	.45
1967	.33
1939	.13
1900	.09

$.09 in 1900 bought goods equal to $1.00 in 1984.

INFLATION DEVASTATES FIXED ASSETS AND SOME OTHER INVEST-
MENTS. LEARN TO MAKE MONEY WHEN TAX AND INFLATION ARE
HIGH.

Government "transfer of wealth" programs to the working poor are offset
by their loss caused by inflation. Training and jobs without inflation is an
alternative. HISTORY SHOWS THAT "RUN AWAY" INFLATION EVENTU-
ALLY RESULTS IN A MONETARY COLLAPSE — POSSIBLY A MAJOR
DEPRESSION FOLLOWS. Are conditions different today or will history repeat?
Some nations have used borrowed money and indexing when inflation has
exceeded 100% yearly.

Our forefathers saved to create the lifestyle which we enjoy today but
we allow government to live above our means and convey debt to our children.

Years of Major Inflation

0- 400
1150-1275
1500-1625
1755-1800
1900-1983 (Some years)

Some inflation has always been present unless the world or country is
experiencing a severe depression. The very high for U. S. inflation rate in the
1980s results from a "cartel" increase in the price of oil. Will other cartels be
formed to control prices of other products which they supply worldwide? We
will share our wealth with developing countries and this is a technique used.

Inflation is a hidden tax which can be very harmful to our economic
health. Cash and long term bonds are probably hurt the most by inflation.
Inflation hurts the wage earner even when wages are increased rapidly. The

businessperson and the investor often recognize the problem and they may have the knowledge to take defensive actions.

The Federal Reserve Board is trying to control inflation. Can it be successful in a worldwide economy?

LONG TERM WAGE AND INVESTMENT TRENDS
WAGE TRENDS IN THE UNITED STATES

Starting around 1940, wages increased rapidly during inflation periods and no adjustments were made in these trends until the "give backs" during the 1980s. These were caused by decreased government regulation and a need to make American industry competitive with the "worldwide economy". The standard of living after adjusting for both taxes and inflation increased rapidly before the 1970s. Since that time, effects of bracket creep caused by inflation and increases in social security taxes have been detrimental. The data show that wages after inflation but before taxes have remained rather constant since 1970 when expressed in constant value dollars. Increasing taxes have actually reduced the living standard of many families. The pay raises make us feel good but the wage earner has, in many cases, become poorer. High taxes and high inflation usually help few individuals or businesses. Study the following charts for details. Also note that there have been substantial changes in the workforce — women and youths entered and older men retired.

YOUR INCOME STATUS
Based on median income in 1983—

If Your Family Income is:	You Fall in This Bracket:
More than $75,000	Top 3%
More than $50,000	Top 13%
More than $40,000	Top 23%
More than $30,000	Top 39%
More than $25,000	Top 49%
Less than $20,000	Bottom 39%
Less than $15,000	Bottom 28%
Less than $10,000	Bottom 16%
Less than $5,000	Bottom 5%

Size of Average Family
Household size has declined

1790	5.79 persons/family
1900	4.78
1920	4.34
1940	3.57
1960	3.33
1980	2.75

Wages increased more rapidly than inflation
Rise of minimum wage in United States

1938	$0.25/hour
1939-45	0.35
1945-50	0.45
1950-56	0.75
1956-61	1.00
1961-63	1.15
1963-67	1.25
1967-68	1.40
1968-74	1.50
1974-75	2.00
1975-76	2.10
1976-78	2.30
1978-79	2.55
1979-80	2.90
1980-81	3.10
1981—	3.35

$3.35/0.25 — 13 fold for period 1939 to 1983.

A JOB IS YOUR BEST SECURITY. ALWAYS HAVE A JOB OR BUSINESS.

Unemployment increases during periods of recession.

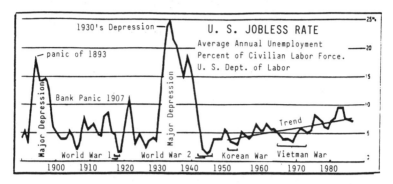

Basic data from government statistics

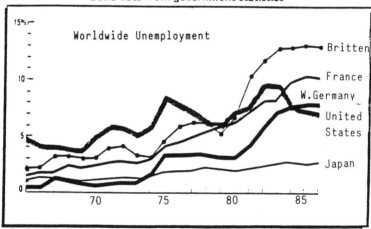

Basic data from government statistics

Investors are satisfied with a return after taxes and inflation of around 2% annually from investments made and retained over many years. More money is made by investing long term and by selling when prices are high and buying again when prices are relatively low. The trader and the short term investor have trouble keeping even over a period of time. You must study long term trends for individual assets and act as needed. Prices in current dollars often show substantial increase because of inflation effects but the true after-inflation and tax return may show a decline or small 2% increase during long periods. Inflation severely damages cash and bonds which are held over long time periods. Taxes damage everyone, including investors. Higher interest rates helps protect cash assets.

The past history often cannot be extrapolated to forecast the future. However, study of the past does provide background information which often helps avoid mistakes in the future.

Wages are our most important asset. Our knowledge and ability are very important investments. A graph showing the change in earnings of workers in the United States follows on page 223.

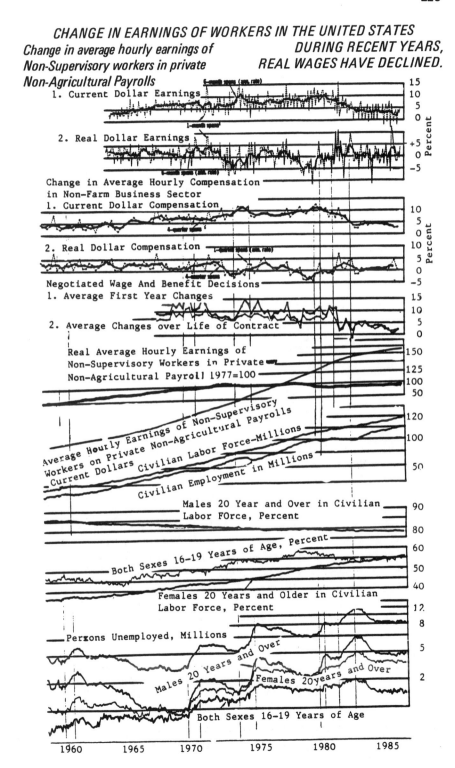

CHANGE IN EARNINGS OF WORKERS IN THE UNITED STATES DURING RECENT YEARS, REAL WAGES HAVE DECLINED.

Change in average hourly earnings of Non-Supervisory workers in private Non-Agricultural Payrolls

High unemployment insurance is blamed for part of the high unemployment. People look longer when they receive income. The increased number of youths and women, who were relatively inexperienced, reduced efficiency and increased costs so that foreign competition was greater. They also may have reduced the quality of the product so that Americans bought more foreign products. The American jobs also changed and training was required to increase costs and reduce efficiency. Regardless of the cause, American industry moved overseas and many jobs may have been permanently lost. As foreign wages increase and fewer new people enter the American workforce, quality and efficiency should improve and some reversal might be seen. Also, Americans might be taught to buy American products again, even at a higher price. We need more high paying, non-service jobs and we need to manufacture our cars and other products so that we have a base in case of war.

INTEREST RATES, OR THE PRICE OF MONEY

Values shown are for a dollar at any desired point in time. The true value of the dollar has declined with time as a result of inflation.

PURCHASING POWER

Year	Cents Required to Purchase Dollar
1984	100
1972	45
1967	33
1939	15
1900	9

RETURN ON LONG TERM BONDS BEFORE INFLATION ADJUSTMENT

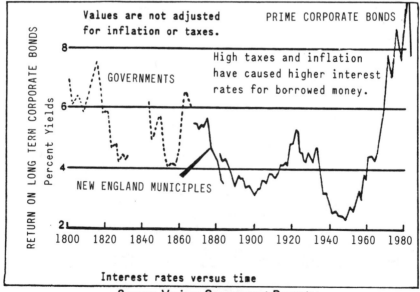

Source: Various Government Reports

Owning dollars or very short-term dollar investments is good during a depression. Most businesses selling on credit are hurt by high interest rates and inflation. Home construction declines when interest rates are high and so do most jobs.

The decline from a peak interest rate occurs within a few months on all interest indicators. Federal Funds decline first, followed by Treasury bills and notes (time to buy corporate bonds), the prime rate, discount rate (time to buy stocks), and mortgage rates. Corporate bond interest often is the last to decline.

HISTORY OF INTEREST RATES

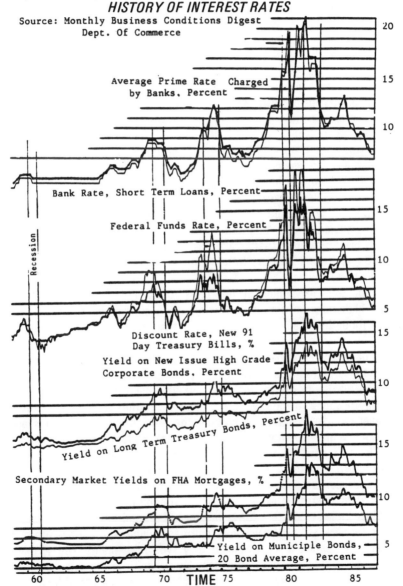

BOND PRICES

Bonds must be bought at the correct time — when interest rates are at high values.

The redemption value at a time specified on the bond and the interest rate to be earned in the period between the time when the bond is issued and the time when the bond is redeemed are both fixed values determined when initially sold. Unfortunately, interest rates in the marketplace vary with values of rates of inflation. The marketplace adjusts the value of the bond if sold at a time other than the redemption date so that the bond has values based on market-place interest rates. Thus, the sales price of the bond may be higher or lower than the face value redemption price shown on the bond.

Inflation also reduces the purchasing power of the dollar so that the money originally invested has less value when purchasing needed items when the bond is converted into cash. The amount is equal to the total amount of the inflation during many years. The interest rate earned on the bond is fixed so that the interest earned is less than the market rates when interest rates and inflation rates are high.

Throughout history, inflation has been present in varying amounts when considered over longer periods of time. There has been some inflation during periods of recession during recent years. A decline in inflation did occur during part of the 1930's depression. Rates of inflation also have tended to increase with time and so have interest rates as shown on curves presented previously.

It is obvious that a long term investment in bonds, if made when interest rates are low, is often a disaster. Investment in short-term, money market fund, bank CDs, and short Treasury bills is superior since these do take advantage of changing interest rates.

Long term investment in long term bonds when interest rates are at an all-time high may be a satisfactory long term conservative investment if the bonds cannot be recalled at a date earlier than that shown on the face of the bond. The investor retains a high interest rate based on the face value and the sales value of the bond has increased as long as interest rates remain lower than the value shown on the bond face.

The maximum loss occurs when bonds bought when interest rates were low must be sold at a time far earlier than redemption date when interest rates are higher than face values. At such time, the selling price of the bond is low and there is a loss on face value. The investor also takes a loss in purchasing power of the dollar as related to overall inflation and he also has received a low rate of interest return. The investor is hit with the worst of all possible factors.

Bonds can be an excellent short term trading device. Bonds are simply bought when interest rates are high or when bond price is low. The bonds are sold when interest rates are lower or when the bond price has increased. The investor receives a capital gain type return although his interest return may be less than that available from other money type investments. Today, there are many types of bonds and performance may differ from the above description.

There are also other factors which influence the behavior of bond type investments. As an example, the company may cease to exist or its bond rating may decline. Bonds usually can be sold at market price.

History of Banking Industry

Banks lend your deposits to others. Their cash reserves are small and they borrow from the Federal Reserve when they need added cash. In 1986, banks are not liquid.

Commercial banks also create money and they lend much more than their actual deposits when complying with Federal Banking Regulations. Some commercial banks are able to lend seven times the cash reserves left in Federal Reserve accounts. In 1987, many banks and savings and loan organizations are financially in trouble as indicated by the following graph showing annual banking losses of troubled banks.

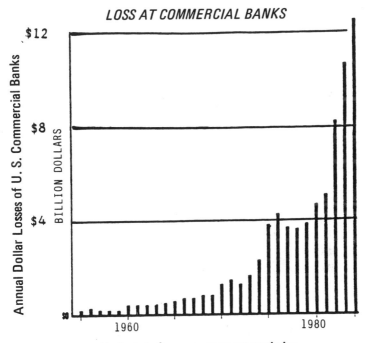

LOSS AT COMMERCIAL BANKS

Basic data from government statistics

Small banks and savings and loan organizations are allowed to fail but large banks are protected by the government. The FDIC will eventually refund your insured deposit up to $100,000 — just like it promised to. *But it never promised to give you your money back when you want it. . .or need it.*

You probably won't be able to retrieve your money all at once. Very large banks are not allowed to default because the effect of a bank holiday on major stock, bond and commodities markets will be drastic. The Dow will plummet 200 to 300 points immediately and all markets will shut down completely. . .at least temporarily while the banking system is being patched back together. When cash is large, use several "banks".

Will inflation follow, or will it be depression?

STOCK PRICES

Stock prices often are low when inflation and interest rates are relatively high. At low interest rates, stock prices depend upon earnings and dividends but bonds compete with stocks when interest rates are high. Stocks also declined during the 1930's depression.

High inflation hurts stocks.

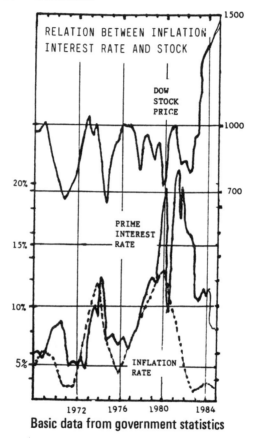

Basic data from government statistics

STOCK PRICES AT TIMES VARY AS AN INVERSE OF THE INTEREST RATE. AT OTHER TIMES, STOCK PRICES IGNORE INTEREST RATES AND RELATE WITH EARNINGS, DIVIDENDS AND OTHER FACTORS. A relation with declining interest rates is often noticed during early stages of an increase in business activity. The relationship with earnings is seen six months to a year before a decline in stock prices.

Stock prices have been increasing in most countries but the increase has not been at the same rates and there are time lags. These differences offer investment opportunities.

In the 25 years ending December 1985, the S&P 500 had a compound annual gain after inflation of 4.2%, while the Solomon High Grade Bond Index during the same 25 year period had a compound annual return after inflation of 0.8%. Values do not adjust for taxes. Taxes are paid on income before adjusting for inflation.

To make money, you cannot simply buy and hold over long time periods. You must learn to "buy near lows" and sell when the prices are high. Alternate investments to conform with expected performance in different economic environments.

Results of the regression analysis shown below suggest that Dow Jones Industrials price relates with the change in dividends, earnings and bond yields.

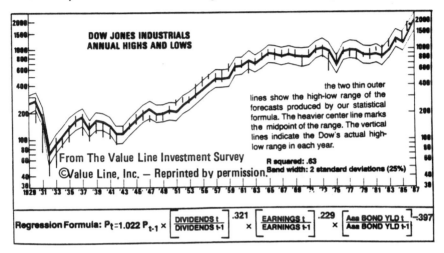

DOW JONES INDUSTRIALS
ANNUAL HIGHS AND LOWS

the two thin outer lines show the high-low range of the forecasts produced by our statistical formula. The heavier center line marks the midpoint of the range. The vertical lines indicate the Dow's actual high-low range in each year.

From The Value Line Investment Survey
©Value Line, Inc. — Reprinted by permission.

R squared: .63
Band width: 2 standard deviations (25%)

Regression Formula: $P_t = 1.022\ P_{t-1} \times \left[\dfrac{DIVIDENDS\ t}{DIVIDENDS\ t-1}\right]^{.321} \times \left[\dfrac{EARNINGS\ t}{EARNINGS\ t-1}\right]^{.229} \times \left[\dfrac{Aaa\ BOND\ YLD\ t}{Aaa\ BOND\ YLD\ t-1}\right]^{-.397}$

MILESTONES FOR STOCKS

January 12, 1906	$ 100.25
March 12, 1956	500.24
November 14, 1972	1003.16
December 11, 1985	1511.70
January 8, 1987	2002.25

Values before tax and inflation

Long term performance trends of a fund are a better indication of future behavior of a fund than the performance during the past six months or a year. Look for long term performance to select a good manager of your funds. He may be able to repeat. Be certain that he continues to manage the fund.

Wars, depressions and inflation, when very high, all hurt stock prices. The effect of recent inflation on stock price is shown on page 230.

Business reflecting use of tools has grown even after adjusting for inflation. Stock market prices in general reflect business growth.

A graph showing stock prices in Great Britain and the United States in the time period 1700 through 2000 follows the Standard and Poors 500 Stock Performance graph on page 230. The 1985 values should be divided by about 10 to obtain values comparable to 1900 values.

Interest rates all move together with a slight delay. Federal funds often decline first; followed by treasury bills, prime rate, discount rate, mortgage rates and corporate bonds. This is shown on the graph on page 231.

STANDARD AND POORS 500 STOCK PERFORMANCE

Sources: New York Stock Exchange for stock prices and Department of Commerce for inflation data. Available from Dow Jones Publications.

Source: London and New York Stock Exchanges

The 1985 values should be divided by about 10 to obtain values comparable to 1900 values.

INTEREST RATES ALL MOVE TOGETHER WITH SLIGHT DELAY
FEDERAL FUNDS OFTEN DECLINE FIRST, FOLLOWED BY
TREASURY BILLS, PRIME RATE, DISCOUNT RATE,
MORTGAGE RATES AND CORPORATE BONDS

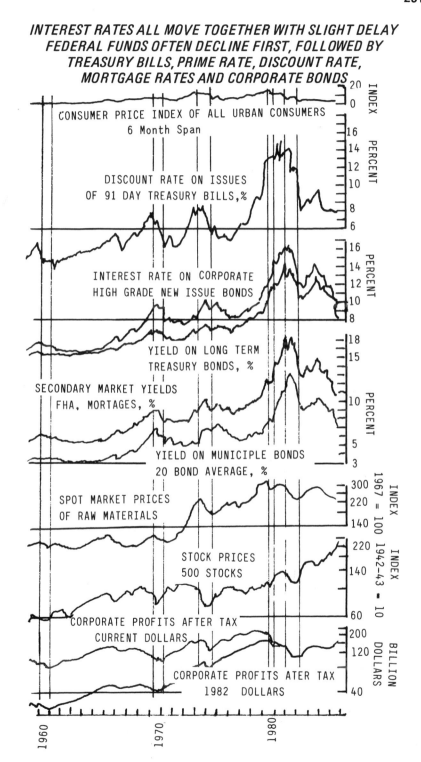

CONSUMER PRICE INDEX OF ALL URBAN CONSUMERS
6 Month Span

DISCOUNT RATE ON ISSUES
OF 91 DAY TREASURY BILLS,%

INTEREST RATE ON CORPORATE
HIGH GRADE NEW ISSUE BONDS

YIELD ON LONG TERM
TREASURY BONDS, %

SECONDARY MARKET YIELDS
FHA, MORTGAGES, %

YIELD ON MUNICIPLE BONDS
20 BOND AVERAGE, %

SPOT MARKET PRICES
OF RAW MATERIALS

STOCK PRICES
500 STOCKS

CORPORATE PROFITS AFTER TAX
CURRENT DOLLARS

CORPORATE PROFITS ATER TAX
1982 DOLLARS

232

Investors use many indexes when evaluating stocks. Several are shown below. Others are given throughout this text.

HISTORY OF SOME INDEXES RELATED TO STOCKS

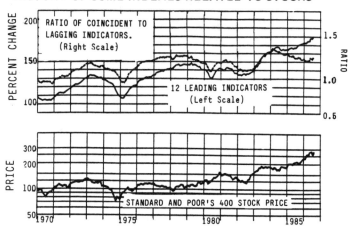

Source: Government and N.Y. Stock market Statistics.

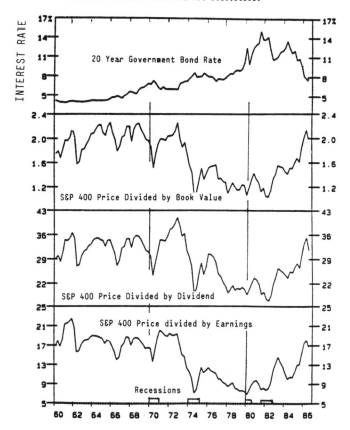

LAND PRICE TRENDS
VERY ROUGH VALUES FOR ILLINOIS FARMLAND

Year	Value Per Acre	Percent of Debt Service Covered By Rents
1960	$ 650	60
1965	750	65
1970	900	50
1975	1750	80
1980	3500	30
1985	1800	50

1986 land prices remain above the top of the long term channel.

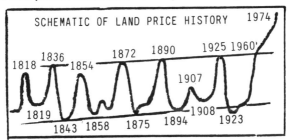

Basic data from government statistics

Land prices have been high for years. Return based on return from crops has been poor since the 1950s. However, appreciation has been substantial and land has been a good investment if bought at the low point of price cycles. Overall, land price increase has exceeded inflation.

Study of curves for long term inflation suggest that the land price channel before 1960 is for a period without major inflation. Also, major inflation often is not entirely corrected by later depression. Thus, the high price increases after 1970 may not require complete correction.

Farm prices, a commodity, increased during the 1970's inflation and so did land prices. An adjustment is noted during the 1980s. In 1985, farmers are learning that excessive debt and expansion cause trouble when land prices are too high. The farmer can make money on his investment or on his work effort. Not both.

HOME PRICE TRENDS

The price of the average home in 1965 was below $25,000. In 1986, the average home is selling for more than $100,000. Values differ substantially by city and location in cities. The Average price increase has been greater than the inflation rates.

The apartment owner, like the farmer, has trouble making a fair return on the necessary investment. Tax shelters are part of the problem since laws enabled the investor to make money by reduction of taxes. The Federal Government simply paid part of the purchase price. Some inflation hedge is also probable in housing prices. These purchases are complicated by housing for the poor, zoning restrictions, foreign investment as well as by the usual supply and demand of the marketplace for both the investor and the renter. A simple desire for security related to real investments also tends to increase prices during times of economic uncertainty.

Values after inflation adjustment are required when seeking true growth in value of investments. Much of the price increase in value of investments is merely the result of inflation without any increase in true values.

RARE COINS AND GOLD PRICES

At a market bottom, gold and silver bullion prices will be low; inflation will be low; coin prices will be at cheap levels; dealers will be broke (some will be going bankrupt); and the last thing on your mind will be purchasing more coins. Note that this scenario is identical to the last two major market bottoms (1976 and 1982).

The price history for gold is shown below:

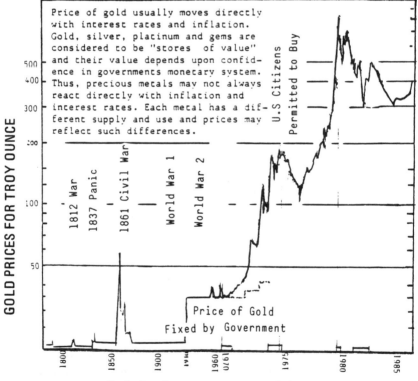

Basic data from government statistics.

Gold may be bought as coins, bars, certificates, mutual funds and other methods, including the Precious Metals Central Fund of Canada and on the American Stock Exchange. Grading of coins is being standardized and they are now bought over the telephone using numbers of the rare coin designated by grading group.

RULES FOR ACCUMULATING WEALTH

Have a sound plan adjusted for taxes, inflation and risks.

Write the goal on paper — then determine whether it meets your needs, is realistic, specific, measurable. MAKE LIFE INTERESTING BY STRIVING FOR A GOAL.

Look at the plan using the general approach — what is my strategy or method for getting it accomplished? How do I get from here to there?

Determine the value of achieving the goal — what are the benefits and rewards which will be received? What unmet needs will satisfy? Are the aims and rewards sufficient to force me to see the plan to its accomplishment? Make a real commitment and stick with the plan.

Determine the activities needed to accomplish the goals — what must I do to reach my goals? How will I know when my goal has been accomplished?

Make a detailed plan or flow sheet — diagram showing the barriers -- both mental and physical — which must be overcome. Recognize the hardships and work needed to reach your goals. Believe that you can achieve the goal which you have determined to be necessary. MAKE YOUR GOAL YOUR HOBBY — A FUN EXPERIENCE.

Review your resources — determine the time, money, people, skills, information, your energy, etc. needed to reach your objectives. What is needed to overcome the obstacles and accomplish the tasks?

Establish a time frame for each part of the required work. Make it realistic but do not be surprised if the actual time is somwhat longer. Unless you have experience, the time required may be twice your estimate.

Keep track in writing of each of your little accomplishments. Ask whether your activities are leading to desired results. Change details when necessary.

Learn to study, assemble information, think, plan and act. There is no "free lunch." Keep trying and work.

Be honest in your evaluations — with yourself and others. Learn to accept your responsibilities. Take care of yourself today and plan for retirement. Plan today. YOU CANNOT ACCOMPLISH WITHOUT TRYING — GIVE LIFE YOUR BEST.

Many investment advisors recommend the relation between investment type and the business cycle as shown on the schematic on page 236. The indicated investments should be bought before business enters a phase and sold near the end of the phase.

There are long term and short term business or economic cycles. You must be aware of their existence and adjust your business and investments as required to profit from them. Your wages also may be dependent upon these cycles. Certainly increases in wages and salary depend upon a successful business climate. It is normal for companies to hire too many during up-turns and fire people during recessions. Managers, too, are lazy and inefficient. They like to play golf and loaf.

History suggests that you should hold cash and interest rate mediums such as bonds, T-bills and money funds during the recession phase. During the growth phase, you should be invested in securities such as growth stocks, mutual funds,

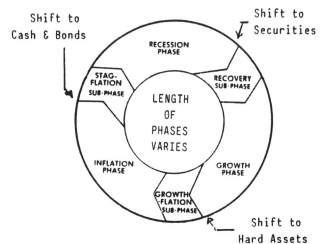

your business commodities and real estate. Hard assets should be held during the inflation phase, such as gold and silver, mining stocks, rare coins, collectibles and possibly foreign currencies. Of course, history may not always repeat.

Real estate and your business are sound investments. They do require steady management and are not saleable on short notice. They are not liquid assets. Each is complicated and their purchase, sale and management require study of many pages. Good books are available in the library and from government commissions. Real estate cannot be taken with you when you move. Even a home can be difficult to sell.

Selecting the broad category of investments for each phase of the business cycle is relatively easy. Picking the specific investment and the time to make the selection is more difficult.

You might manage your investments using the above business cycle or using many other techniques. Value Line Investment Service has developed a statistical technique giving results shown on the figure on page 237.

Value Line, in 1984, offered monthly disks with data for 32 variables on 1650 stocks. Their software permits ranking of stocks based on nine variables. Also, changes in rank on the graph on page 237 are published weekly in Value Line reports. They also have a fund using the techniques and published screens.

You may also have others manage your money. Mutual funds is one possibility. Value Line and Danforth Associates offer personal management services. Other groups such as Wall Street Digest offer supervision of assets.

Organizations of professional planners include:

1. International Association for Financial Planning, 5775 Peachtree Dunwoody Road, N.E., Atlanta, Georgia 30342

2. The Institute of Certified Planners, 3443 South Galena, Denver, Colorado 80231.

3. National Association of Personal Financial Planners, 125 Wilke Road, Arlington Heights, Illinois 60005.

Write them if you need help.

REMEMBER THAT INFLATION IS ALWAYS REDUCING THE VALUE

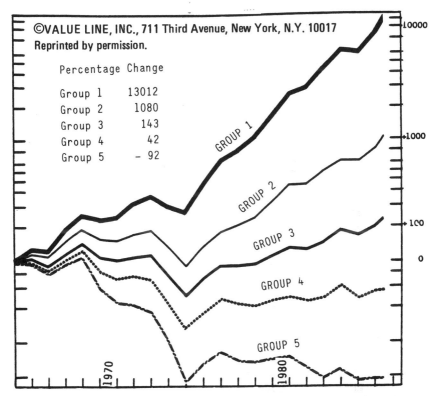

PERFORMANCE OF STOCKS
VALUE LINE RANKING FOR TIMELINESS
ALLOWING FOR CHANGES IN RANK

237

©VALUE LINE, INC., 711 Third Avenue, New York, N.Y. 10017
Reprinted by permission.

Percentage Change

Group 1   13012
Group 2   1080
Group 3   143
Group 4   42
Group 5   − 92

OF YOUR ASSETS WHILE YOU ARE LOOKING AT THE OTHER INFLU-
ENCES. TAXES WILL ALSO CATCH UP WITH YOU WHEN YOU SELL.

The public, market technicians, stockbrokers, etc. all seem to be ultra-bullish at market tops and very bearish or pessimistic at bottoms of the business cycle. Investor's intelligence has found that stocks on average are cheap when 65% of investment advisory services publish negative recommendations. When they are over 75% negative, it is likely that a major reversal will occur within several months. The same applies on upside. If 65% of the advisory services issue favorable recommendations, be ready to sell stock or place stop orders carefully. If over 70% are favorable, sell stocks in expectation of a decline during a few months. Likewise, a cash position of 10% by mutual funds suggests a rise in market prices. Mutual funds are near 100% invested in stocks and bonds at market tops.

The stock trader who tries to make a profit from short time swings in the market — emotions of the marketplace — usually loses money. Trends which indicate recessions versus good times are easier to detect but the detection may be late since the stock market is a leading indicator.

Exercise care when buying stocks selling at historic highs or lows. Most of the highs will back off for a better buying opportunity, and the lows are better bought after they have started up again.

Beware of small, obscrue O-T-C stocks. They are super when they make it, but the risks are higher than most people think. The majority of these companies lack the management depth and the capital necessary to turn good products or services into great ones.

Stay away from most stocks selling under $10.00 a share.

Make certain that at least three to five researchers follow each company.

Look up the historic P/E ratios. Most companies tend to have multiples that fluctuate in a fairly narrow range. When the P/E ratio is above the norm, be sure it's justified. When the stock is selling below its average multiple — and there is no particular reason for it — you may get an extra kicker.

Watch under-leveraged companies for the potential mergers, acquisitions, leveraged buyouts, stock buy-back programs.

Make sure the expected earnings increases come from regular operations and not from one-shot accounting changes.

Three consecutive changes in the same direction in the Gross National Product — GNP - is considered to confirm a change in the direction of the economy.

Unfortunately for the investor, the stock market is a leading indicator and the bond loan rate is a lagging indicator. The investor must find other indexes. Some of these include:

1. Charts for stocks may be studied using plots prepared by Value Line and others in the hope of finding a very few stocks which seem to be free of business cycles. Several other assets seem to do well regardless of the state of the economy. Land in well located cities, rare coins, a few stocks are possible candidates. You may find others, including your business.

2. Some investment advisors use computers to screen many investments and indexes and try to develop theory and indexes which give the time for an investment such as the stock market. Cross-plots of indexes can give relationships if adjusted for time lags.

    The cross plot showing stock market performance and interest rates presented earlier should be reviewed.

3. Some assets have price changes related with the rate of inflation. The rate of change in the inflation index might then prove useful.

4. Experience has shown that business cycles often have a life of around 4-5 years and that uptrend is somewhat longer than the decline. Stocks often show three upward stages and two downward.

5. Some investments and some stocks lag the economy and they can be related to the economy. There is a definite rotation of the leadership of stock groups and such relations are used by the knowledgeable investor.

6. Most investors do not have the ability to successfully speculate with stocks. To reduce risks, some investors place 90% of their money in safe investments and speculate with 10% in the options market.

You cannot expect to be an expert investor after reading this short section. You might also study many specialized books available from your library. Study screens and charts — Value Line.

7. Since most money is made by the average stock market investor when the "market as a whole" is moving rapidly, you might make your selections early in the economic cycle and wait for the move which will occur at the proper time on the investment clock. You may catch the major profit intervals while making a modest gain during the holding period when the market is dull. As a minimum, you should always be prepared to react quickly when a major market move begins. As an example, during many past years, a major stock market move follows three changes in the "discount rate" within 3 to 9 months. The Fed's recent emphasis on money supply may distort this index.

8. Study the past indexes of the market for probable range in indexes at market tops and bottoms. Also, use the past trends or channels for individual stocks to determine probable buy and sell prices.

Summarizing, you should:

1. Know what you are doing.
2. Diversify, but not too much. Use 10 to 15 stocks in at least eight industry groups.
3. Buy when prices are relatively low. Investment cost is lower.
4. Sell when prices become too high.
5. Keep tax at minimum values. Know tax law or hire experts.
6. Let your profits run but do keep track of trends and sell near tops.
7. Remember the 90% of all short investors lose money eventually.
8. Try to avoid loss of capital by knowing risks and using "stops".
9. Have the necessary patience. Delay buying for price pull-backs but do learn to act when appropriate in both buying and selling. Study stock trends and values. When buying, remember that there are other stocks and that market values do change.

Know the value of money as related with time. THE MOST IMPORTANT FACT THAT YOU WILL EVER LEARN IS ON THE GRAPH ON PAGE 240. STUDY IT CAREFULLY. LEARN THE VALUE OF MONEY AND KNOW HOW THE INTEREST EARNED ON THE INVESTED DOLLAR GROWS. LEARN HOW TO ADJUST FOR TAXES, INFLATION AND RISK. USE YOUR HIGHEST TAX BRACKET IN YOUR DECISIONS.

The graph does not include adjustments for risk, taxes or inflation. Recognizing the compound growth of investments and interest on money is basic to accumulation of wealth. Always consider effects of taxes, risks and inflation in all decisions.

Following the 1986 tax law revisions, REIT investments may be attractive. Contact Sierra Capital Realty Trust and The Cedar Income Fund. For stocks, review data from Value Line and Long Term Values, Box 24933, Las Nageles, California 90024.

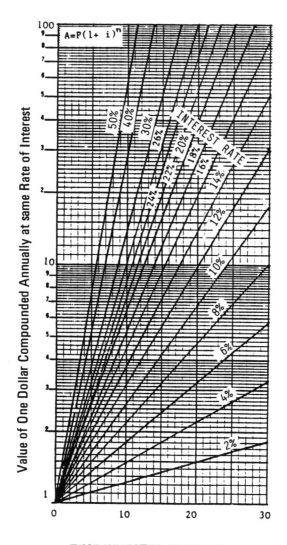

TIME INVESTED IN YEARS

Know growth and its determination. Plot your data on the graph shown on page 241. Draw the best possible straight line through data points. Determine with triangles the slope on the existing graph which best matches the data so plotted. This slope is the growth rate.

LOOK FOR ASSETS WHICH HAVE A SOUND, LONG TERM GROWTH RATE. ALWAYS KNOW YOUR CASH FLOW AND VALUE OF YOUR TOTAL ASSETS BUT DO NOT TELL OTHERS.

Know average values for important parameters affecting your business, such as the values for stocks, as shown on page 241.

React promptly to major changes in inflation, interest rates, business cycles, political trends, etc.

DETERMINATION OF GROWTH RATE

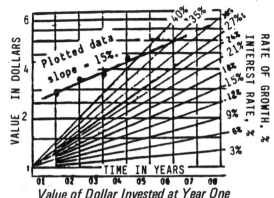

Value of Dollar Invested at Year One
Base Curves Plotted From Interest Tables
Plotted Data Have Same Slope as 15% Interest Line

AVERAGES FOR YEARS 1920 to 1981 – Dow Jones Industrials
(Some data exclude years 1921, 1931 and 1933)

Price/Earnings ratio	13.7%	–	Range since 1950	7-22%*
Price/Dividend ratio	22.5			13.30%*
Cash/Total Invested:				
Money Managers				8-17%
Mutual Funds				7-12%
Earned on Book Value	11.3			8-13%*
Earnings yield	7.7			5-15%*
Dividend yield	4.7			3-6%*
Earnings Growth Rate	5.5			
Dividend Growth Rate	4.4		*Lows occur at bottoms of business	
Book Value Growth Rate	5.2		Highs near crests.	
Earnings Yield/Earnings Growth	13.2%			
Dividend Yield/Dividend Growth	9.1%			
Moody's Aaa Bond Yield	5.0%			
Inflation rate CPI	2.5			

Recognize that investments have differing cycles and sell high and buy low.

The investment world presents many good opportunities for the knowledgeable and astute investor as shown on the figures on page 242.

TAKE ADVANTAGE OF THE CHANGE IN PRICES. Note that the peaks and lows do not all occur at the same time. Prices of commodities rotate. The same is true for different stock and bond groups.

STUDY CYCLES FOR INDIVIDUAL SELL AND BUY POINTS. TRY TO BUY NEAR LOWS AND SELL NEAR HIGHS. PRICE OF A SINGLE ASSET OR STOCK RISES AND FALLS IN CYCLES AND THE NET GROWTH USUALLY IS NOT SUFFICIENT TO OFFSET THE DETRIMENT OF INFLATION AND POSSIBLY TAXES.

242

INVESTMENT MEDIUMS PEAK AND EBB AT DIFFERENT TIMES

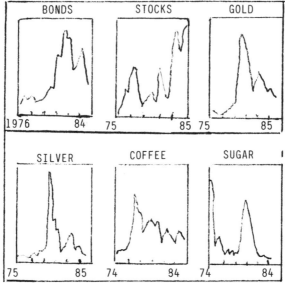

Basic data from government statistics

Average Annual Total Return During Various Time Periods
Before Taxes and Inflation — Starting in 1986

Time Period	S&P 500	Bonds	Treasury Bills
Last 40 Years	11.2%	3.8%	4.8%
Last 30 Years	9.5	5.3	5.8
Last 20 Years	8.7	6.7	7.3
Last 10 Years	14.3	9.8	9.0
Last 5 Years	14.7	17.8	10.3

Over the long term, the annual return on stocks is higher than on bonds or Treasury Bills. The exception is during the last 5 years when interest rates declined rapidly.

A lender and investor usually does not make an investment in a company unless return is 10% to 15% before tax and inflation depending upon expected minor risks. The conservative investor and lender demands around 2% return after adjusting for taxes and inflation.

Learn to recognize business cycles and adjust your actions accordingly. Patience and longer term viewpoint are involved. See chart on the inflation and business cycles on page 243. CHANGE YOUR INVESTMENTS TO TAKE ADVANTAGE OF BUSINESS CYCLES.

See also how investments fare in different economic environments when the cycle is divided into recessionary, growth and inflation phases as shown on the table on page 243. CYCLES ARE NOT ALWAYS IDENTICAL. Prices of commodities usually increases during growth and inflation phases. Labor in the past has not responded to any part of the cycle but in 1984, with deregulation, the price of labor has declined.

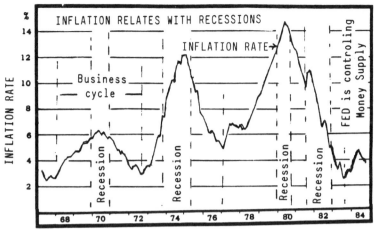

Basic data from government statistics

HOW INVESTMENTS FARE IN DIFFERENT ECONOMIC ENVIRONMENTS WHEN THE CYCLE IS DIVIDED INTO RECESSIONARY, GROWTH AND INFLATION PHASES

	Recession	Growth	Inflation
Rare Coins	Good	Excellent	Excellent
Bullion	Poor	Marginal	Excellent
Mining Stocks	Poor	Marginal	Good
Foreign Currencies	Poor	Poor	Good
Real Estate	Poor	Marginal	Good
Common Stocks	Poor	Excellent	Marginal
Penny Stocks	Marginal	Excellent	Good
Growth Stocks	Poor	Excellent	Marginal
Mutual Funds	Marginal	Excellent	Good
Bonds	Good	Marginal	Poor
T-Bills	Good	Marginal	Poor

CAN THE FEDERAL RESERVE BOARD CONTROL CYCLES BY AD-JUSTING MONEY SUPPLY OVER THE LONG TERM?

Recognize how inflation is created by banks. Whenever the government fails to balance the budget, it must find money elsewhere to finance its deficits. Historically, the government's favorite method of financing or "monetizing" the debt is by creating money "out of thin air". The Federal Reserve does this by writing checks to buy government bonds — checks that are backed by nothing and end up being deposited in American banks. The checks then become "bank reserves" that allow commercial banks to "create" billions of dollars that never existed before and loan them to private citizens, business and to the *government.*

Devise a workable strategy such as the five shown on the graph on page 244 for stocks. Combinations of several strategies may be desired.

There are many types of investments and the strategies used are many

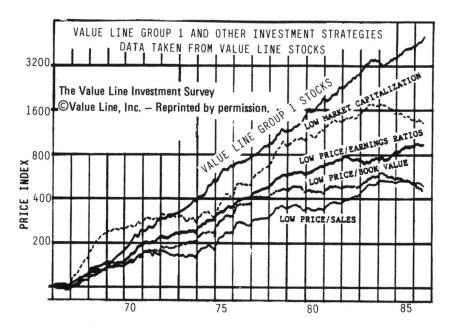

and depend upon individuals. Business cycles and investment environment also are important.

Know the basic rules, such as the following:

Learn the art of *"buying near long term lows and selling near long term highs".*

Beware of investments that look too good for risks involved.

Be patient. Do not switch too often. Select properly instead.

When everyone agrees, they are likely wrong. No money is left to buy.

Always consider effects of taxes and inflation in decisions.

Study behavior of people — the majority run with the crowd and do not think. Practical thinkers are successful.

Know all the rules of the investment medium in which you invest.

Learn from successful investors — follow the methods of the rich.

Getting rich is a do-it-yourself effort. You must try.

You can make money in both good and bad markets.

Believe that you, too, can make a million — keep trying.

Owning your single family home is the best investment.

Learn leveraging — the art of making money on bor-
rowed assets.
Make investing a hobby creating fun, satisfaction and
wealth.
Learn to take advantage of inflation — it is always
present.
Learn to reduce your taxes legally. Know tax laws.
Save — You need money to make money — Know
interest rates.
Know values and indexes for your investment me-
diums.
Be certain that your bank is safe.

To find out whether your bank is safe, obtain a recent annual statement and financial statement. Then check these figures:

Net operating income to average assets. An acceptable ratio for regional banks is 1 percent; for money-center banks, 0.5 percent; for savings and loans, 0.25 percent.

Net operating income to average equity. Average is 14 percent to 15 percent for banks and 6.8 percent for S&Ls.

Loan losses. Anything above 0.5 percent is above normal.

Non-performing assets to total loans. The FDIC's bank standard is 1 percent.

Loan-loss allowance to total loans. For banks, 1 percent is considered adequate; for S&Ls, 1 percent to 1.5 percent.

Primary capital (capital plus loan-loss allowance) to assets. The FDIC considers 5 percent a minimum for banks, 3 percent for S&Ls.

Loans to deposits. The FDIC considers anything over 70 percent unhealthy; 5 percent of deposits should be in cash or short-term investments.

Since deregulation, theft and fraud seem to be easier. Commercial banks use "reserves" as basis for loans which greatly exceed "reserves" as allowed under existing laws. "Reserves" allow banks to "print" money legally by making loans far in excess of their deposits. Is this the same as trading in futures and sale of "naked"options when security is poor?

Manage mutual funds when money/time/experience are limited. Learn and keep trying — do not allow a defeat to deter you. Use successful specialists — do not spend money educating your lawyer, accountant, broker, etc. They should know their specialty and offer sound guidance. Diversify to ten stocks to reduce risks. Always retain the ability to repay current obligations.

The big secret about millionaires is that they keep their wealth a secret. Most don't drive a Cadillac, Mercedes or other luxury car, and most don't even live in a big, expensive home. When asked why they live such low profile lives, the overwhelming majority said it was because they are basically conservative, modest folks who believe in hard work, family values and religious principles. They prefer quiet evenings at home with the family to racing in the fast lane.

Many people live beyond their ability to repay. A monthly income can be used to obtain loans and mortgages. The money can be used for daily living rather than investments. Unless the debt is also supported by saleable assets, hard times and possibly bankruptcy should be anticipated during periods of low economic activity since jobs may be lost and other income may be less during recessions. Jobs are often lost. Price of all assets rises and falls with time. Beware when you borrow.

Timing of Investments. The time at which investments are made often determines success. Mr. Martin Zweig, a successful investment advisor, gives the following advice in a book "Winning on Wall Street." He suggests use of monetary, momentum and crowd indicators as follows:

Monetary Indicators

1. Prime rate.

    A buy signal is given by a cut in prime rate of banks when the value is less than 8%. If the prime rate is higher than 8%, two cuts or a cut of 1% is required.

    A sell signal is indicated by an increase in prime rate when the prime rate is 8% or more. If the prime rate is below 8%, a sell signal is given by two consecutive hikes or by a full 1% change at a single date.

2. The FED Indicator.

    This indicator has been used by many analysts for years. The indicator is today based on changes in the discount rate and in reserve requirements of banks combined.

    a. Discount rate. About 3 changes occur during an average year. A cut in the discount rate that follows a rise in the discount rate or comes after a stable period of two years is a buy signal.

    b. The same procedures are followed when changes are made in reserve requirements of banks supervised by the Federal Reserve Board. Change in margin requirements of stockbrokers is omitted since such changes are too rare today.

    The FED indicator is calculated by adding the values for the discount rate and reserve requirements. The scoring technique varies. Mr. Zweig's book and articles by others should be studied.

3. Installment Debt Indicator. Use year-to-year basis using monthly data. Basic data are obtained from Federal Reserve Statistical Release G-19, obtained from Publications Department, Federal Reserve Board, Twentieth and Constitution Avenues, NW, Washington, DC 20551. The simple procedure divides the value of a year ago by this month's value. Subtract one from the result so that you have values in percent.

    When values have been falling and reach 9%, a buy signal is indicated. When the past change is upward and values reach 9%, a sell signal is given.

Momentum Indicators

1. Advance-Decline Indicator.

    Record daily NYSE stocks which advance and decline in price. Divide daily advances by the daily declines. Review a 10 day record. A strong but rare move upward in momentum is indicated when the ratio reaches 2 to 1. This signal is a rare occurrence and is a strong buy signal. The reverse also is a sell signal. Lower values for the ratio are poorer signals. False signals can occur.

2. Volume Indicator.

Record daily NYSE uptick volume and downtick volume. Divide the ups by the downs. A ratio of 9 to 1 upside often is a buy signal but there have been reverses or false signals.

3. The 4% Model Indicator.

Record the weekly closes of the VALUE LINE INDEX and determine the weekly change expressed as a percent. A buy signal is indicated when the value is 4% upward and a sell signal is given when the change downward exceeds 4%. Watch for small changes in the 4% change which may be false signals.

These three indicators may be combined, as proposed by Mr. Zweig.

Crowd Indicators

The crowd is often wrong and following indexes are useful.

1. Mutual Fund Indicator.

Use ratio of cash divided by assets as shown in Barron's weekly reports. When the ratio reaches an undetermined low value, a market top may be approaching. A value of 10% may be a buy signal.

2. Barron's Ads.

Simply count ads appearing in each issue and record bearish and bullish nature. When bullish ads exceed about 13 per issue, expect a bear market.

Seasonal Indicators

For reasons which are often not understood, the market tends to rise when:

1. The first trading day is after Thanksgiving and Christmas.
2. When the day is before a major holiday such as Labor Day and New Year.
3. A rise often occurs on Fridays.
4. A rise often occurs during December, January, July and August.
5. A rise often occurs the last day of the month and the first four days of the month.
6. Governments arrange for good times the year which starts two years and ends one year before elections.
7. The year before the election is also often good.

The market often tends to fall on Mondays and during the first two weeks of December.

Insider Trading

A buy signal may be given when three or more insiders buy and no insiders sell during a three month period of time. When three sell with no buys, consider selling the stock.

Advice

Use stop orders and hope that stock can be sold near your set price. Use 10% to 20% below the advancing market price of the owned stock.

Do not be afraid to sit on your cash.

Diversify:

> Buy a no-load fund with small charges for operation when you have only $5,000.
>
> Invest in five stocks if you have $5,000 to $20,000.
>
> With $250,000, be invested in 20 stocks with 8 industries as defined by VALUE LINE.
>
> Selected stocks should be carefully selected and hopefully are expected to perform well.
>
> Study the statistics found in Value Line, Standard and Poors or other sources provided by advisors and brokers. Learn to use prepared charts.

NOTE: Some of these comments have been provided by reviewers, including the authors. Ideas used in the text are based on experience and reading advice of others.

Most advisors are crowd followers. Many advisors and newsletter writers make it a point to be followers since their liability for mistakes is less when they are part of a large group. These groups become more and more bullish as prices go up and more and more bearish when prices go down. Many advisors also use 10 week moving averages to smooth the curves. You should know some of these indexes and the values which indicate market increase and decline.

Insider Sell/Buy Record

An 8 month moving average is often used since number of sales is often limited. A value of about 3 for the insider sell/buy ratio often reflects a sell signal. A value of 1 suggests a buy signal. The normal ratio is 2 sell to 1 buy.

Advisory Services Record

A 10 week moving average is often used to smooth the data. Here a sell is indicated when more than 75% of the services have a firm opinion that the market should go up. A 40% favorable opinion often suggests a buy signal.

Excess Cash of Mutual Funds

Mutual funds must retain a portion of their assets in cash equivalents so that payments can be made when money is withdrawn. The amount retained depends upon economic conditions being assumed by fund managers. When the cash to assets ratio of mutual funds drops to around 6%, the market may be in trouble. A value around 10% suggests that a market rise may be approaching. Mutual funds must keep invested if they are to maximize returns. Some analysts work with excess reserve ratios which may offer some refinement.

There are dozens of indexes and the reader might discuss with a good broker for details. The experts or advisors often are wrong in their selection of market peaks and lows as evidenced by put/call ratios, floor specialists, odd lots, etc.

Barron's, in their Market Laboratory, presents data for other indexes on a weekly basis. Study reports published by the federal government, Moodys and Standard and Poors. If you need more information, review indexes in the American Statistics Index which lists statistical publications prepared by thousands of economists. The amount of statistical data available is extremely large.

Price earnings ratios are often high when stock owners are optimistic and

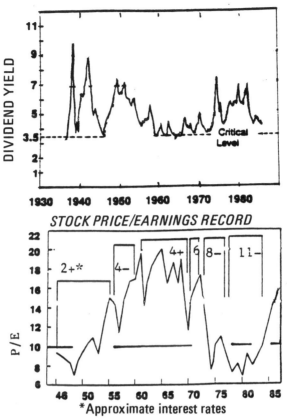

expect rapid increases in dividends and improvement in the economy. There are too many buyers relative to sellers. Too much money chases too few stocks. The reverse is true when values are low.

After a substantial move in stock price, a correction of 30% to 50% of previous move should be expected, followed by a second move of about original move.

MEASURED MOVE METHOD

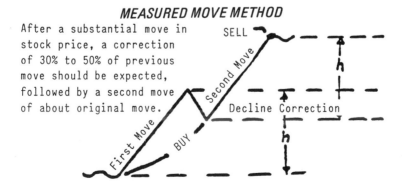

After a substantial move in stock price, a correction of 30% to 50% of previous move should be expected, followed by a second move of about original move.

Buyers and sellers often trade at support levels. They may have bought or sold at these prices before.

SUPPORT LEVEL METHOD

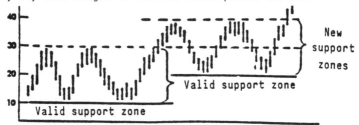

Price changes often occur at support levels.

VARIOUS CHANNELS

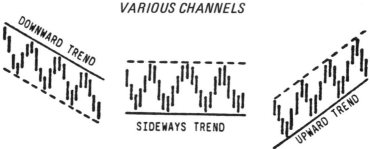

A major reversal often follows the third substantial reversal.

GAPS

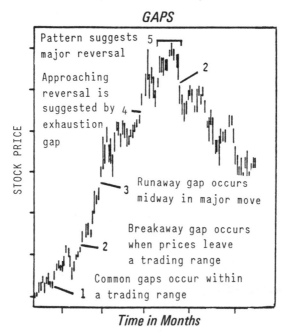

Breaks in trading range for successive days. The common gap in thinly traded stock may not be important. The break-away gap often occurs when prices are leaving the trading range. A major trend line may be broken at the same time, which signals a reversal of a trend.

The run-away gap often occurs in the middle of a price movement. If price moves below this value, the price trend has probably been broken.

The exhaustion gap suggests that the price trend is nearing its end and it is probably a time to sell.

Reduction of risks. Know the rules of probability.

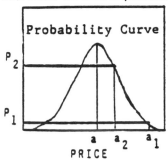

Assume that the current price is at point "a". The probability of the price reaching another price becomes less as the amount of price difference increases. As an example, the probability "P_1" that the price "a_1" will be reached is much lower than the probability "P_2" that price "a_2" will be reached. Both probabilities are greater than zero.

Risks can be reduced if you believe in yourself and have confidence in your ability. You need to study, know what you are doing, decide and then act. Risks might include:

1. Waiting until the markets have reached either exact lows or highs to act. You cannot successfully pick exact highs and lows. Try for near highs and near lows. If you wait for ideal situations before you act, your actions may be zero. Inaction is the biggest risk of all.

2. Using a buy, hold and pray strategy is often a disaster. Performance of investments changes with time and you must accept change and act to make money rather than take losses.

3. Leaving your money in the bank. See sections dealing with inflation to see what will happen to your assets. They will soon approach zero if you do not consider inflation.

4. Allowing other people to handle your assets. People watch out for their self-interests. Seldom will a manager watch out for your interest. Most fiduciaries such as banks are very conservative because of laws governing their actions. Your best friend will take your money if you allow him to control your assets. We are all selfish and must look out for ourselves.

5. Ignoring tax consequences. The tax collector also likes your assets. Take advantage of tax "loopholes" by knowing tax law. Pay no more than legally required.

6. Putting all of your assets in one basket. Are you perfect in making selections? If not, diversify. For example, buy at least 10 stocks in 8 best performing industries. One in each.
7. Acting out of fear and greed. This practice causes you to "buy high and sell low. You are doing exactly the opposite of what you must do to make money. You must "buy near lows and sell near highs" if you want to successfully handle your investments. You need to protect your assets rather than waste your hard-earned savings.
8. Churning your assets. Have patience but do buy and sell when necessary. Find a discount broker to reduce commissions. Do not be a day-to-day trader but when holding "long term", take advantage of major price swings. Sell when price is too high based on fundamentals and buy when prices are low. Study cycles of investments and the economy.
9. Track the flow of money throughout the world. Watch the first hour of trading, possibly European money, on New York Stock Exchange. Prices increase when money is invested and prices decline when money is withdrawn. A rapid withdrawal of foreign money can cause a depression.

You might find the following to be useful:
1. Don't trust a person because of an affiliation. Members of a club or a religious group may not be knowledgeable and they can be used by the "con artist".
2. Do not accept deals which "can't miss", particularly when the salesman suggests an urgency. He is trying to get you to act on emotion rather than rational logic.
3. If a deal sounds too good, it is likely it is a fraud.
4. Know what you are doing. Remember that every deal in commodities means that a dollar is lost by someone for every dollar of profit. Few traders can make money. The odds are stacked.
5. Always study and read the prospectus before investing. Do not rush.
6. The salesman gets his commission even when you are sold at a loss. Your economic interets and risks differ.
7. Never give money to a telephone salesman or a television sales ad. First study facts.
8. Do not accept high pressure sales. If you do not understand details of a deal, do not sign.
9. It is better to pay taxes than enter into a deal where everything is lost.

All deals should make economic sense before considering tax and inflation, and also after.

Methods which may beat averages. The best method is to study so that you learn and use the technique of "buying near lows" and selling "near price tops".

VALUE LINE has been successful with a method using momentum and other indexes. For years, the conclusion that VALUE LINE category 1 was composed of stocks with strong price growth history has been known. Value Line also uses other techniques and these should enable them to find strong upward trending price stocks at an earlier date than simple observation of the price and relative strength lines on plots of Value Line data. Daily plots might help.

If the above is true, the small individual has a set of techniques which cannot be used by the fund manager effectively and the individual can beat the stock market averages. The method is simply a search of the VALUE LINE plots — or those from other companies using daily plots — for strong, upward trend lines for the price and relative strength lines. After buying the stocks, the trends must be watched daily and the stocks should be sold after a break in the trends is observed. Sale should be immediate. This is the same as placing "stops" at 5%-15% of the peak price reached before downward move from a high is observed.

Capital gains were removed from the 1987 tax but they might again be included. Value Line admits that use of its Category 1 technique, which has a track record much superior to averages — involves frequent sales so that sale and buy commissions must be low. Also, it is obvious that careful supervision — possibly daily review of stock prices — is required.

In daily practical operations, the proposed method is simple. Select stocks in VALUE LINE Category 1 classification. Go to Value Line or other plots of prices and relative strength and select 10 or more stocks in eight VALUE LINE industrial groups which have the highest upward price trend in stock price. Buy and watch price daily so that sale is made when trend line is broken or when price dips below a previously set value. The reverse should be available for use in short sales. Hope trends continue during time sufficient to obtain "capital gains" tax treatment. One might beat the VALUE LINE performance since they use 100 stocks and you can select higher growth with reduced risks if you use only 10-30 stocks. For profits, trend must continue during considerable time. If bought when price is much above the trend line long term, risks are increased and somewhat different techniques may become appropriate. Examples of the Sawtooth Method and the Free Wheeling Method are on page 254.

Money is made if stock is bought and stock advances with the trend base-line regardless of time. Do not buy when price is far above trend line or when relative strength line is declining. For the Free Wheeling Method, stock should be on "new highs" lists and have safety, high growth earnings. Reduce loss by using "Stops". Sell when line is broken on downside. Sales should be considered when upside line of channel is approached.

Other basic rules for selection of stocks should not be ignored. Select stocks whose price is above previous all-time highs, etc. for Free Wheeling. The trick is to find a valid trend early by using all available data. As an example, growth might be determined by plotting, on semi-log paper, items such as earnings, dividends, book value and various ratios discussed earlier.

Always use "stop orders" to protect against declines.

As alternatives, completely covered puts and calls, warrants, convertibles might be investigated. Some of these techniques can increase return without

EXAMPLE OF SAWTOOTH METHOD

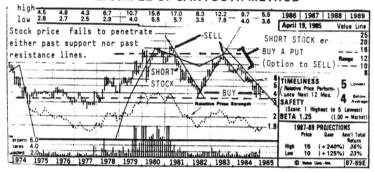

EXAMPLE OF FREE WHEELING METHOD

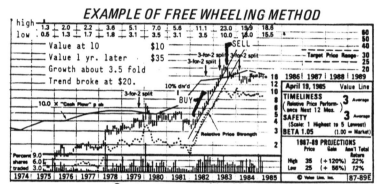

Curves constructed by Value Line
711 Third Avenue, New York, NY 10017

added risks and do fit into a conservative investment. The procedures and theories involved require special detailed study. Contact an investment stockbroker.

The above methods work for some but are not for everyone. These methods are probably more risky than methods based on basic value. You should use all available information and you alone are responsible for the results obtained.

You may also hire a professional manager who has a record of being successful. Remember that you must select a mutual fund with care since most do not beat the market averages. Also, most stockbrokers, lawyers, bankers and accountants place their personal interest first. They are interested in commissions and fees and may not give sound advice. If you have investments in the $25,000 to $100,000 range, you might investigate the following money managers as alternates.

PERFORMANCE HISTORY OF SEVERAL MANAGERS OF INVESTMENTS FOR LARGE INVESTORS

Manager	Performance 1st half 1986	Longer term performance History
Astrop Advisory Corp.	29.7%	25.3% From 1/79 to 6/30/86
Rittenhouse Financial Serv.	23.2%	22.12 From 1/81 to 12/85

RNC Capital Management	23.0	23.0	From 1/76 to 12/85
Van Deventer & Hoch	21.1	23.2	From 1/80 to 12/85

Contact "The Wall Street Digest", 101 Carnegie Center, Princeton, NJ 08540

There are other good managers and you should select with utmost care.

Major profits are made when "turn-arounds" in the fortunes of a company can be accurately forecast. A complete study of company performance and a little luck are required. The risk is that the company will not survive and all invested money is lost. Alternatively, the company might improve rather than decline.

Some investors try to reduce the risks by comparing long term curves of moving averages with current values for stock prices. The moving average for each Friday's price for a period of time up to 30 weeks is plotted with each Friday's closing prices. Stocks show four stages in a cycle:

1. The first stage occurs when the daily stock price begins to be higher than the 30 week moving average. This is a signal to watch for a rise in the price of the stock or an average index.
2. If the daily price "surges" above the 30 week moving average, buy immediately. Wait for this surge before buying if you are a conservative investor. Your gain is reduced but your risks are much lower.
3. The surest sign of a market top for the stock or index occurs when the daily price is no longer consistently above the 30 week moving average. If price movement is above and below the 30 week average and volume rises, consider selling immediately.
4. When the daily price is below the 30 week moving average, do not own the stock or index.

Other investors use various economic and sentiment indexes to determine possible turns in stock and asset prices. You should become familiar with these techniques by asking brokers for studies — basic graphs and curves — of their analyst. Study the basics of these studies. Some are informative and valuable.

There is no magic formula for overnight riches. Successful management of your assets is a long-term proposition requiring self-discipline and a reasonable investment of time and effort. Analysts have determined that during the 50 years beginning with 1926, $1.00 invested in the S&P 500 stocks would have grown to $279.00 (excluding taxes and reinvesting dividends). During the same period, $1.00 invested in the smallest 20% of companies on the NYSE would have grown to $1,241. The smaller companies were generally purchased by individuals rather than institutions and this is but one piece of evidence that the serious individual can out-perform the institutions and the popular market averages. Individuals can obtain better investment results than most professionals — if they are willing to spend the necessary time and exert the necessary effort — because small transactions seldom influence prices.

Buying stocks is relatively easy since past trends and history are available for companies and the economic conditions for industry can be determined from statistics available from the federal government and other sources. Curves showing price performance history and other statistics are available from Value Line and other sources. Such advisory services also present useable information relative to the condition of the national economy. You might simply select stocks with good past earnings and price history or you might dig deeper into the performance of the company to determine real worth which is preferable and less risky. If you have cash, spending it is rather simple. Buy a performing mutual fund if amounts for overall investment are small and if you need management. This reduces risks but does cost fees. Select with care since most funds do not beat the market averages.

Selling Assets. Determining when to sell is more complicated both emotionally and practically. It is difficult to determine when the company is faltering since management tends to use accounting to cover up its deficiencies. Forecasting the future for the economy also is not easy since even the leading indicators are subject to forecast errors and often do not trend in the same direction at an early date. The stock market often reacts to the economy as much as six or more months before the economy actually turns around. Also, tax considerations always enter into the decision. If taxes are paid as a result of a sale, the money left to invest is always less than before the sale and payment of taxes. Sale of losers is relatively easy since a tax loss is involved and we actually have more money to spend as a result of a sale, although there is an overall loss.

A very rapid change in price of an asset will usually be partly corrected. Land prices during the 1980s are a longer term example and the history of prices of many stocks offer many short-term examples. Try to sell when the price is near highs and buy again when the prices are near low values. Know probable price ranges. This is not easy and study and work is involved.

The best approach to selling is use of "stop loss orders". A selling price should be determined for all assets and this price should advance as the price of the asset increases. The selling price might be 5% to 20% less than current market price depending upon tax and emotions. Always sell when the value drops below this previously determined selling price and do not vacillate or find excuses for delay.

Assets should also be sold when the countrywide economic indicators indicate a major change is imminent. Remember that different assets behave differently in various economic climates.

If reliance is placed on others, remember that all recommendations other than buy are actually sell recommendations. Watching insiders and managers of large funds may be a better indicator than brokers and stock letters.

Watch earnings and forecasts of earnings of individual companies. Earnings usually grow when stock prices are increasing.

Watch company managements. Experience has shown that companies are in trouble when:

1. There is greed at the top. Salary of management level should not differ more than 30%. High salary differentials usually suggest that there is fighting among the managers and that needed teamwork is lacking.
2. Decisions are not based on facts relative to market, a products potential and technology rather than financial considerations. After

facts are established, financial considerations and methods are used to determine whether returns are adequate for action.

3. Decisions are not made after all alternative possibilities have been evaluated. Consider best case environment, average possibilities and worse case conditions before making decisions. Plan for each possibility but if action is taken to implement, use best case plan until proven wrong.

4. Decisions are based on quick acclamation. Always explore all alternatives. Ask for and carefully consider contrary ideas before making decisions. Managers should ask staffs for written reports based on all alternatives before deciding.

If the management fails in any of the above, stay away from their stock.

Watch Federal Funds Rates for possible long term or major reversal of a trend. Also, watch money supply for major changes. Recessions in past years have been associated with higher interest rates and reduced money supply.

Watch for evidence of excessive speculation. Speculation is often indicated when:

1. Volume of low price stocks increases rapidly compared with DOW.

2. Watch flow of funds. Cash and bonds of major funds may reach 25% of total assets at market peaks. About 30% of household assets, other than homes, may be in stocks at tops. Start to worry when over 50% of investment letters are bullish and sell when figure exceeds 65%.

3. Public interest as evidenced by newspaper space is high at economic tops.

4. The market is less secure when new highs are less than 300 on a weekly basis.

5. Stocks may be at a high when NYSE member shorts exceeds 78% of total NYSE short sales. These values re changing since Options — calls and puts — are replacing shorts.

6. A declining trend in ten week moving averages often indicates a lower price for stocks.

7. Watch first hour sales and prices. These often reflect European Trading.

8. Reduction in money supply, reductions in "free reserves", reduction in strength of economy, increases in interest rates and an increase in bond value compared with stocks all suggest a downturn in stock prices. Many other ratios might be studied to analyze decline of fortunes of a company.

9. There are many mood indicators which should be watched for downward changes.

INFLATION IS ALWAYS REDUCING THE VALUE OF YOUR ASSETS WHILE YOU ARE LOOKING AT OTHER INFLUENCES. TAXES WILL ALSO CATCH UP WITH YOU WHEN YOU SELL ASSETS. Never take a risk which will cause you to go bankrupt. Spread risk and do necessary "homework". Diversify.

SUMMARY

1. Recognize that the value of all investments and groups of assets rises and falls with time. Change the mix of your investments to conform.
2. Determine the time on the economic clock for each of your investments. No two sets of conditions are exactly the same and history or business cycles do not always repeat. Asset management does take time and effort.
3. Use patience but do act when necessary. Use "stop orders". Try for near tops and near bottoms. Remember that the crowd is often wrong, especially at "turn-around" times. Successful "experts" or advisors are few.
4. Diversify and obtain liquidity by owning securities, mutual funds and trust instruments rather than owning entire companies, real estate and bulk gold, etc. Consider risks, inflation and taxes in your decisions.
5. Control and management of your assets is your business and no one else is responsible for your decisions and actions. All advice is at times wrong and you must decide alone what is proper for you. You must decide alone and cannot make anyone else responsible for your decisions. Your assets grow when you decide properly and shrink when you make an error. All advice given to you depends upon your decisions and you alone must decide what is to be used by you in the management of your assets. You alone live with the results and you alone are responsible. Don't blame others nor give others credit when you are successful. Be calculating. Use no emotions.
6. Save you must. Have fun managing assets. Give it a try and find out the joys of management and benefits of a savings account and investments. You will be glad that you did as you grow older.

LEARN AND KEEP TRYING — DO NOT ALLOW DEFEAT TO DETER YOU.

REFERENCES

Many groups prepare statistics. Please consult:

Department of Commerce, Washington, D.C.

    Bureau of Economic Analysis

    Bureau of Census

Department of Labor

Federal Reserve System, Head Office and Regional Banks

Congressional Information Service, U. S. Congress

Standard and Poors, Index to Surveys, 25 Broadway, New York NY 10004

The American Statistics Index, often available in the library, gives names of research groups.

Contact owner of the local bookstore. Discuss with the head of the library.

Write Executive Books Summaries, 5 Main Street, Bristol, VT 05443 for summaries of latest books related to business.

Contact local businessmen, teachers, religious leaders.

Index

260